# Communications
# in Computer and Information Science     2470

Series Editors

Gang Li , *School of Information Technology, Deakin University, Burwood, VIC,
Australia*
Joaquim Filipe, *Polytechnic Institute of Setúbal, Setúbal, Portugal*
Zhiwei Xu, *Chinese Academy of Sciences, Beijing, China*

AF172577

### Rationale

The CCIS series is devoted to the publication of proceedings of computer science conferences. Its aim is to efficiently disseminate original research results in informatics in printed and electronic form. While the focus is on publication of peer-reviewed full papers presenting mature work, inclusion of reviewed short papers reporting on work in progress is welcome, too. Besides globally relevant meetings with internationally representative program committees guaranteeing a strict peer-reviewing and paper selection process, conferences run by societies or of high regional or national relevance are also considered for publication.

### Topics

The topical scope of CCIS spans the entire spectrum of informatics ranging from foundational topics in the theory of computing to information and communications science and technology and a broad variety of interdisciplinary application fields.

### Information for Volume Editors and Authors

Publication in CCIS is free of charge. No royalties are paid, however, we offer registered conference participants temporary free access to the online version of the conference proceedings on SpringerLink (http://link.springer.com) by means of an http referrer from the conference website and/or a number of complimentary printed copies, as specified in the official acceptance email of the event.

CCIS proceedings can be published in time for distribution at conferences or as post-proceedings, and delivered in the form of printed books and/or electronically as USBs and/or e-content licenses for accessing proceedings at SpringerLink. Furthermore, CCIS proceedings are included in the CCIS electronic book series hosted in the SpringerLink digital library at http://link.springer.com/bookseries/7899. Conferences publishing in CCIS are allowed to use Online Conference Service (OCS) for managing the whole proceedings lifecycle (from submission and reviewing to preparing for publication) free of charge.

### Publication process

The language of publication is exclusively English. Authors publishing in CCIS have to sign the Springer CCIS copyright transfer form, however, they are free to use their material published in CCIS for substantially changed, more elaborate subsequent publications elsewhere. For the preparation of the camera-ready papers/files, authors have to strictly adhere to the Springer CCIS Authors' Instructions and are strongly encouraged to use the CCIS LaTeX style files or templates.

### Abstracting/Indexing

CCIS is abstracted/indexed in DBLP, Google Scholar, EI-Compendex, Mathematical Reviews, SCImago, Scopus. CCIS volumes are also submitted for the inclusion in ISI Proceedings.

### How to start

To start the evaluation of your proposal for inclusion in the CCIS series, please send an e-mail to ccis@springer.com

Ludovico Boratto · Allegra De Filippo ·
Elisabeth Lex · Francesco Ricci
Editors

# Recommender Systems for Sustainability and Social Good

First International Workshop, RecSoGood 2024
Bari, Italy, October 18, 2024
Proceedings

 Springer

*Editors*
Ludovico Boratto (iD)
University of Cagliari
Cagliari, Italy

Allegra De Filippo (iD)
University of Bologna
Bologna, Italy

Elisabeth Lex (iD)
Graz University of Technology
Graz, Austria

Francesco Ricci (iD)
Free University of Bozen-Bolzano
Bolzano, Italy

ISSN 1865-0929        ISSN 1865-0937 (electronic)
Communications in Computer and Information Science
ISBN 978-3-031-87653-0        ISBN 978-3-031-87654-7 (eBook)
https://doi.org/10.1007/978-3-031-87654-7

# Advances in Recommender Systems for Sustainability and Social Good: Preface

The First International Workshop on Recommender Systems for Sustainability and Social Good (RecSoGood 2024) was held as part of the 18th ACM Recommender Systems Conference (Recsys 2024) on October 18, 2024. RecSoGood 2024 was held in Bari, Italy, with support for remote attendance. The workshop was jointly organized by the University of Cagliari (Italy), the University of Bologna (Italy), the University of Graz (Austria) and the Free University of Bozen–Bolzano (Italy).

This first edition of the workshop was mainly motivated by pressing global sustainability issues for technology and innovation within the field of Recommender Systems. By exploring how recommendation technologies can be leveraged to support sustainability objectives, we open up opportunities for research, development, and experimentation in this emerging area. Engaging the Recommender Systems community in discussions around sustainability fosters awareness and collaboration on this topic.

The workshop counted 35 submissions from different countries. All submissions were double-blind peer-reviewed by at least three internal Program Committee members, ensuring that only high-quality work was then included in the final workshop program. The pool of reviewers included researchers in the field from industry and academia. The final program included 8 full papers and 6 short papers.

The program of the workshop included interesting paper presentations and a final discussion to highlight open issues, research challenges, and briefly summarize the outcomes of the workshop. The collected novel contributions fell into three main topics. The first topic focused on Recommender Systems for Sustainable Development grouped by Sustainable Development Goals. Papers included in the second topic analyzed Energy and Carbon Efficiency in Recommender Systems, with particular attention to modeling these systems to reduce the carbon footprint and the environmental impact. Finally, the third topic targeted novel perspectives and conceptualizations of diversity and personalization in recommendations. More than 50 attendees participated.

In addition to the paper presentations, the program also included one keynote talk. Alan Said from the University of Gothenburg (Sweden) examined the current panorama of Recommenders for Social Good by reflecting on the role of accountability and sustainability with practical examples and open perspectives.

This workshop confirmed the emerging relevance of the topic, with an increasing level of engagement thanks to the return to in-presence events. RecSoGood 2024 strengthened the community that works on sustainability and social good in recommender systems, aiming to represent a key event where ideas and solutions for current challenges can be discussed. This success motivates us to organize the second edition of the workshop next year. The organizers would like to thank the authors, the reviewers for helping to shape an interesting program, and the attendees for their participation.

November 2024

Ludovico Boratto
Allegra De Filippo
Elisabeth Lex
Francesco Ricci

# Organization

## Workshop Chairs

Ludovico Boratto — University of Cagliari, Italy
Allegra De Filippo — University of Bologna, Italy
Elisabeth Lex — Graz University of Technology, Austria
Francesco Ricci — Free University of Bozen–Bolzano, Italy

## Program Committee

Robin Burke — University of Colorado, Boulder, USA
Iván Cantador — Universidad Autónoma de Madrid, Spain
Federica Cena — University of Turin, Italy
Marco de Gemmis — University of Bari, Italy
Gaetano Di Benedetto — University of Bari, Italy
Karlijn Dinnissen — Utrecht University, Netherlands
Michael Ekstrand — Drexel University, USA
Alexander Felfernig — TU Graz, Austria
Dongmin Hyun — Yahoo Research, USA
Hanna Hauptmann — Utrecht University, Netherlands
Dietmar Jannach — University of Klagenfurt, Austria
Bart Knijnenburg — Clemson University, USA
David Massimo — Public Value Technologies, Germany
Giacomo Medda — University of Cagliari, Italy
Alessandro Petruzzelli — University of Bari, Italy
Marco Polignano — University of Bari, Italy
Erasmo Purificato — Joint Research Centre EC, Italy
Amon Rapp — University of Turin, Italy
Giuseppe Spillo — University of Bari, Italy
George Stalidis — International Hellenic University, Greece
Alain Starke — University of Amsterdam, Netherlands
Helma Torkamaan — Delft University of Technology, Netherlands
Wolfgang Wörndl — Technical University of Munich, Germany

Chairs and program committee members are in alphabetical order by last name.

# Contents

# Recommender Systems for Social Good: The Role of Accountability and Sustainability

Alan Said[(⊠)]

University of Gothenburg, Gothenburg, Sweden
alansaid@acm.org

**Abstract.** This work examines the role of recommender systems in promoting sustainability, social responsibility, and accountability, with a focus on alignment with the United Nations Sustainable Development Goals (SDGs). As recommender systems become increasingly integrated into daily interactions, they must go beyond personalization to support responsible consumption, reduce environmental impact, and foster social good. We explore strategies to mitigate the carbon footprint of recommendation models, ensure fairness, and implement accountability mechanisms. By adopting these approaches, recommender systems can contribute to sustainable and socially beneficial outcomes, aligning technological advancements with the SDGs focused on environmental sustainability and social well-being.

**Keywords:** sustainability · accountability · fairness · recommender systems · sustainable development goals

## 1 Introduction

Recommender systems have become integral to our digital experiences, guiding us in selecting content, products, and services across domains such as entertainment, e-commerce, and health. With their expanding influence, these systems are uniquely positioned to contribute to societal goals beyond personalization and engagement, aligning with frameworks like the United Nations Sustainable Development Goals[1]. However, this potential comes with responsibility: as these systems grow, so do concerns regarding their environmental footprint, fairness, and accountability.

This work explores how recommender systems can be aligned with SDGs focused on sustainability, social responsibility, and accountable use of technology. Specifically, it addresses the need for strategies to mitigate the carbon impact of recommender systems, enhance fairness across user groups, and establish accountability mechanisms to increase transparency and trust. These approaches

---

[1] https://sdgs.un.org/goals.

support goals like SDG 10—*Reduced Inequality*, SDG 12—*Responsible Consumption and Production*, SDG 13—*Climate Action*, and SDG 16—*Peace, Justice, and Strong Institutions*, demonstrating how technological advancements in recommender systems can be steered towards social good.

## 2     Recommender Systems Through the Lens of the SDGs

Recommender systems play a significant role in shaping digital consumption, offering a pathway to support the SDGs. As these systems influence user choices and behaviors, they can either drive positive societal change or exacerbate existing challenges. Here, we explore how recommender systems can be designed to align with specific SDGs, primarily focusing on social responsibility, sustainability, and accountability.

### 2.1     SDG 10: Reduced Inequality

Fairness in recommender systems is essential to prevent the reinforcement of social biases, aligning with SDG 10's goal of reducing inequalities. Biased algorithms in sensitive domains like criminal justice and finance can perpetuate unequal access to opportunities. For instance, automated systems in judicial sentencing [7] and financial scoring [8] have raised concerns due to potential demographic biases, underscoring the importance of fairness in recommendation and decision-support applications with significant real-world implications. Achieving fairness in this space, however, is complex, as there is no universally agreed-upon definition. Abu Elyounes [1] notes that much of the research on fairness in AI involves justifying why one notion is "fairer" than others, reflecting the diversity of fairness interpretations. Li et al. [5] emphasize that fairness needs vary by context, with metrics like demographic parity and equalized odds presenting trade-offs that impact perceived fairness.

A study by Kecki and Said [4] demonstrates that public perceptions of fairness are context-dependent, with preferences shifting based on the stakes involved, further highlighting the need for contextual sensitivity in fairness-aware systems. An adaptable approach to fairness is essential: high-stakes applications like healthcare may prioritize accuracy, while applications emphasizing equal access could focus on demographic parity. By adopting such adaptive, context-aware approaches, recommender systems can support SDG 10 by fostering equitable access and reducing inequalities across various domains.

### 2.2     SDG 12: Responsible Consumption and Production & SDG 13: Climate Action

Recommender systems can support responsible consumption by guiding users towards sustainable choices. However, these systems often rely on large-scale, deep learning models with substantial environmental impacts. Recent studies show that the average carbon footprint of a single deep learning recommender system paper can exceed 3,000 kg of $CO_2$ equivalents—a figure comparable to long-haul flight emissions [9].

In 2023 alone, over 17,000 papers were published on deep learning recommenders[2], placing the cumulative emissions of this field on par with those of smaller nations [3]. This environmental cost prompts questions about whether high-emission models are necessary for every use case.

"Good old-fashioned AI" models, like neighborhood-based methods, can offer competitive recommendation accuracy without deep learning's energy demands. For some applications, the incremental accuracy of deep learning may not justify its carbon footprint. For instance, recommending digital content (e.g., music or movies) has low environmental impact even if recommendations are suboptimal, i.e., skipping to the next track or selecting a different movie causes negligible $CO_2$ emissions. However, in fashion e-commerce, poor recommendations can lead to significant environmental costs from shipping and returns, e.g., up to half of fashion e-commerce orders in Europe are reportedly returned [6]. Here, accurate recommendations could reduce unnecessary shipments, directly supporting SDG 12 by encouraging responsible consumption.

To mitigate environmental impact, practitioners can explore energy-efficient algorithms, optimize resources, and consider carbon offsets. Additionally, recommender systems can align with SDG 13 by prioritizing sustainable options, such as local products or eco-friendly items, fostering environmentally conscious behaviors across different application contexts.

## 2.3   SDG 16: Peace, Justice, and Strong Institutions

Accountability and transparency in recommender systems are foundational to building trust, aligning with SDG 16's focus on strong institutions. Users benefit from knowing how and why recommendations are made, as transparency fosters trust and allows users to make informed choices. Accountability mechanisms—such as transparency, explainability, and reproducibility—enable stakeholders to monitor and audit these systems, ensuring they act fairly and justly.

One approach to promoting accountability in recommender systems is through reproducibility, which strengthens research validity and builds trust within the research and practitioner communities as well as with users [2]. Furthermore, accountability allows for identifying and addressing biases, supporting ethical and socially responsible recommendations. This practice aligns recommender systems with the principles of justice and fair treatment, reinforcing their role as trusted digital facilitators.

---

[2] https://scholar.google.com/scholar?as_ylo=2023&as_yhi=2023& q=%22deep+learning%22+%22recommender+system%22%7C %22recommender+systems%22%7C%22recommendation+system%22%7C %22recommendation+systems%22.

# 3    Conclusions

Recommender systems research and practice offer many opportunities to support the SDGs by making choices that promote accountability, transparency, and context-aware design. Through careful consideration of these principles, the research and practitioner communities can align recommender systems with the goals of reducing inequalities (SDG 10), fostering responsible consumption and production (SDG 12), advancing climate action (SDG 13), and strengthening justice and institutions (SDG 16). However, achieving these outcomes requires a nuanced and contextual approach; there is no "one size fits all" solution, as different applications and environments demand tailored strategies to ensure effective and sustainable outcomes.

While this work focused on SDGs 10, 12, 13, and 16, many other SDGs can be linked to recommender systems, from promoting good health to supporting quality education and beyond. This highlights the importance of researchers and practitioners in the recommender systems field to adopt societal good as a guiding principle, continually reflecting on the broader impacts of their work on global well-being.

# References

1. Abu Elyounes, D.: Contextual Fairness: A Legal and Policy Analysis of Algorithmic Fairness (2019). https://doi.org/10.2139/ssrn.3478296
2. Bellogín, A., Said, A.: Improving accountability in recommender systems research through reproducibility. User Model. User-Adap. Inter. **31**(5), 941–977 (2021). https://doi.org/10.1007/s11257-021-09302-x
3. European Commission and Joint Research Centre, Crippa, M., et al.: GHG emissions of all world countries - 2023. Publications Office of the European Union (2023). https://doi.org/10.2760/953322
4. Kecki, V., Said, A.: Understanding fairness in recommender systems: a healthcare perspective. In: Proceedings of the 18th ACM Conference on Recommender Systems, RecSys 2024, pp. 1125–1130. Association for Computing Machinery, New York (2024). https://doi.org/10.1145/3640457.3691711
5. Li, Y., et al.: Fairness in recommendation: foundations, methods, and applications. ACM Trans. Intell. Syst. Technol. **14**(5), 95:1–95:48 (2023). https://doi.org/10.1145/3610302
6. Marketing Yocabè: Guida ai resi nel mondo dell'e-commerce, March 2023
7. Polonski, V.: AI is convicting criminals and determining jail time, but is it fair? World Economic Forum, November 2018
8. Tolan, C., Ash, A., Marsh, R.: The nation's largest credit union rejected more than half its Black conventional mortgage applicants | CNN Business. CNN, December 2023
9. Vente, T., Wegmeth, L., Said, A., Beel, J.: From clicks to carbon: the environmental toll of recommender systems. In: Proceedings of the 18th ACM Conference on Recommender Systems, RecSys 2024, pp. 580–590. Association for Computing Machinery, New York, October 2024. https://doi.org/10.1145/3640457.3688074

# Decoupled Recommender Systems: Exploring Alternative Recommender Ecosystem Designs

Anas Buhayh$^{(\boxtimes)}$ (iD), Elizabeth McKinnie (iD), and Robin Burke (iD)

Department of Information Science, University of Colorado, Boulder, USA
{anas.buhayh,elizabeth.mckinnie,robin.burke}@colorado.edu

**Abstract.** Recommender ecosystems are an emerging subject of research. Such research examines how the characteristics of algorithms, recommendation consumers, and item providers influence system dynamics and long-term outcomes. One architectural possibility that has not yet been widely explored in this line of research is the consequences of a configuration in which recommendation algorithms are decoupled from the platforms they serve. This is sometimes called "the friendly neighborhood algorithm store" or "middleware" model. We are particularly interested in how such architectures might offer a range of different distributions of utility across consumers, providers, and recommendation platforms. In this paper, we create a model of a recommendation ecosystem that incorporates algorithm choice and examine the outcomes of such a design.

**Keywords:** multistakeholder recommendation · recommender systems · decentralized recommender ecosystems

## 1 Introduction

An implicit architectural assumption in recommender systems research is the item data/recommendation platform monolith: a single centralized database of all items that can be recommended, a single recommendation algorithm operating over them, and a single centralized database of consumer profiles resulting from user interactions with those items. Fielded systems often contain multiple recommenders operating over different items within the same application: think recommending posts and recommending users to follow in a social media system, or session-oriented and long-term recommendations coexisting in an e-commerce setting. However, these are still monoliths, enabled by a central representation of the user profile and item catalog.

As a personalization technology, recommender systems have historically had a strong focus on the consumers, for whom the experience is personalized, and the evaluation of recommender systems has, appropriately, taken this perspective. In a multistakeholder approach [2], the field of view is expanded to consider

© The Author(s), under exclusive license to Springer Nature Switzerland AG 2025
L. Boratto et al. (Eds.): RecSoGood 2024, CCIS 2470, pp. 5–18, 2025.
https://doi.org/10.1007/978-3-031-87654-7_2

how the recommender system impacts providers of recommended items and others, in addition to item consumers. But even when adopting a multistakeholder lens, the idea of the monolithic recommender remains. We believe this architectural design enforces a "one-size-fits-all" recommender system objective on both consumers and providers on the platform. Even in peer-to-peer recommendation, for example [20], the user data is moved to the client but we do not see algorithmic diversity as a goal.

Rajendra-Nicolucci et al. [8] introduce the *friendly neighborhood algorithm store* model, which emphasizes user choice among third-party algorithms for recommendation designed to meet individual needs. This model creates opportunities for innovation and empowerment for both consumers and providers, fostering healthy competition among algorithm designers. For instance, algorithm designers could develop tools that focus on niche products, ensure the quality of verified content, or create more governable spaces for communities by deploying special content moderation or re-ranking strategies. This work echoes calls from Fukuyama et al. [11] and others that call for solutions that separate user interface functions from back-end platform operations, especially for social media platforms, an approach they term *middleware*.

This work was also inspired by the work of Yao et al. [24], who used simulations to show that recommender ecosystems tend towards low utility for consumers interested in niche content because such systems incentivize providers to alter their content in the direction of mainstream, popular material.

In this paper, we use simulations to study the implications of the friendly algorithm store – or generally, a collection of third-party recommender systems – to address one of the problems identified in [8] and confirmed in [24], which is the inability of a single dominant algorithm to meet the needs of all users. To the best of our knowledge, no prior work has simulated recommender ecosystems with decoupled architectures. Our research aims to address the following questions:

- How do multiple recommender systems interact and evolve within an ecosystem, and what insights can we glean from these interactions?
- In a decoupled ecosystem, how is utility distributed among providers, consumers, and recommender platforms, and what implications does this distribution have for system dynamics and outcomes?
- How are these properties influenced by domain- and application-specific characteristics such as the long-tail properties of item popularity, the specific properties of different recommendation algorithms, and the distribution and stability of consumer interests?

To begin to explore these questions, we developed the Simulator for MOdular Recommendation EcoSystems (SMORES) that models the complex interactions between consumers, providers, and recommender platforms in a recommender ecosystem, focusing on how utility is distributed among these three classes of stakeholders. Figure 1 shows a schematic depiction of the different ecosystem structures that we consider: a typical monolithic configuration versus a decoupled one. In this paper, we present our preliminary investigations using SMORES to

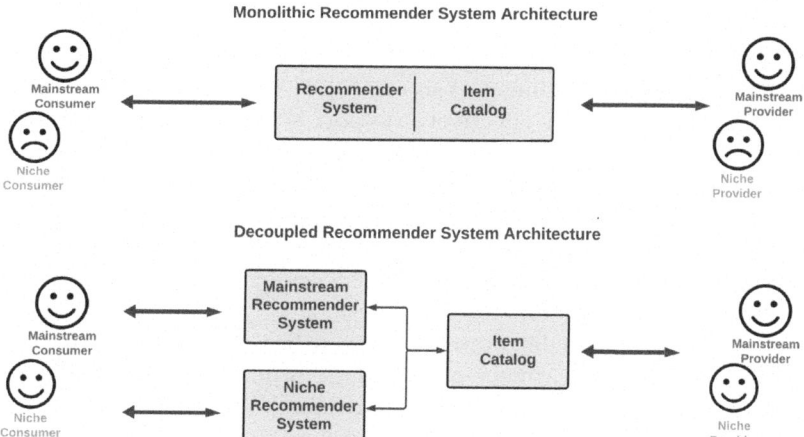

**Fig. 1.** The monolithic vs decoupled recommender system architecture. In the decoupled scenario, consumers can choose among recommender systems and both consumers and providers benefit.

study the impact of consumers switching among recommender platforms. Our findings demonstrate that introducing a specialized niche recommender system can significantly enhance the utility for both consumers interested in niche items and the providers who produce them. The key contributions of our work are as follows:

1. We describe SMORES and show how it enables the study of the dynamics of decoupled recommender ecosystems.
2. Using SMORES, we construct a simple recommender choice scenario to mimic the interaction between a consumer and multiple recommender platforms.
3. Under this scenario, we demonstrate that recommendation platform choice provides better outcomes for both niche providers and niche consumers.

## 2    Related Work

Our work contributes to the trajectory of exploring and evaluating multistakeholder recommendation systems, focusing on all groups and individuals interacting with and affected by these systems [2,6]. The multistakeholder recommendation concept delineates the ecosystem into three primary components: *consumers*, who consume the recommendations; *providers*, who produce the items to be recommended; and the *system*, encompassing the recommendation algorithm and the platform operating it [2]. Previous research in this domain has predominantly focused on understanding and addressing fairness and disparities among the diverse populations interacting with recommender systems [3,19,22,23]. Building on this foundation, our work examines the question of recommender algorithm choice from a multistakeholder perspective, looking at how different classes of consumers and providers are impacted by this architectural configuration.

In their simulated experiment, Yao et al. [24] demonstrate that traditional top-k recommendations can effectively support social welfare for content creators (providers) when these creators adapt their strategies and content to align with market demands. However, we contend that this approach may lead to an unhealthy, homogeneous market and impose costs on providers who may find it challenging to chase popular tastes by constantly adapting their output. These incentives serve to marginalize niche providers and consumers, further isolating them from the mainstream [9].

Research on recommender systems fairness has shown that these systems often exhibit disparate treatment of providers, primarily driven by popularity bias inherent in collaborative filtering algorithms [1,4]. Such biases can create barriers to entry for new providers [13], thereby impacting the inclusivity and diversity of recommender ecosystems. Notably, many businesses and individuals rely on platforms housing recommender systems as their primary source of income [5,10]. Additionally, recommender systems serve as essential content moderation tools on social media platforms [12]. While these moderation techniques effectively reduce the visibility of harmful content and protect providers from abusive comments, they also risk suppressing marginalized voices and limiting the reach of providers' content [14,17]. The diverse roles of recommender systems underscore the complex interplay between algorithmic decision-making, platform governance, and societal equity.

Our work is grounded in the principles of the "pluriverse" - a concept delineating a diverse world composed of a myriad of smaller worlds, and "the very small online platforms," as well as "the friendly neighborhood algorithm store," as articulated in [8]. While these concepts have traditionally been associated with Decentralized Online Social Networks, often referred to as the Fediverse [18], this architectural approach emphasizes decentralized and community-driven governance, albeit with accompanying challenges [7]. In our adaptation, we integrate recommender systems into this decentralized framework, thereby empowering consumers to exert greater control over the recommendation algorithms shaping their online interactions.

This work also has a close connection to the *middleware* proposal from [11], which envisions recommender systems as a form of middleware that sit on top of existing social media platforms. They envision this as a new dimension of commercial competition, describing it as *"a competitive layer of new companies with transparent algorithms [who] would step in and take over the editorial gateway functions currently filled by dominant technology platforms whose algorithms are opaque."*

## 3   Methods

### 3.1   Simulation Architecture

We developed the SMORES simulation architecture, inspired by RecSim [16], to model different versions of a multistakeholder recommender ecosystem shown in

Fig. 1. Key elements of this model are our representations of an item $i \in I$ where $I$ is the set of all items; consumer $j \in J$ where $J$ is the set of all consumers; recommender system $k \in K$ where $K$ is the set of all recommender algorithms; and provider $v \in V$ where $V$ is the set of all providers.

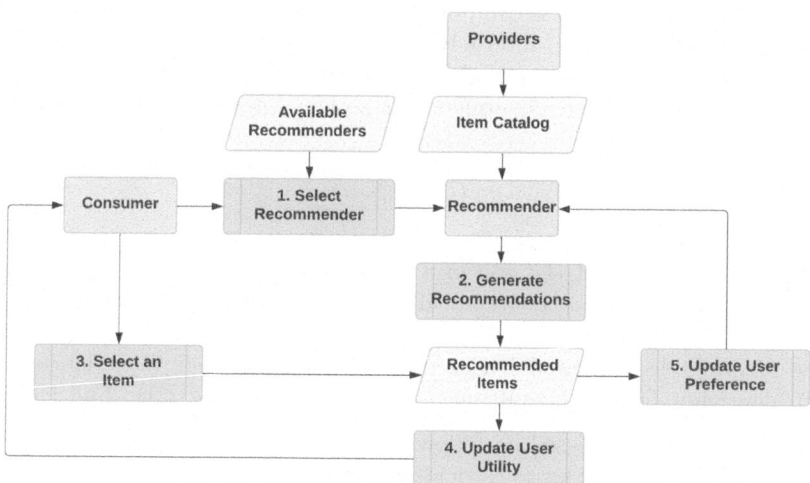

**Fig. 2.** The simulation environment process highlighting the stakeholders in green, processes in blue, and the inputs/outputs in pink. (Color figure online)

As shown in Fig. 2, the basic operation of the simulation involves a consumer $j$ choosing a recommender system $k$ with which to interact, consulting the recommender, being delivered a list of recommended items $[i_0..i_n] = \ell_{j,k}$, and then selecting a particular item $\bar{i}_{j,k}$. In our model, the consumer can only consult one recommender per iteration. We also assume that there is some inertia in consumers' recommender algorithm choices and they update their algorithm choice only periodically, not every time they seek a recommendation. The algorithm produces recommendation lists from the items made available to it by the providers. For these experiments, we assume that all items are available to all recommenders. A sequence in which every user obtains recommendations is termed a *day* and 30 such sequences are a *cycle*. Consumers update their recommender preferences at the end of each cycle.

Consumers choose an item every time a recommendation list is produced and they obtain utility from that recommendation – for example, by watching the recommended movie they chose. Providers obtain utility when their items are shown on recommendation lists and when they are selected or clicked on by consumers. The recommender systems also obtain utility in our simulation, but we do not include an analysis of recommender utility in this paper for reasons of space. We detail the simulation calculations below.

## 3.2    Selection Models

**Recommender Selection Model.** We experiment with two different recommender selection models. The first is a simple threshold-based model. In this model, the consumer computes their utility towards a recommender system over the entire experiment so far and compares it to a threshold $\tau$. The utility score for the recommender system is computed with a recency bias parameter $\beta$, which assigns more weight to recent interactions. Let $u_{j,\ell,k}$ be the utility that consumer $j$ associates with a given recommendation list $\ell$ from recommender $k$, and let $U_{j,k}$ be the utility calculated for recommender $k$ so far. An updated $U'_{j,k}$ is computed as:

$$U'_{j,k} = \frac{U_{j,k} \times \beta + u_{j,\ell,k}}{1 + \beta} \tag{1}$$

If $U'_{j,k}$ falls below $\tau$ at the end of a given cycle and there is another recommender to switch to, the consumer will choose the other recommender for the next cycle.

The second selection model uses the well-known Upper Confidence Bound (UCB) algorithm from the multi-armed bandit literature [21]. The UCB formula with decay is expressed as follows: $\text{UCB}_{j,k} = U_{j,k} + \frac{\sqrt{2\log(t)/n_{j,k}}}{1+t}$, where $U_{j,k}$ represents the utility score associated with recommender $k$ based on historical interactions with the recommender and updated using the formula above, $t$ denotes the current day of interaction, and $n_{j,k}$ is the number of times recommender $k$ has been selected by consumer $j$. This approach ensures that the exploration rate diminishes over time, allowing for more focused exploitation of the best-performing recommenders. At the end of each cycle, consumer $j$ will select the recommender with the greatest $\text{UCB}_{j,k}$ value.

**Item Selection Model.** When a recommendation list $\ell$ is presented to the consumer, the utility $u_{j,i}$ of each item $i \in \ell_{j,k}$ is computed as the dot product of the consumers' feature interests and the selected item's features: $f_i \cdot p_j$ where $f_i$ is the feature vector associated with item $i$ and $p_j$ is the preference over the same features associated with consumer $j$. This utility score is then normalized by the size of the feature set and converted into selection probabilities using the softmax function:

$$\pi_{j,i} = \frac{\exp(u_{j,i} - \max(u_\ell))}{\sum_{x \in \ell} \exp(u_{j,x} - \max(u_\ell))} \tag{2}$$

The selected item $\bar{i}$ is chosen at random using the $\pi_i$ values as probabilities. This item is identified as the *clicked* item for provider utility calculation. Note that a consumer *must* choose an item each day. This design decision implies that even if an entire set of recommendations does not match the user preferences, some selection will be made and some provider will gain utility from that choice. In future work, we plan to explore decision models in which consumers have the null option of not clicking on any item.

### 3.3 Utility Models

**Consumer Utility Model.** Although the consumer always selects a single item in each recommendation list, their utility is computed from the recommendation list as a whole using the feature-based model discussed above: the utility of a single item is computed as the dot product of the user's feature preferences and the item's features, normalized by the feature count. The average of these values is computed over all of the items in the list, yielding the overall list utility $u_{j,\ell,k}$. The overall utility of a particular recommender is updated as given in Eq. 1.

**Provider Utility Model.** At each cycle, the provider's utility is updated based on fees charged by the connected recommender systems. This fee structure includes a display fee (or utility cost) $\delta_d$, charged when the provider's item appears on a recommendation list, and a click fee $\delta_c$, charged when a consumer selects the provider's item. There is also utility associated with having one's item appear on a recommendation list, $\phi_d$, and having one's item clicked on, $\phi_c$. The total utility for provider $v$ relative to recommender $k$ is calculated as: $u_{v,k} = (\phi_d - \delta_d) \times n_{d,v,k} + (\phi_c - \delta_c) \times n_{c,v,k}$ where $n_{d,v,k}$ is the number of times that an item from provider $v$ has been displayed by recommender $k$ and $n_{c,v,k}$ is similar but for clicks.

**Recommender System Utility Model.** The utility accrued by each recommender algorithm is computed based on the fees assessed on providers. We do not focus on or report recommender system utility in this paper but we expect that, in a decoupled recommendation architecture, different recommendation platforms might have different business models and we plan to explore a diversity of such options in future work.

### 3.4 Dataset

We chose to anchor our simulated results on data from a real-world dataset, the well-known MovieLens 100k dataset [15]. The items are movies and the features for each movie are the movie's associated genre labels.

We sampled 600 users from the dataset as our consumers and, calculated consumer preference vectors based on the frequency of genres in their preferred items. However, to highlight the concept of *niche consumers* and *niche items*, we manipulated these profiles as follows. We selected the *Western* genre, one of the genres less prevalent in the dataset, as our niche genre. For the 10% of users with an affinity for this genre, we enhanced their affinity by multiplying the *Western* feature by 4, while reducing the features for other genres proportionately. We did the opposite for our *mainstream* users, shrinking their interest in the *Western* genre by a factor of 1/4.

### 3.5 Providers

We generated 10 providers: nine of these providers each offered a random, equal sample of items (n=100) to ensure that our focus remained on the impact of content type rather than quantity. The tenth provider specialized exclusively in the niche items, offering a collection comprised of movies from the *Western* genre.

## 3.6   Recommenders

We implemented a content-based *Mainstream* recommender. The recommender uses a naive Bayes model to update consumer preferences over genres based on clicks and then populates the recommendation list with the most popular movies of these genres. To explore outside of the most popular movies of these genres, the recommender uses an exploration probability (%20) to randomly select movies of the same genres the consumer historically interacted with to create their recommendation list. We plan to explore additional recommendation algorithms in future work, including collaborative techniques. The *Niche* recommender was implemented similarly, however, concentrating exclusively on the *Western* genre.

## 3.7   Experiments

We conducted three experiments using this simulation framework:

1. **Single recommender**: A single recommender (the *Mainstream* recommender) provides recommendations to all consumers: the standard monolithic design.
2. **Decoupled recommenders with threshold**: We introduce the *Niche* recommender in parallel with the *Mainstream* recommender; consumers switch between recommenders using the threshold criterion described above.
3. **Decoupled recommenders with UCB**: The same pair of recommenders as above provide recommendations, but the consumers use the upper confidence bound (UCB) criterion to decide between recommenders.

Other simulation parameters include: days per cycle, 30; cycles per experiment, 60; recommendation list size, 5; click utility ($\phi_c$), 0.4; display utility ($\phi_d$), 0.1; click fee ($\delta_c$), 0.1; display fee ($\delta_d$), 0.01; switching threshold ($\tau$), 0.04.

## 4   Results

### 4.1   Single Recommender Experiment

The results for the first experiment are shown in Fig. 3. The figures at the top provide two different representations of consumer utility, broken down by mainstream and niche consumers. The box plot on the left shows the distribution of utility during the *last day* of the last cycle, representing the final state of the simulation. We see that niche consumers have a much lower utility than the more mainstream consumers of the system. The figure at the right confirms this outcome over the course of the experiment. It shows the average consumer utility (cumulatively) for each type of consumer and again we see that mainstream consumers have much higher utility.

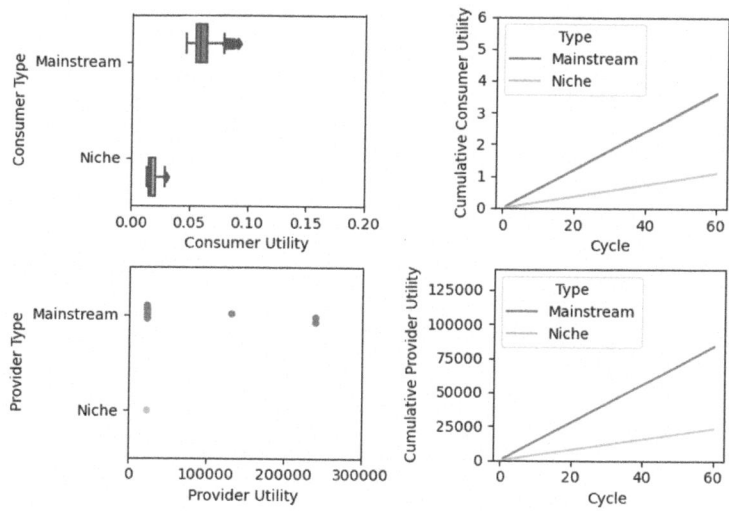

**Fig. 3.** Single recommender experiment: Consumer and provider utility, distribution and cumulative results. The top left box plot shows consumer utility on the last day, while the bottom left strip plot shows provider utility on the last day. The right column line plots depict cumulative consumer utility and provider utility over all cycles.

For providers (lower part of the figure), the story is very similar. The single niche provider has much lower utility both at the end of the simulation snapshot and the cumulative plot.

## 4.2 Threshold-Based Switching Experiment

Figure 4 is in the same format as Fig. 3 but for the threshold-based switching experiment. At the start of the experiment, all consumers were initially connected to the *Mainstream* recommender. Consumers will switch between recommenders if their utility falls below the threshold $\tau = 0.04$ at the end of a cycle.

The decoupled recommender configuration provides an avenue for niche consumers dissatisfied with the *Mainstream* recommender. We see that the utilities are much improved for niche consumers and the mainstream consumers are relatively unaffected.

The story for providers is a bit different. We see more equity across the providers, but the mainstream providers lose utility because their items are not being forced on niche consumers who are not that interested in them, and now that the niche provider has an avenue to reach interested consumers, they can become one of the more profitable providers.

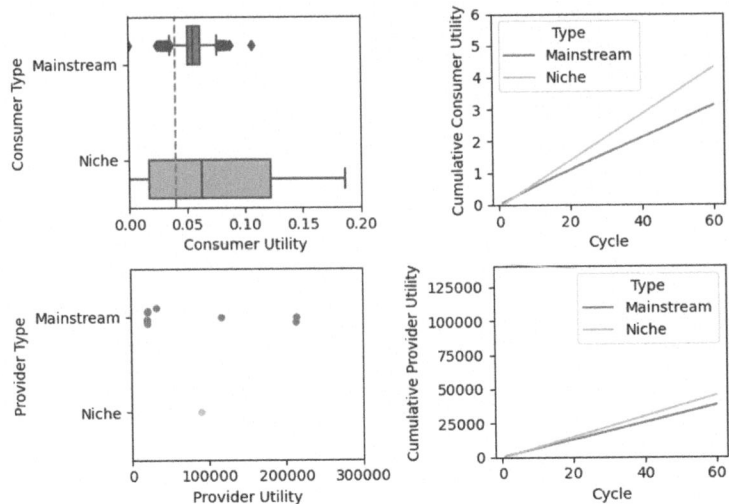

**Fig. 4.** Decoupled recommender with threshold-based switching experiment. The dashed line in the top left plot represents the switching threshold. The provider utility is the sum of the two recommenders' utility for that provider.

### 4.3  UCB Switching Experiment

The third experiment was very similar to the second but the switching criterion is based on the upper confidence bound (UCB) technique described in Sect. 3.2. This technique allows consumers to select the best model for them, based on their own experiences, rather than having to wait until their experience is so bad that it hits the threshold before switching.

The results from this experiment are shown in Fig. 5 and are similar to the threshold-based switching experiment results for user utility. A bigger difference is shown in the utility for the *Niche* provider. This is most likely because the exploration mechanism of UCB means that more *Mainstream* consumers end up in the *Niche* recommender for at least one cycle, and while there, are required to click on (and can *only* click on) the niche provider's items. We note that the cumulative utility curve becomes linear (and more like that of Experiment 2) after about 20 cycles. Presumably by this point, the exploration phase is more or less complete, *Mainstream* consumers stay where they are, and the *Niche* provider is receiving utility just based on Niche consumers' clicks.

### 4.4  Comparing Experiment Results

To further validate our results and provide a contrast between the three experimental conditions, we ran our three experiments on five random seeds and recorded the mean per-day utilities for the niche and the mainstream consumers and for the niche and mainstream providers. See Fig. 6. As the individual experiment results have indicated, niche consumer utility is greatly enhanced by the

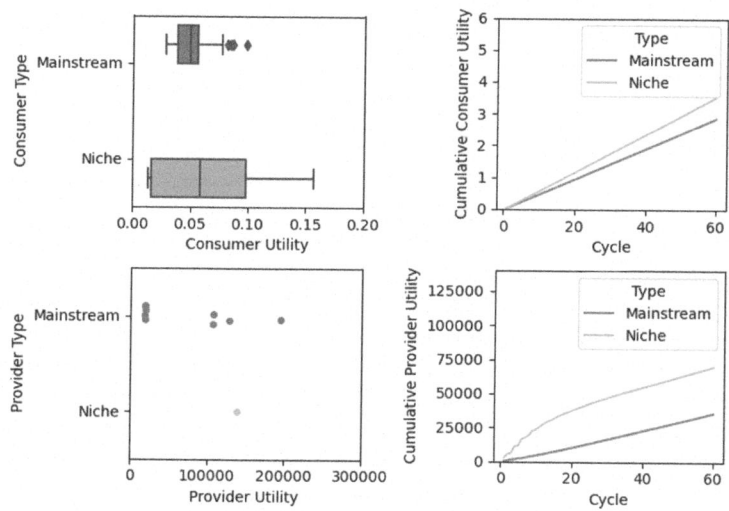

**Fig. 5.** Decoupled recommender with UCB-based switching.

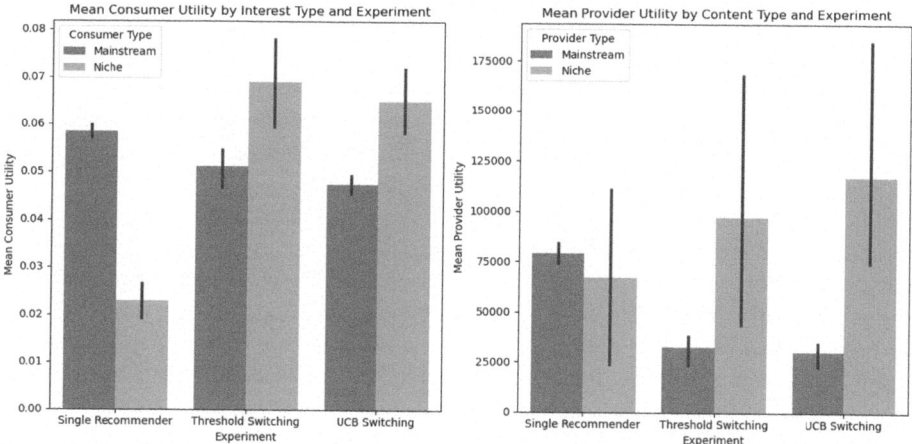

**Fig. 6.** Mean utility scores on the last day for five random seeds of the three experiments for providers and consumers.

decoupled design, and the type of switching criteria (threshold-based or UCB-based) makes little difference. The mainstream consumers do see a bit of utility loss under these conditions, probably because they switch to the niche recommender and do not get good results.

The provider story is different. Niche providers gain in the decoupled environment but within the variability of the simulation, it is hard to say how significant this increase is in general. The mainstream providers do lose out because they have fewer captive consumers than in the monolithic case. We expect this difference to be reduced if consumers could opt out of clicking when presented with low-utility items.

## 5    Conclusion

In this paper, we use our recommender ecosystem simulation SMORES to study the concept of *decoupled recommendation*, where recommender algorithms compete for recommendation consumers. We confirm findings from prior ecosystem work, which show that niche consumers and niche providers tend to do poorly in monolithic systems. The decoupled alternative is better for both providers and consumers but is particularly beneficial for niche consumers with marginal costs for mainstream consumers. This work therefore lends support to calls made in policy and governance circles that envision an algorithm marketplace, allowing consumers to choose algorithms to be applied to the platforms that they use.

The work described here represents an initial exploration of this concept with a great deal of additional study that can be performed. We have constructed an artificial setting where niche consumers are quite selective of and mainstream consumers are quite averse to niche items. Also, there is only one niche genre and only one recommender alternative. We expect to relax these assumptions in future work. We have only explored a content-based mainstream recommender and a niche-specific recommender, but there is room to explore additional designs including collaborative recommendation. We are also interested in exploring how robust our findings are relative to changes in the selection models and utility models.

There are many directions in which to explore different algorithmic utility models. In our current model, the recommenders are free to consumers and provider-supported but all providers are associated with all recommenders. We do not currently model the interaction between the item catalog platform and the recommenders or the variety of business models that recommenders might pursue. This is an important avenue to consider if such decoupled recommender system architectures are to be implemented and supported.

## References

1. Abdollahpouri, H.: Popularity bias in ranking and recommendation. In: Proceedings of the 2019 AAAI/ACM Conference on AI, Ethics, and Society, AIES 2019, pp. 529–530. Association for Computing Machinery (2019). https://doi.org/10.1145/3306618.3314309
2. Abdollahpouri, H., et al.: Multistakeholder recommendation: survey and research directions. User Model. User-Adapted Interact. **30**(1), 127–158 (2020). https://doi.org/10.1007/s11257-019-09256-1
3. Abdollahpouri, H., Burke, R.: Multi-stakeholder recommendation and its connection to multi-sided fairness, 30 July 2019. https://doi.org/10.48550/arXiv.1907.13158

4. Abdollahpouri, H., Mansoury, M., Burke, R., Mobasher, B.: The unfairness of popularity bias in recommendation, 19 September 2019. http://arxiv.org/abs/1907.13286
5. Alvarez De La Vega, J., Cecchinato, M., Rooksby, J.: 'Why lose control?' a study of freelancers' experiences with gig economy platforms. In: Kitamura, Y., Quigley, A., Isbister, K., Igarashi, T., Bjørn, P., Drucker, S. (eds.) Proceedings of the 2021 CHI Conference on Human Factors in Computing Systems, p. 455. ACM, New York (2021). https://doi.org/10.1145/3411764.3445305
6. Burke, R.: Multisided fairness for recommendation. In: 2017 Workshop on Fairness, Accountability and Transparency in Machine Learning (FAT/ML 2017) (2017)
7. Bustamante, P., et al.: On the governance of federated platforms. SSRN Scholarly Paper, August 2023. https://doi.org/10.2139/ssrn.4528712
8. Chand, R.-N., Michael, S., Ethan, Z.: The three-legged stool: a manifesto for a smaller, denser internet, 29 March 2023. https://publicinfrastructure.org/2023/03/29/the-three-legged-stool/
9. Choi, Y., Kang, E.J., Lee, M.K., Kim, J.: Creator-friendly algorithms: behaviors, challenges, and design opportunities in algorithmic platforms. In: Proceedings of the 2023 CHI Conference on Human Factors in Computing Systems, pp. 1–22 (2023)
10. Dalal, S., Chiem, N., Karbassi, N., Liu, Y., Monroy-Hernández, A.: Understanding human intervention in the platform economy: a case study of an indie food delivery service. In: Proceedings of the 2023 CHI Conference on Human Factors in Computing Systems, pp. 1–16. ACM, Hamburg, Germany (2023). https://doi.org/10.1145/3544548.3581517
11. Fukuyama, F., Richman, B., Goel, A.: How to save democracy from technology: ending big tech's information monopoly. Foreign Aff. **100**, 98 (2021)
12. Gillespie, T.: Do not recommend? reduction as a form of content moderation. Social Media + Society **8**(3), 20563051221117552 (2022). https://doi.org/10.1177/20563051221117552
13. Gope, J., Jain, S.K.: A survey on solving cold start problem in recommender systems. In: 2017 International Conference on Computing, Communication and Automation (ICCCA), pp. 133–138 (2017). https://doi.org/10.1109/CCAA.2017.8229786
14. Haimson, O.L., Delmonaco, D., Nie, P., Wegner, A.: Disproportionate removals and differing content moderation experiences for conservative, transgender, and black social media users: marginalization and moderation gray areas. Proc. ACM Hum.-Comput. Interact. **5**(CSCW2), 1–35 (2021). https://doi.org/10.1145/3479610
15. Harper, F.M., Konstan, J.A.: The Movielens datasets: history and context. ACM Trans. Interact. Intell. Syst. **5**(4), 1–19 (2015)
16. Ie, E., et al.: Recsim: a configurable simulation platform for recommender systems. arXiv, September 2019. http://arxiv.org/abs/1909.04847
17. Kingsley, S., Sinha, P., Wang, C., Eslami, M., Hong, J.I.: 'give everybody [..] a little bit more equity': content creator perspectives and responses to the algorithmic demonetization of content associated with disadvantaged groups. Proc. ACM Hum.-Comput. Interact. **6**(CSCW2), 1–37 (2022). https://doi.org/10.1145/3555149
18. La Cava, L., Greco, S., Tagarelli, A.: Understanding the growth of the fediverse through the lens of mastodon. Appl. Netw. Sci. **6**(1), 64 (2021). https://doi.org/10.1007/s41109-021-00392-5

19. Ranjbar Kermany, N., Zhao, W., Yang, J., Wu, J., Pizzato, L.: A fairness-aware multi-stakeholder recommender system. World Wide Web **24**(6), 1995–2018 (2021). https://doi.org/10.1007/s11280-021-00946-8

20. Ruffo, G., Schifanella, R.: A peer-to-peer recommender system based on spontaneous affinities. ACM Trans. Internet Technol. (TOIT) **9**(1), 1–34 (2009)

21. Slivkins, A., et al.: Introduction to multi-armed bandits. Found. Trends® Mach. Learn. **12**(1-2), 1–286 (2019)

22. Smith, J.J., et al.: The many faces of fairness: exploring the institutional logics of multistakeholder microlending recommendation. In: Proceedings of the 2023 ACM Conference on Fairness, Accountability, and Transparency, FAccT 2023, pp. 1652–1663. Association for Computing Machinery (2023). https://doi.org/10.1145/3593013.3594106

23. Wu, H., Ma, C., Mitra, B., Diaz, F., Liu, X.: A multi-objective optimization framework for multi-stakeholder fairness-aware recommendation. ACM Trans. Inf. Syst. **41**(2), 47:1–47:29 (2022). https://doi.org/10.1145/3564285

24. Yao, F., Li, C., Nekipelov, D., Wang, H., Xu, H.: How bad is top-$k$ recommendation under competing content creators? In: International Conference on Machine Learning, pp. 39674–39701. PMLR (2023)

# Enhancing Tourism Recommender Systems for Sustainable City Trips Using Retrieval-Augmented Generation

Ashmi Banerjee(✉), Adithi Satish, and Wolfgang Wörndl

Technical University of Munich, Munich, Germany
{ashmi.banerjee,adithi.satish}@tum.de, woerndl@in.tum.de

**Abstract.** Tourism Recommender Systems (TRS) have traditionally focused on providing personalized travel suggestions, often prioritizing user preferences without considering broader sustainability goals. Integrating sustainability into TRS has become essential with the increasing need to balance environmental impact, local community interests, and visitor satisfaction. This paper proposes a novel approach to enhancing TRS for sustainable city trips using Large Language Models (LLMs) and a modified Retrieval-Augmented Generation (RAG) pipeline. We enhance the traditional RAG system by incorporating a sustainability metric based on a city's popularity and seasonal demand during the prompt augmentation phase. This modification, called Sustainability Augmented Reranking (SAR), ensures the system's recommendations align with sustainability goals. Evaluations using popular open-source LLMs, such as *Llama-3.1-Instruct-8B* and *Mistral-Instruct-7B*, demonstrate that the SAR-enhanced approach consistently matches or outperforms the baseline (without SAR) across most metrics, highlighting the benefits of incorporating sustainability into TRS.

**Keywords:** Tourism Recommender Systems · Sustainability · Retrieval-Augmented Generation · Large Language Models

## 1 Introduction

Tourism Recommender Systems (TRS) have been widely used to assist travelers by providing personalized suggestions for accommodations, activities, destinations, and more [25]. Previously, these systems have largely been centered around the user's perspective, with their needs being the only criteria for their evaluation. However, in recent times, they have evolved into platforms that must balance the interests of multiple stakeholders, creating a multistakeholder environment [2]. Tourism has far-reaching effects beyond its direct stakeholders, impacting the environment, local businesses, and residents. Thus, a TRS should incorporate sustainable options and practices to address these diverse effects

---

A. Banerjee and A. Satish—These authors contributed equally.

L. Boratto et al. (Eds.): RecSoGood 2024, CCIS 2470, pp. 19–34, 2025.
https://doi.org/10.1007/978-3-031-87654-7_3

and promote responsible tourism. This is particularly important in this domain, as it faces unique challenges such as seasonality, travel regulations, and limited resources like airline tickets and hotel availability [6].

The United Nations World Tourism Organization defines sustainable tourism as *"tourism that takes full account of its current and future economic, social and environmental impacts, addressing the needs of visitors, the industry, the environment, and host communities"* [21]. The significance of sustainable tourism development has become increasingly evident, especially with the growing threat of climate change [4,12,37,55], emphasizing the need to integrate sustainability into TRS. Although much work has been exploring the multistakeholder nature of TRS [46,50,57,60], work focusing on generating sustainable recommendations is limited [8].

Recent studies have increasingly explored the potential of Large Language Models (LLMs) to provide personalized user recommendations [14,36]. However, given the dynamic nature of tourism data, a TRS using LLM must adapt to frequent updates and changes. Fine-tuning LLMs to address these changes is unfeasible and resource-intensive due to the substantial computational costs and time needed for each update [47]. Moreover, LLMs are prone to hallucinations, where they provide answers that contradict real-world knowledge or are irrelevant to user prompts [27,64]. One effective way to address these challenges, is to implement a Retrieval-Augmented Generation (RAG) pipeline, which has proven successful in dynamic content scenarios [16,17]. This approach enhances LLMs by integrating additional information from external databases [30].

This paper proposes a novel way to generate sustainable recommendations by leveraging LLMs using RAG. We aim to recommend sustainable European cities based on natural language user queries on vacation planning. To achieve this, we create a knowledge base of tourism information for 160 European cities, covering attractions, hotels, and restaurants. We refine the traditional RAG system by incorporating a sustainability metric based on a city's popularity and seasonal demand during the prompt augmentation phase. This enhancement, termed Sustainability Augmented Reranking (SAR), ensures that recommendations prioritize sustainability. We evaluate our system with and without the SAR enhancement using two popular open-source LLMs, *Llama-3.1-Instruct-8B* and *Mistral-Instruct-7B*. Results show that SAR consistently matches or outperforms the baseline across most metrics, underscoring the efficacy of integrating sustainability into TRS. Our approach helps mitigate hallucinations and allows for a multi-stakeholder perspective in recommendations, balancing user preferences with sustainability principles.

This paper is organized as follows: Sect. 2 reviews the related work, Sect. 3 describes our approach, Sect. 4 presents the results of our evaluation, comparing our method with and without the SAR enhancement using *Llama-3.1-Instruct-8B* and *Mistral-Instruct-7B*, and Sect. 5 concludes the paper by summarizing the key findings and suggesting directions for future research.

# 2    Related Work

In the tourism domain, research on recommender systems is primarily centred around the user's perspective, with their historical preferences used in tour recommendation and their subsequent evaluation. User attributes like location history, geo-tagged photographs, and check-in behavior have previously been used to identify Points of Interest (POIs) that align with user interests [13, 33, 34, 38, 40, 51]. This section surveys the existing work across Retrieval-Augmented LLMs for Recommender Systems and Sustainable TRS.

## 2.1    Retrieval-Augmented LLMs for Recommender Systems

A new tangent of research in recommender systems has emerged over the past decade, which involves utilizing the generation and reasoning capability of LLMs to provide recommendations [1, 11, 15, 26, 35, 65]. In tourism, fine-tuning remains the primary approach to enable LLMs to generate personalized recommendations that cater to the end-user's preferences [31, 56].

To address the challenge of hallucinations in LLMs, recent studies focus on augmenting LLMs with the retrieved user history and find that this combination of retrieval and text generation shows comparable performance with multiple baselines [16, 20]. This approach of using the RAG architecture to enrich LLM prompts with user-item information enhances the LLM's reasoning and conversational abilities, improving the quality and veracity of its recommendations by providing suitable explanations from the context [39, 54, 59].

## 2.2    Sustainable Tourism Recommender Systems

Findings by Banerjee et al. [8] reveal the recent emergence of a promising dimension of research that considers Society or the environment as one of the stakeholders in the recommendation process. For example, Merinov [41] incorporates sustainability into a multistakeholder recommender system by modeling an objective to rearrange tourist flows to prevent overcrowding. Other sustainability objectives considered in prior work include economic sustainability [43], food security [42], air pollution [23], eco-friendly accommodations [24], and carbon emissions of different modes of transportation [9].

In contrast to this state-of-the-art research in sustainable TRS, which predominantly involves formulating different sustainability objectives, the novelty of our research lies in taking advantage of the inherent abilities of LLMs to process textual information and generate explanations for each recommended destination. This allows us to simultaneously consider the user's preferences and ensure that sustainability objectives are met.

# 3   Approach

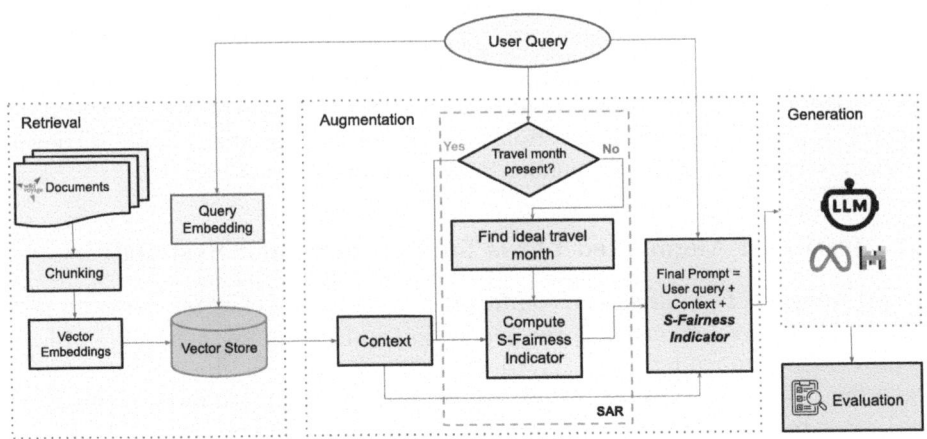

**Fig. 1.** Pipeline of our proposed modified RAG system. The green dotted box shows the modified augmentation phase with the addition of the sustainability metric. (Color figure online)

We assume users visit our system seeking recommendations for European cities to travel to for vacation. To effectively meet their needs, it is essential to implement a TRS that can adapt to the dynamic nature of tourism data, accommodating frequent updates and changes [2,6]. Continuously fine-tuning an LLM for these changes is not feasible, as it is inefficient and expensive to re-train the model every time the information is updated [47]. Therefore, we opt to use a modified Retrieval-Augmented Generation (RAG) pipeline as it demonstrates promising results in scenarios with frequently changing content [16].

Typically, a naive RAG system comprises of three main phases—information Retrieval, prompt Augmentation, and Generation [30]. We modify the conventional naive RAG system by incorporating a sustainability metric (S-Fairness indicator) based on the popularity and the monthly seasonal demand of the city to re-rank the retrieved context during the prompt augmentation phase [9]. This enhancement, termed Sustainability Augmented Reranking (SAR), ensures that the generated results prioritize sustainability considerations. While Fig. 1 visually represents our system's workflow, the subsequent sections offer a detailed explanation of this process.

## 3.1   Data Preparation

For our knowledge base, we use data from Wikivoyage[1], an online travel guide offering detailed information on travel destinations. Each city on Wikivoyage has

---

[1] https://www.wikivoyage.org/.

a dedicated article with extensive details on transportation, weather, and tourist attractions, organized into various headings and subheadings. We specifically utilize two datasets from Wikivoyage: the *Articles* and *Listings* datasets.

The *Articles*[2] dataset consists of XML files containing the full text of articles for various cities on Wikivoyage. It provides a broad textual overview of each city, highlighting key tourist-related information and city characteristics. For instance, Fig. 2a presents a word cloud of the most common terms in the Paris article from our dataset. Frequent terms such as "train," "price," "ticket," "hours," "directions," "louvre," "eiffel tower", "notre dame", and "museum" highlight the essential tourist details and reflect the city's unique features.

The *Listings*[3] dataset, on the other hand, offers detailed descriptions of POIs, accommodations, and dining options. For our study, we focus on European cities, selecting a curated list of 160 cities across 41 countries from this dataset. As illustrated in Fig. 2b, the top 10 clusters generated using BERTopic [22] encompass a diverse range of POI categories, including culture, religion, natural landscapes, and wildlife from the *Listings* dataset.

Together, these datasets provide a comprehensive textual landscape of travel destinations by combining general overviews with more detailed information about the cities.

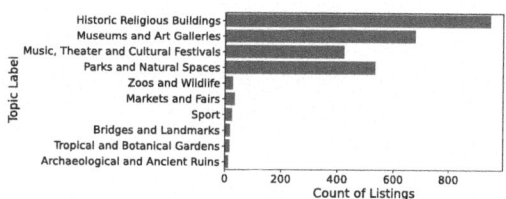

(a) Wordcloud of the Wikivoyage Article page for Paris

(b) Counts of the Topic Clusters of POIs in the Wikivoyage Listings dataset

**Fig. 2.** Exploratory Data Analysis for Wikivoyage Articles and Listings

To calculate the popularity and seasonality indices for the sustainability metric, described in Sect. 3.3, we use data from Tripadvisor API[4] to determine the aggregated number of POIs in each of the 160 cities. Monthly visitor footfall data is based on publicly available information from the https://www.whereandwhen.net/ website. These counts are then normalized on a scale from 0 to 1 using Min-Max normalization technique [44] to establish each city's relative popularity and seasonality.

In our data, London ranks highest in popularity, followed by Paris, Rome, and Barcelona. The overall trend in seasonality indicates that most European

---

[2] https://dumps.wikimedia.org/enwikivoyage.

[3] https://github.com/baturin/wikivoyage-listings.

[4] https://tripadvisor-content-api.readme.io/reference/overview.

cities experience high footfall during the summer months, although some cities exhibit specific spikes at particular times. For instance, Munich shows a significant increase in visitor counts in September, coinciding with Oktoberfest. Conversely, Brussels, a city with many business travelers [49], has low seasonality indices during the summer months (May-August), a period typically associated with vacation in Europe.

## 3.2 Information Retrieval

The Information Retrieval phase in a RAG system involves extracting data from a large repository and storing it as embeddings in a vector database to provide context for generating accurate responses. In this paper, we utilize LanceDB[5], an open-source vector database, to store these embeddings and compute similarities during retrieval. To efficiently manage document storage and ensure the retrieved context fits within the LLM's context window, we chunk Wikivoyage documents by subheadings, dividing them into smaller, logically coherent pieces to enhance retrieval and maintain contextual relevance [61].

To compute embeddings, we utilize the `all-MiniLM-L6-V2` model[6], which leverages the pre-trained MiniLM model to map text into a 384-dimensional dense vector space [53]. Using this model, we generate embeddings for the chunked documents and transform the user query from natural language into embeddings. Cosine similarity [58] is then used to measure the similarity between the query embedding and the embeddings of the chunked documents. The top ten most similar cities with their respective chunks, which serve as the context, are subsequently returned.

## 3.3 Sustainability Augmented Reranking (SAR)

After retrieving the context, the next step involves augmenting the user query with this context. The novelty in our approach lies in incorporating sustainability considerations during this phase. The sustainability of a destination is represented by its S-Fairness, or Societal Fairness, which reflects the equitable distribution of tourism's benefits and impacts on the non-participating stakeholders (Society) such as environment, residents and local businesses, involved in the recommendation process [7].

To compute this metric, we use a simplified approach based on a normalized weighted combination of popularity and seasonality indices for each destination and travel month, based on our prior work [9]. We adapt the equation for calculating the sustainability metric $\psi(c_i^j)$, or S-Fairness indicator, for a destination city $c_i$ in month $j$ as the following:

$$\psi(c_i^j) = 0.334 \cdot \rho(c_i) + 0.385 \cdot \sigma(c_i^j) \tag{1}$$

---

[5] https://lancedb.github.io/lancedb/.
[6] https://huggingface.co/sentence-transformers/all-MiniLM-L6-v2.

where $\rho(c_i)$ indicates the popularity and $\sigma(c_i^j)$ seasonality indices, respectively. The weight coefficients are derived from the original work [9], where we conducted a user survey to assess the importance of various factors influencing travel destination choices. A lower $\psi(c_i^j)$ value indicates a more sustainable option for the given month. If the user does not specify a travel month, we calculate the S-Fairness indicator for the month with the lowest seasonality index for each destination retrieved in the context, and recommend that month as the ideal time to visit.

---

**System Prompt for Augmentation**

You are an AI recommendation system.
Your task is to recommend European cities for travel based on the user's question. You should use the provided contexts to suggest the city best suited to the user's question.
You recommend a list of the top three most sustainable cities to the user and the best month of travel. If the user has already provided the month of travel in the question, use the same month; otherwise, provide the ideal month.
A sustainable city is defined as a city with low overall popularity and low footfall for the intended month of travel. Each recommendation should also explain why it is being recommended on sustainability grounds. The context contains a sustainability score for each city, also known as the S-Fairness indicator, along with the ideal month of travel. A lower S-Fairness value indicates that the city is a better destination for the month provided. A city without a sustainability score should not be considered. You should only consider the S-Fairness indicator values while choosing the best city. However, your answer should not contain the numeric score itself.
Your answer must begin with "I recommend, " followed by the city name and why you recommended it. Your answers are correct, high-quality, and written by a domain expert. If the provided context does not contain the answer, state, "The provided context does not have the answer."

---

**Fig. 3.** System prompt used for augmentation. The text in Sepia represents the default prompt (without sustainability scoring information), and the text in green represents the additional sustainability information to include SAR.

Thus, the S-Fairness indicator aims to recommend more sustainable cities by considering their popularity and monthly visitor counts, thereby balancing tourist flow throughout the year and addressing issues of over- and under-tourism. This paper focuses exclusively on the impact of popularity and seasonality on sustainability, in contrast to the original model, which also accounted for emissions from travel to the destination. This adjustment was made due to challenges in interpreting natural language queries to determine users' starting points and the limited availability of relevant data on public transport. However, the coefficients from the original model are retained as they were normalized in the initial equation.

We define a city's popularity by the number of POIs it has normalized between 0 and 1 across all cities, while seasonality refers to the normalized monthly footfall for the city. Although the popularity index provides a general measure, it may not reflect unique characteristics or visitor trends in specific months. Therefore, with its monthly granularity, the seasonality index offers a more accurate depiction of crowd levels, ensuring that recommendations include less popular yet appealing and less crowded destinations [9].

Once the sustainability data is added to the context, we instruct the LLM to balance user preferences (as outlined in the query) with sustainability concerns. We aim to determine whether including explicit sustainability information in the context and prompt leads to more sustainable recommendations than when the LLM provides recommendations without explicit sustainability scores. We use two prompts to achieve this: one with explicit sustainability information (SAR) and one without (baseline). We employ a "role-playing" prompting technique [29], where the system describes the role and responsibilities of the LLM, along with the user query and retrieved context. Figure 3 illustrates the prompts used for both scenarios. For the SAR prompt, explicit sustainability information is included, as shown in Fig. 3 in green, whereas the baseline prompt omits this information. By comparing the outcomes from these two prompts, we aim to assess the impact of incorporating explicit sustainability information on the quality and sustainability of the recommendations provided by the LLM.

### 3.4 Response Generation

The final stage of a RAG pipeline involves response generation by the LLM, which uses the augmented prompt with the retrieved context to produce an output. Here, the LLM performs two tasks—selecting the three most suitable and sustainable cities based on the user query and generating an appropriate response using the provided context. It functions as a mediator in a multistakeholder scenario, balancing user preferences with sustainability concerns in its responses. Furthermore, we instruct the LLM to explain each city chosen in its recommendation. This capability of LLMs to generate human-like explanations improves the overall quality and transparency of the recommendations compared to more traditional methods. Finally, to evaluate this pipeline, we conduct a comparative analysis of the answer generation using two different open-source instruction-tuned LLMs, *Llama-3.1-Instruct-8B* and *Mistral-Instruct-7B*, as described in Sect. 4, for both the SAR and baseline scenarios.

# 4    Evaluation

In this section, we evaluate the effectiveness of our proposed approach by comparing it against a baseline method, i.e., without the SAR enhancement. We utilize two popular open-source instruction-tuned LLMs—*Llama-3.1-Instruct-8B* [18] and *Mistral-Instruct-7B* [28] to conduct this comparison, aiming to assess the impact of incorporating SAR on the quality of the generated recommendations. Section 4.1 describes our experimental setup, including the use of other LLMs to generate synthetic test cases for evaluation. In Sect. 4.2, we discuss the different metrics used for evaluation and present the corresponding results.

## 4.1    Setup: Synthetic Test Case Generation

To effectively evaluate the pipeline, a diverse set of test queries reflecting various user preferences is essential, and recent research suggests using LLMs to create synthetic test data for different domains [10,32], including recommender systems [45]. We use state-of-the-art LLMs, including GPT-4 [3] and Gemini-1.5-Pro [48], to generate 200 diverse test queries about European travel destinations for different months and seasons, such as recommending winter destinations for hiking and skiing. Each of the 200 queries is passed to both models twice — once using the basic system prompt (baseline) and once with the sustainability prompt and S-Fairness indicators (SAR), as illustrated in Fig. 3. This results in a total of 800 responses for analysis.

As evident from Fig. 4, we can see a sample generated test prompt using GPT-4 and the corresponding responses for both baseline and SAR using *Llama-3.1-Instruct-8B*. The top recommendation for SAR, Strasbourg, has the lowest S-Fairness indicator among the ten retrieved cities, indicating that the model effectively balances user preferences with sustainability concerns.

## 4.2    Evaluation Metrics

Since RAG systems often consist of multiple independent components, evaluating the system can be challenging, as different phases need to be evaluated. For the scope of this paper, we only consider the final LLM-generated response for both baseline and SAR for evaluation. Our metrics are inspired by the RAGAS framework proposed by Es et al. [19]. The research questions we aim to address through our evaluation, along with their updated results after further optimization (as presented in Table 1), are discussed in the following subsections.

**Answer Relevance.** Answer Relevance measures how well the LLM-generated response answers the question [19]. In situations where manual evaluation is infeasible, LLMs have previously been shown to perform remarkably well in judging answers in a human way when provided with a suitable grading scheme [52,66].

---

**Example Prompt and Model Response**

**Prompt:**
*I'm interested in culture and architecture; suggest cities in Europe for a trip in autumn.*

**Baseline:**
1. I recommend Sibiu, Romania. I recommend Sibiu, Romania because it is a city rich in history and culture. The city has a well-preserved medieval old town with narrow streets and colorful buildings, which is perfect for exploring. The city also has a strong cultural identity, with many festivals and events throughout the year, including the famous Sibiu International Theatre Festival.
...

**SAR:**
I recommend Strasbourg, Sibiu, and Plovdiv. I recommend these cities because they have lower s-fairness scores, which indicates that they are more sustainable options for travel in November. Strasbourg is a historic city with a well-preserved city centre that is a UNESCO World Heritage Site. Sibiu is a charming city with a rich cultural heritage, featuring a mix of Gothic and Romanesque architecture. Plovdiv is a vibrant city with a rich history, offering a glimpse into Bulgaria's past. All three cities offer a unique cultural experience, and their lower s-fairness scores make them more sustainable options for travel in November.

---

**Fig. 4.** Example of a prompt generated by *GPT-4o-mini* and responses generated by *Llama-3.1-Instruct-8B*. The response contains the top choice recommended by the model for the **baseline** and SAR. The top recommendation for SAR, Strasbourg, has the lowest S-Fairness indicator among the ten retrieved cities, indicating that the model effectively balances user preferences with sustainability concerns.

**Table 1.** Table comparing the performance of the *Llama-3.1-Instruct-8B* and *Mistral-Instruct-7B* models across 200 prompts, evaluating both baseline and SAR scenarios using different metrics.

| Models | Method | Evaluation Metrics | | | | |
|---|---|---|---|---|---|---|
| | | Relevance | | Sustainability (%) | | Faithfulness (%) |
| | | *GPT-4o-mini* | *Claude-3-5-sonnet* | Accuracy | Frequency | |
| *Llama-3.1-Instruct-8B* | Baseline | $8.16_{\pm 1.78}$ | $6.29_{\pm 2.27}$ | – | – | 0 |
| | SAR | $7.69_{\pm 1.73}$ | $5.50_{\pm 2.29}$ | 10.5 | 42.5 | 0 |
| *Mistral-Instruct-7B* | Baseline | $3.85_{\pm 2.72}$ | $3.05_{\pm 2.45}$ | – | – | 14.0 |
| | SAR | $3.96_{\pm 2.65}$ | $2.97_{\pm 2.35}$ | 7.5 | 36.5 | 9.5 |

We employ two LLMs to judge Answer Relevance—*GPT-4o-mini* [3] and *Claude-3-5-sonnet* [5] by instructing them to grade the answer on a scale of 0–10, where 0 means that the answer is completely irrelevant and 10 implies that the answer is relevant and completely answers the question[7]. We compute the mean and standard deviation (indicated by the $\pm_{values}$) for both *Llama-3.1-Instruct-8B* and *Mistral-Instruct-7B* for the baseline and SAR, as shown in Table 1.

Responses generated by *Llama-3.1-Instruct-8B* have higher average scores than those generated by *Mistral-Instruct-7B*, regardless of the judge, indicating *Mistral-Instruct-7B* often struggles to provide answers of high quality. Furthermore, our observations reveal that the average scores exhibit consistency upon incorporating SAR, maintaining similar levels as before its inclusion. Notably, when evaluating *Mistral-Instruct-7B* alongside *GPT-4o-mini*, for SAR, there is even a marginal improvement in the average scores. This suggests that the introduction of SAR preserves the overall quality and relevance of the answers to the question while taking into consideration sustainability during response generation.

**Sustainability.** As discussed in Sect. 3.3, the main goal of SAR is to help models consider the societal impact of recommended cities during the reranking process. For our evaluation, we focus on the S-Fairness ranks of the retrieved cities, where a better rank indicates a lower S-Fairness indicator value. To extract the list of recommended cities, we tokenize the generated response and then compare it with the list of retrieved cities from the context. We measure the *accuracy* of our methodology by measuring how often each model selects the city with the lowest sustainability score as its top choice. Our results, as described under "Sustainability" in Table 1, show that *Llama-3.1-Instruct-8B* recommends the most sustainable city as a top candidate 10.5% of the time, compared to *Mistral-Instruct-7B* at 7.5%.

Since SAR instructs the LLMs to rerank the retrieved context and select the top 3 cities, we also measure the *frequency* with which the model's top choice is the most sustainable among the recommended cities. This approach helps us account for scenarios where cities more aligned with user preferences may not be the most sustainable but ensures sustainability is still a factor in ranking the top choices. Here, the results are more favorable for both *Llama-3.1-Instruct-8B* and *Mistral-Instruct-7B*, with the top choice having the lowest relative S-Fairness rank 42.5% and 36.5% of the time, respectively. This suggests that while the models may not always prioritize the most sustainable cities, sustainability still plays a significant role in their reranking process.

**Model Agreement and Faithfulness.** We also investigate whether the models agree in their responses when given the same prompts and context. Our analysis shows that the overall agreement between the baseline models is low,

---

[7] https://huggingface.co/learn/cookbook/en/llm_judge.

with both models recommending the same set of cities only 4% of the time. However, the partial agreement is significantly higher, at 49%, indicating that the models recommend at least one common city almost half the time.

Furthermore, we observe an increase in partial agreement (60.5%) when SAR is included in the prompt. The S-Fairness indicator introduced by SAR encourages the models to consider cities with the lowest scores, which may lead to more frequent alignment in their recommendations compared to the baseline method. However, the total agreement decreases upon including SAR (1%).

Evaluating the faithfulness of LLM-generated text has largely relied on the availability of reference answers that can be compared with the candidates to compute similarity or conditional probability-based metrics [62,63]. However, in the context of RAG, faithfulness can be defined in terms of the generated answer and the retrieved context [19]. We compute the faithfulness by counting the prompts with out-of-context (OC) responses, which indicate complete model hallucination.

Our results, listed under "Faithfulness" in Table 1 show that *Llama-3.1-Instruct-8B* performs exceptionally well, with no OC responses in the baseline model, outperforming *Mistral-Instruct-7B*, which hallucinates 14% of the time. Introducing SAR reduces hallucinations in *Mistral-Instruct-7B* to 9.5%, further supporting its effectiveness. With *Llama-3.1-Instruct-8B*, neither the baseline nor the SAR-enabled models recommend any OC responses.

## 5    Conclusion and Future Work

This paper presents a novel approach to enhancing TRS by incorporating sustainability metrics during the prompt augmentation phase of an RAG pipeline, ensuring that sustainability is prioritized in the recommendation process. Our findings using two popular open-source models—*Llama-3.1-Instruct-8B* and *Mistral-Instruct-7B* indicate that the addition of the Sustainability Augmented Reranking (SAR) generally matches or enhances model performance, without compromising answer quality.

Future research could further refine this approach by expanding the knowledge base to include more diverse, real-time datasets and exploring additional sustainability metrics, such as carbon footprint and local economic impact, to provide a more holistic assessment of sustainable travel recommendations. Examining the effects of various prompts and incorporating popularity and seasonality indices into the context, or using S-Fairness ranks rather than absolute values, could provide valuable insights into LLM performance. Ranking sustainability during the retrieval phase may also enhance alignment with sustainability goals, ensuring that potential sustainable destinations are not overlooked.

Currently, there is no user information available, posing a cold-start problem. Future work could address this by developing a conversational recommender system that tailors recommendations based on user preferences and profiles. Moreover, response generation currently occurs in a zero-shot setting; future iterations might explore few-shot learning and in-context learning to improve recommendation relevance and alignment with sustainability goals. These refinements could potentially improve the effectiveness of LLMs in delivering recommendations that are both relevant and aligned with sustainability objectives.

# References

1. Abbasi-Moud, Z., Vahdat-Nejad, H., Sadri, J.: Tourism recommendation system based on semantic clustering and sentiment analysis. Expert Syst. Appl. **167**, 114324 (2021)
2. Abdollahpouri, H., et al.: Multistakeholder recommendation: survey and research directions. User Model. User-Adap. Inter. **30**(1), 127–158 (2020). https://doi.org/10.1007/s11257-019-09256-1
3. Achiam, J., et al.: Gpt-4 technical report. arXiv preprint arXiv:2303.08774 (2023)
4. Anne Hardy, R.J.S.B., Pearson, L.: Sustainable tourism: an overview of the concept and its position in relation to Conceptualisations of tourism. J. Sustain. Tourism **10**(6), 475–496 (2002). Publisher: Routledge _eprint: https://doi.org/10.1080/09669580208667183
5. Anthropic, A.: The claude 3 model family: Opus, sonnet, haiku. Claude-3 Model Card 1 (2024)
6. Balakrishnan, G., Wörndl, W.: Multistakeholder recommender systems in tourism. In: Proceeding of Workshop on Recommenders in Tourism (RecTour 2021) (2021)
7. Banerjee, A.: Fairness and sustainability in multistakeholder tourism recommender systems. In: Proceedings of the 31st ACM Conference on User Modeling, Adaptation and Personalization, UMAP 2023, pp. 274–279, New York, NY, USA. Association for Computing Machinery (2023)
8. Banerjee, A., Banik, P., Wörndl, W.: A review on individual and multistakeholder fairness in tourism recommender systems. Front. Big Data **6**, 1168692 (2023)
9. Banerjee, A., Mahmudov, T., Adler, E., Aisyah, F.N., Wörndl, W.: Modeling sustainable city trips: integrating CO2 emissions, popularity, and seasonality into tourism recommender systems (2024). arXiv:2403.18604 [cs]
10. Bao, J., et al.: A synthetic data generation framework for grounded dialogues. In: Proceedings of the 61st Annual Meeting of the Association for Computational Linguistics (Volume 1: Long Papers), pp. 10866–10882 (2023a)
11. Bao, K., Zhang, J., Zhang, Y., Wang, W., Feng, F., He, X.: Tallrec: an effective and efficient tuning framework to align large language model with recommendation. In: Proceedings of the 17th ACM Conference on Recommender Systems, pp. 1007–1014 (2023b)
12. Butler, R.W.: Sustainable tourism: a state-of-the-art review. Tour. Geogr. **1**(1), 7–25 (1999)
13. Cheng, A.-J., Chen, Y.-Y., Huang, Y.-T., Hsu, W.H., Liao, H.-Y.M.: Personalized travel recommendation by mining people attributes from community-contributed photos. In: Proceedings of the 19th ACM international conference on Multimedia, pp. 83–92 (2011)
14. Dai, S., et al.: Uncovering chatgpt's capabilities in recommender systems. In: Proceedings of the 17th ACM Conference on Recommender Systems, pp. 1126–1132 (2023a)
15. Dai, S., et al.: Uncovering ChatGPT's capabilities in recommender systems. In: Proceedings of the 17th ACM Conference on Recommender Systems, RecSys 2023, pp. 1126–1132, New York, NY, USA. Association for Computing Machinery (2023b)

16. Di Palma, D.: Retrieval-augmented recommender system: Enhancing recommender systems with large language models. In: Proceedings of the 17th ACM Conference on Recommender Systems, pp. 1369–1373 (2023)

17. Ding, H., Pang, L., Wei, Z., Shen, H., Cheng, X.: Retrieve Only When It Needs: adaptive retrieval augmentation for hallucination mitigation in large language models (2024). arXiv:2402.10612 [cs]

18. Dubey, A., et al.: The llama 3 herd of models. arXiv preprint arXiv:2407.21783 (2024)

19. Es, S., James, J., Espinosa-Anke, L., Schockaert, S.: Ragas: automated evaluation of retrieval augmented generation. arXiv preprint arXiv:2309.15217 (2023)

20. Gao, Y., Sheng, T., Xiang, Y., Xiong, Y., Wang, H., Zhang, J.: Chat-rec: towards interactive and explainable llms-augmented recommender system. arXiv preprint arXiv:2303.14524 (2023)

21. Gössling, S.: Tourism, information technologies and sustainability: an exploratory review. J. Sustain. Tour. **25**(7), 1024–1041 (2017)

22. Grootendorst, M.: Bertopic: neural topic modeling with a class-based tf-idf procedure. arXiv preprint arXiv:2203.05794 (2022)

23. Herzog, D., Sikander, S., Wörndl, W.: Integrating route attractiveness attributes into tourist trip recommendations. In: Companion Proceedings of The 2019 World Wide Web Conference, pp. 96–101 (2019)

24. Hoffmann, F.J., Braesemann, F., Teubner, T.: Measuring sustainable tourism with online platform data. EPJ Data Sci. **11**(1), 41 (2022)

25. Isinkaye, F., Folajimi, Y., Ojokoh, B.: Recommendation systems: principles, methods and evaluation. Egyptian Inf. J. **16**(3), 261–273 (2015)

26. Ji, J., et al.: Genrec: large language model for generative recommendation. In: European Conference on Information Retrieval, pp. 494–502. Springer (2024)

27. Ji, Z., et al.: Survey of hallucination in natural language generation. ACM Comput. Surv. **55**(12), 1–38 (2023)

28. Jiang, A.Q., et al.: Mistral 7b. arXiv preprint arXiv:2310.06825 (2023)

29. Jin, J., et al.: Lending interaction wings to recommender systems with conversational agents. Adv. Neural. Inf. Process. Syst. **36**, 27951–27979 (2023)

30. Lewis, P., et al.: Retrieval-augmented generation for knowledge-intensive NLP tasks. Adv. Neural. Inf. Process. Syst. **33**, 9459–9474 (2020)

31. Li, B., Zhang, K., Sun, Y., Zou, J.: Research on travel route planning optimization based on large language model (2024)

32. Li, Z., Zhu, H., Lu, Z., Yin, M.: Synthetic data generation with large language models for text classification: potential and limitations. arXiv preprint arXiv:2310.07849 (2023)

33. Lim, K.H., Chan, J., Karunasekera, S., Leckie, C.: Tour recommendation and trip planning using location-based social media: a survey. Knowl. Inf. Syst. **60**, 1247–1275 (2019)

34. Lim, K.H., Chan, J., Leckie, C., Karunasekera, S.: Personalized trip recommendation for tourists based on user interests, points of interest visit durations and visit recency. Knowl. Inf. Syst. **54**, 375–406 (2018)

35. Lin, J., et al.: How can recommender systems benefit from large language models: a survey. arXiv preprint arXiv:2306.05817 (2023)

36. Liu, J., Liu, C., Lv, R., Zhou, K., Zhang, Y.: Is chatgpt a good recommender? a preliminary study. arXiv preprint arXiv:2304.10149 (2023)

37. Liu, Z.: Sustainable tourism development: a critique. J. Sustain. Tour. **11**(6), 459–475 (2003)

38. Lu, E. H.-C., Chen, C.-Y., Tseng, V.S.: Personalized trip recommendation with multiple constraints by mining user check-in behaviors. In: Proceedings of the 20th International Conference on Advances in Geographic Information Systems, pp. 209–218 (2012)
39. Lu, Y., et al.: Revcore: review-augmented conversational recommendation. arXiv preprint arXiv:2106.00957 (2021)
40. Majid, A., Chen, L., Chen, G., Mirza, H.T., Hussain, I., Woodward, J.: A context-aware personalized travel recommendation system based on geotagged social media data mining. Int. J. Geogr. Inf. Sci. **27**(4), 662–684 (2013)
41. Merinov, P.: Sustainability-oriented recommender systems. In: Proceedings of the 31st ACM Conference on User Modeling, Adaptation and Personalization, pp. 296–300 (2023)
42. Pachot, A., Albouy-Kissi, A., Albouy-Kissi, B., and Chausse, F.: Multiobjective recommendation for sustainable production systems. In: MORS Workshop held in Conjunction with the 15th ACM Conference on Recommender Systems (RecSys), vol. 2021 (2021)
43. Patro, G.K., Chakraborty, A., Banerjee, A., Ganguly, N.: Towards safety and sustainability: designing local recommendations for post-pandemic world. In: Fourteenth ACM Conference on Recommender Systems, pp. 358–367, Virtual Event Brazil. ACM (2020)
44. Patro, S.: Normalization: a preprocessing stage. arXiv preprint arXiv:1503.06462 (2015)
45. Rahmani, H.A., Craswell, N., Yilmaz, E., Mitra, B., Campos, D.: Synthetic test collections for retrieval evaluation. In: Proceedings of the 47th International ACM SIGIR Conference on Research and Development in Information Retrieval, pp. 2647–2651 (2024)
46. Rahmani, H.A., Deldjoo, Y., Di Noia, T.: The role of context fusion on accuracy, beyond-accuracy, and fairness of point-of-interest recommendation systems. Expert Syst. Appl. **205**, 117700 (2022)
47. Rajbhandari, S., Rasley, J., Ruwase, O., He, Y.: Zero: Memory optimizations toward training trillion parameter models. In: SC20: International Conference for High Performance Computing, Networking, Storage and Analysis, pp. 1–16. IEEE (2020)
48. Reid, M., et al.: Gemini 1.5: Unlocking multimodal understanding across millions of tokens of context. arXiv preprint arXiv:2403.05530 (2024)
49. Santos, A., Cincera, M.: Tourism demand, low cost carriers and European institutions: the case of brussels. J. Transp. Geogr. **73**, 163–171 (2018)
50. Shen, Q., Tao, W., Zhang, J., Wen, H., Chen, Z., Lu, Q.: Sar-net: A scenario-aware ranking network for personalized fair recommendation in hundreds of travel scenarios. In: Proceedings of the 30th ACM International Conference on Information & Knowledge Management, pp. 4094–4103 (2021)
51. Takeuchi, Y., Sugimoto, M.: Cityvoyager: An outdoor recommendation system based on user location history. In: International Conference on Ubiquitous Intelligence and Computing, pp. 625–636. Springer (2006)
52. Wang, J., et al: Is chatgpt a good nlg evaluator? a preliminary study. arXiv preprint arXiv:2303.04048 (2023)
53. Wang, W., Wei, F., Dong, L., Bao, H., Yang, N., Zhou, M.: Minilm: deep self-attention distillation for task-agnostic compression of pre-trained transformers. Adv. Neural. Inf. Process. Syst. **33**, 5776–5788 (2020)
54. Wang, Z.: Empowering few-shot recommender systems with large language models-enhanced representations. IEEE Access (2024)

55. Weaver, D.: Sustainable tourism. Routledge (2007)
56. Wei, Q., Yang, M., Wang, J., Mao, W., Xu, J., Ning, H.: Tourllm: enhancing llms with tourism knowledge. arXiv preprint arXiv:2407.12791 (2024)
57. Weydemann, L., Sacharidis, D., Werthner, H.: Defining and measuring fairness in location recommendations. In: Proceedings of the 3rd ACM SIGSPATIAL International Workshop on Location-Based Recommendations, Geosocial Networks and Geoadvertising, pp. 1–8 (2019)
58. Wikipedia contributors. Cosine similarity — wikipedia, the free encyclopedia (2024). https://en.wikipedia.org/wiki/Cosine_similarity
59. Wu, J., et al.: Coral: collaborative retrieval-augmented large language models improve long-tail recommendation. arXiv preprint arXiv:2403.06447 (2024)
60. Wu, Y., Cao, J., Xu, G., Tan, Y.: Tfrom: a two-sided fairness-aware recommendation model for both customers and providers. In: Proceedings of the 44th International ACM SIGIR Conference on Research and Development in Information Retrieval, pp. 1013–1022 (2021)
61. Yepes, A.J., You, Y., Milczek, J., Laverde, S., Li, L.: Financial report chunking for effective retrieval augmented generation. arXiv preprint arXiv:2402.05131 (2024)
62. Yuan, W., Neubig, G., Liu, P.: Bartscore: evaluating generated text as text generation. Adv. Neural. Inf. Process. Syst. **34**, 27263–27277 (2021)
63. Zhang, T., Kishore, V., Wu, F., Weinberger, K.Q., Artzi, Y.: BERTScore: evaluating text generation with BERT. arXiv:1904.09675 [cs]
64. Zhang, Y., et al.: Siren's song in the AI ocean: a survey on hallucination in large language models. arXiv preprint arXiv:2309.01219 (2023)
65. Zheng, B., et al.: Adapting large language models by integrating collaborative semantics for recommendation. In: 2024 IEEE 40th International Conference on Data Engineering (ICDE), pp. 1435–1448. IEEE (2024a)
66. Zheng, L., et al.: Judging llm-as-a-judge with mt-bench and chatbot arena. In: Advances in Neural Information Processing Systems, vol. 36 (2024b)

# Simulating the Impact of Recommendation Salience on Tourists Experienced Utility

Pavel Merinov$^{(\boxtimes)}$ (ID) and Francesco Ricci (ID)

Free University of Bozen-Bolzano, Bolzano, Italy
{pmerinov,fricci}@unibz.it

**Abstract.** When visiting a busy urban area and its attractions, tourists often experience discrepancies between their expected and actual satisfaction. In fact, popular attractions tend to be crowded, forcing visitors to spend extra time in queues or cramped spaces, which negatively impacts their actual experience. Recommender systems that guide tourists to less crowded attractions could alleviate this problem. However, for the system to be effective, the recommendations must have sufficient salience to convince tourists to accept them at decision time (trip plan). Recommender systems may produce different levels of salience, and therefore will influence tourists in different ways. This raises the question of how the salience of recommendations can quantitatively affect tourists behaviour and satisfaction.

In this paper, we propose a data-driven simulation protocol to model the impact of recommendation salience on the expected utility of the recommended items and ultimately on the users' choices. It is based on the Plackett-Luce choice model, with a utility function that is decomposed in three components: popularity bias, topic preferences, and distance to attraction. By clearly separating these components of the decision utility, we can better model how recommendation induced salience affects user utility perception: by temporarily increasing the popularity of the recommended items. Using a case study in the city of Verona we simulate how a non personalised recommender system that promotes less crowded sites impacts on the users' choices and ultimately on the actual experience of tourists. Our simulation approach provides insights for destination managers looking to implement similar systems on-site.

**Keywords:** Non personalised Recommendations · Simulations · Decision and Experienced Utilities · Urban Tourism · Overcrowding and Congestion

## 1 Introduction

Behavioural studies have shown [23] that human decision makers may overestimate the value of an item when assessing its quality. That is, the decision utility of an item (aka expected utility), as a measure of the expected satisfaction for the item, is at odds with the actual hedonic experienced utility, i.e., the real

L. Boratto et al. (Eds.): RecSoGood 2024, CCIS 2470, pp. 35–51, 2025.
https://doi.org/10.1007/978-3-031-87654-7_4

satisfaction produced by consuming the item. In urban tourism, for example, this can lead to a situation where a tourist decides to visit a popular point of interest (POI), but, especially during peak hours, the visit is unsatisfactory and even frustrating, because of the overcrowding.

Recommender systems (RS) are machine learning technologies and software tools designed to assist users in decision making [26], and can address the above mentioned problem. In fact, recommendations can increase the perceived salience of items, making them more attractive to the decision maker, i.e., they can increase their expected utility. This can be achieved, for example, by giving reasons and explanations for the recommendations, by using nudging techniques to promote the recommendations, or simply because recommendations reduce the "search costs" and users tend to trust them. In other words, salience increases the chances that a decision maker will buy or try a recommended item. Salience is a key factor in the success of an RS [10]. However, the direct relationship between salience and its impact on user choice, and consequently on the actual user experience, has not been thoroughly investigated. In the tourism domain, this information is highly relevant to destination managers who design and implement recommendation policies. Before deploying these policies in operational systems, it is essential for them to understand (forecast) how the developed policies may impact user decision making and the visit experience.

In this paper, we propose an offline simulation protocol. This protocol aims at estimating the final impact of recommendation salience, which is measured as the resulting conversion rate, on the utility experienced by tourists, without the need for online testing. We follow a data-driven protocol that leverages behavioural logs (users' choices) from the environment of interest for calibration. Although it may not be as accurate as online testing, this method is cost effective and carries significantly less risk than deploying an operational system and testing it with real users.

To demonstrate the practical usage of our protocol, we present a case study from the city of Verona, a popular tourist destination in northern Italy. In the city centre, some points of interest (POIs) are crowded at peak times. Visiting these attractions when they are crowded is likely to results in a lower quality experience compared to visiting them at quieter times. Our stylised RS is designed to address this issue by suggesting next POIs that are somewhat popular but also less crowded. With a dataset of more than five years of observations of how tourists make decision, i.e., which POIs they visit and in which order they visit them, we build a generative model of user sequential choice behaviour. Given this model, we simulate the impact of such an RS on user choices and user experienced utility. We measure the RS impact by a) manipulating, in a realistic way, the salience of the recommendations, which results in an increase of their expected utility at decision time, and b) discounting the experienced utility when a POI is visited during peak (crowded) hours.

Our simulation results produce a dependence plot that illustrates the relationship between salience and experienced utility; an important information, required by destination managers. The shape of this dependence plot follows common sense logic: increased recommendation salience brings additional experienced satisfaction even for small levels of simulated satisfaction penalty for visiting overcrowded POIs. Still precise quantitative results depend on the particular simulated environment configuration. However, the proposed simulation protocol to model user behaviour is quite general, and has a broader applications in urban tourism beyond the specific case of the city of Verona.

## 2   Related Works

The relevant literature is here classified into three topics: (1) decision vs. experienced utility, (2) discrete choice models, and (3) evaluation of interventions and simulations.

### 2.1   Decision Vs. Experienced Utility

Researchers distinguish decision (also known as expected) utility, which is a subjective measure of the value of an item estimated by the decision maker when making a choice, from experienced utility, which is a measure of the satisfaction derived from the item when it is actually consumed [16,23]. The importance to distinguish between them is empirically motivated by the observed mismatch between decision and experienced utilities. For economists, decision utility is crucial because it contributes to explaining user behaviour. For behavioural scientists, however, experience utility is more important because it reflects the actual hedonic satisfaction. Even though some analyses show fundamental correlation between the two [7], in experience markets like POI advertisement, it is important to make a distinction. Related to tourism, in [9], the authors analyse the impact of sudden weather changes on users satisfaction. In [15], the authors empirically evaluate the distribution mismatch between the two utilities. Related to overcrowding impact on user satisfaction, the in [34] the authors explore reviews, applying a text analysis approach. We base our simulations on this literature, assuming that a crowded place penalises the experienced utility, resulting in less satisfaction.

### 2.2   Discrete Choice Models

Discrete choice models are mathematical models that explain user behaviour when making choices. The most well-known choice model is the multinomial [20], which has been revisited and extended numerous times in the economics literature [31]. Very often, a decision process is not just a single choice, but rather a sequence of choices. These problems are known as sequential decision tasks. An example of such a task is the process that generates (explains) the trajectory of the POIs visited by a tourist. There is an extensive literature devoted to the study of modelling methods for this type of task [3], including reinforcement learning [29], inverse reinforcement learning [1,19,22] to recover the unknown reward (utility) function from observed behaviours, and various ranking methods [18,25]. Following the recent literature [30], in this paper we use the Plackett-Luce (PL) parametric ranking model to approximate the sequential choice behaviour of tourists. According to the PL model, each subsequent decision step (number of steps equal to number of sequential choices) obeys Luce's axiom of choice [18], which states that the probability of choosing one item over another is not affected by the presence or absence of other items in the pool. This axiom is frequently cited in economics for modelling consumer decision behaviour.

### 2.3   Evaluation of Interventions and Simulations

Taking aside A/B tests and user studies [6,12,17], that by design involve real or prototype systems launched on the bunch of real users, researchers focus on cheaper alternative to estimate the impact of recommender systems. Simulation is a solution. In the recommendation literature, this is an evolving approach to validate long-term dynamic properties of an environment affected by the recommendation policy. Accuracy [32], additional consumption [11,14], item diversity [5,8,10,13], impact of sustainable ads [24], and popularity bias [33], all this is simulated with different behavioural (domain-specific) assumptions. Here, in particular, we simulate the impact of the recommendation salience [10] on the experienced utility of tourists in a crowded environment.

## 3   Simulation Methodology

In this section, we discuss the key modelling components needed to simulate the impact of recommendation salience on a population of tourists. Here, we (i) estimate decision utility of a population of tourists, (ii) define how recommendations can change it, (iii) formalise experienced utility, and (iv) design a simulation protocol to observe how recommendations impact on experienced utility. The simulation protocol is data-driven and relies on collected feedback from tourists (visit logs). Steps (i) and (iii) specifically depend on a data set. In our case study, we use behavioural logs that track the trajectories tourists take to visit POIs in Verona. However, one may employ alternative data sources, as long as they reveal information about sequential decision making.

### 3.1   VeronaCard Data

The dataset used in our case study was collected in the city of Verona, Italy, over a period of more than five years[1]. Specifically, we use data from 2014 to 2018. It contains trajectories of tourists who have visited the main attractions in Verona. The data collection was facilitated by the VeronaCard system, a pre-paid city pass ticket with an embedded chip. Each time a tourist uses a ticket to enter a

---

[1] https://dati.veneto.it/catalog/VeronaCard.

POI, the electronic system records the visit. Specifically, in our experiment, we use 14 POIs in Verona downtown (the most popular locations that performed consistently throughout the data collection period). All of the POIs are within walking distance of each other. The VeronaCard dataset contains about 2M visits performed by circa 400K tourists. A typical visitor check-ins log contains 5 POIs, but there are also both less and more active tourists. Cumulative statistics of visits are presented in Table 1. For more information about this data, we refer the reader to the original paper [21]. This is an implicit feedback data set.

**Table 1.** POIs in the VeronaCard dataset.

| Id | POI | # Visits |
|----|-----|----------|
| 0  | Arena | 344026 |
| 1  | Casa Giulietta | 309734 |
| 2  | Torre Lamberti | 239734 |
| 3  | Castelvecchio | 222118 |
| 4  | Santa Anastasia | 190022 |
| 5  | Duomo | 167887 |
| 6  | Teatro Romano | 115567 |
| 7  | Palazzo della Ragione | 90574 |
| 8  | Tomba Giulietta | 85330 |
| 9  | San Fermo | 73796 |
| 10 | San Zeno | 72590 |
| 11 | Museo Lapidario | 32689 |
| 12 | Giardino Giusti | 25849 |
| 13 | Museo Storia | 11139 |

### 3.2 User Choice Model

Here, we outline the learning process of the proposed choice model, which is designed to accurately capture the visit trajectories observed in the VeronaCard data. This model is used to simulate tourist decisions both with and without the influence of recommendations. Since each user makes decisions sequentially, this can be framed as a ranking problem. Following the literature [18, 25, 30], we use the Plackett-Luce (PL) model to learn this sequential user behaviour.

Let $r$ be a ranking of $J$ POI items, that is a permutation of $J$ indices. This ranking is determined by the decision utilities $\{u_j\}$ that the decision maker, the user of the RS, assigns to each POI item, but with some error due to the user's inability to estimate these utilities accurately. This uncertainty may be due to incomplete information or to the user's reluctance to spend time making accurate assessments. The PL model accounts for this uncertainty and defines a probability distribution over all possible rankings of $J$ items. We can write this joint probability of observing a ranking $r$ in a population as:

$$\mathrm{PL}(r \mid \{u_j\}) = \prod_{i=1}^{J} \left[ \exp(u_{r[i]}) / \sum_{k=i}^{J} \exp(u_{r[k]}) \right]. \tag{1}$$

The PL model offers an intuitive way to interpret the ranking process. At each step, a user's behaviour is modelled as a multinomial choice. Once a POI is selected, it is removed from the list of available options. And the process repeats for as many steps as the user decides to visit POIs in the city. In our context, the ordered choices form an itinerary that a tourist follows in the VeronaCard data. The model assumes that each POI can only be selected once (or not at all), which is a reasonable assumption for tourists visiting a city.

Given the PL model, we specify the utility structure $\{u_j\}$. Here, the utility function is assumed to be a linear combination of three components:

$$u_j = \left[\, \text{bias}_j \cdot \alpha \,\right] + \left[\, \sum_{d=1}^{D} \text{attr}_{jd} \cdot w_d \,\right] + \left[\, \text{distance}(*, j) \cdot \beta \,\right]. \tag{2}$$

The first component measures the user preference (bias) for popular POIs. Obviously, more popular POIs are highly sought after. The second one is a linear utility function that measure the item attractiveness by using the dot-product similarity between selected POI attributes $\{\text{attr}_{jd}\}$ and user preferences towards these attributes $\{w_d\}$. We discuss later how we have selected the POI attributes. The third one is a dynamic distance attribute that depends on the user's current POI $(*)$ location and the next POI $(j)$ location. This component is included because tourists often exhibit exploratory behaviour, favouring nearby locations over more distant ones.

To estimate $\{\text{bias}_j\}$ from the data, we normalise the total number of visits to a particular POI by the total number of visits to all POIs. This simple statistic mimics the spread of information in the population, which can influence the user's opinion about the item. Intuitively, more popular POIs receive more attention from users and therefore receive a higher decision utility component.

To select the POI attributes and estimate $\{\text{attr}_{jd}\}$ from the data, we use a topic modelling approach. The idea is to introduce attributes that capture thematic user preferences, not contaminated by popularity bias. We have collected texts (10 documents per POI) from the web; simple information provided on websites when searching for a particular POI title. We then have applied Latent Dirichlet Allocation (LDA) clustering to these texts with 3 topics. We note that the best number of topics was determined by visual inspection, and this number may depend on the specific case [4]. Information about the learned topics can be found in Fig. 1. Thus, each POI is encoded as a distribution over these three topics.

We have finally considered in the decision utility calculation the distance between the current tourist position (the position of the POI currently visited) and the next POI the tourist is choosing to visit. In fact, tourists tend to prefer to move to POIs that are closer, assuming that all the other attributes are equal. We extracted the distance between each pair of POIs using geo-spatial services that measure pedestrian street lengths.

We have finally calibrated the parameters $\{\alpha, w_d, \beta\}$ to accurately model the VeronaCard data and, in turn, explain tourist decision making behaviour. For this purpose we have applied gradient ascent to log-likelihood of the PL model.

```
Top-k words of topic #0
    museum       0.034199    garden       0.020996    collection   0.020022
    room         0.013096    history      0.012663    theater      0.011905
    roman        0.011473    area         0.010066    1CENTURY     0.008983
    inscription  0.008767    building     0.008334    ancient      0.008009
    20CENTURY    0.007793    amphitheatre 0.007360    large        0.007252
    natural      0.007252    public       0.007035    place        0.006927
    18CENTURY    0.006819    city         0.006386    stage        0.005953


Top-k words of topic #1
    church       0.052286    san          0.022479    fresco       0.017201
    saint        0.017104    basilica     0.012413    facade       0.012217
    large        0.010947    chapel       0.010654    14CENTURY    0.010360
    cathedral    0.009774    santa        0.009090    12CENTURY    0.009090
    gothic       0.008992    window       0.008797    zeno         0.008797
    arch         0.008797    nave         0.008308    romanesque   0.008308
    15CENTURY    0.008210    portal       0.007819    13CENTURY    0.007624


Top-k words of topic #2
    city         0.026413    building     0.019949    tower        0.018274
    house        0.011092    family       0.010853    wall         0.009656
    complex      0.009097    courtyard    0.008938    place        0.008858
    time         0.008858    architecture 0.008140    palace       0.007661
    piazza       0.007342    medieval     0.007262    art          0.007262
    20CENTURY    0.006783    castle       0.006703    famous       0.006703
    ragione      0.006703    restoration  0.006624    19CENTURY    0.006544
```

**Fig. 1.** LDA results. There are 3 topics extracted from texts. Each topic is a distribution over the vocabulary of words (top words with their importance weights are depicted).

Due to space limits, we omit technical details in this paper. Interested reader can find these details in paper [30]. After training we have obtained Recall@1 = 0.34, Recall@2 = 0.52 for each next POI prediction sample, averaged over the dataset, and the calibrated weights shown in Table 2. While one cannot expect that a stochastic choice model exactly reconstruct the observed choices, its accuracy is a matter of concern, and we leave to future work the analysis of the dependency between choice model precision and simulation results stability.

The sign and magnitude of each weight encodes a positive (or negative) user preference for a particular attribute; positive weight indicate that the user will favour POIs that have larger values of the attribute, while negative values imply that the user will tend to avoid items with larger attribute values. As a result of the calibration process, we can state that the most important contributors to user decision utility are the popularity bias weight and the distance to the POI. Topic preferences, although not zero, appear to be less important in explaining the tourists choices. This is somewhat understandable, by considering that all the considered POIs are distinguished attractions in Verona. Therefore, the final calibrated utility model disentangles: (1) popularity bias, (2) topic interests, and (3) distance attributes. This disentangled representation will be important for understanding the recommendation effect.

**Table 2.** Learned user parameters.

| $\alpha$ | $w_1$ | $w_2$ | $w_3$ | $\beta$ |
|---|---|---|---|---|
| 2.18 | 0.10 | 0.61 | 0.38 | −5.28 |

### 3.3  Recommendation Effect

Given the calibrated user choice model introduced in the previous subsection, we now describe the assumptions on how recommendation salience impacts on user decision utility and therefore alters the default choice behaviour (without any recommendation). The main role of an RS is to inform a user about potentially interesting (relevant) POIs. Therefore, it is reasonable to conjecture that an RS can primarily increase the popularity bias of the recommended POI, but it does not significantly influence how the user evaluates the appropriateness of the content or the distance to the POI. Therefore, we here assume that recommendation salience increases only the popularity component of the decision utility $\{bias_j\}$ of the recommended POIs:

$$\text{RS impact} : bias_j \rightarrow bias_j + \delta. \tag{3}$$

It is important to note that the $\delta$ ($>0$) effect persists only during the decision process [10]. It temporarily increases the decision utility, potentially altering user behaviour by making certain POIs more attractive at the moment of choice, and it does not change the way the user will measure the item utility while experiencing the POI.

Exploring how alternative values of $\delta$ impact users is the purpose of this study. In the experiments section we will consider a grid of values and record the impact for each value.

### 3.4  Simulation Protocol

Our simulation protocol is shown in Fig. 2 and discussed in the rest of the Section. It is important to note that we simulate users' choices both when tourists are exposed to recommendations and when they are not influenced by the RS; then we compare the experienced utilities measured in the two cases. We simulate the Verona visit scenario with realistic POI locations and arrival times recorded in the VeronaCard data. For our case study, we test the impact of the crowdedness-aware RS that is described below.

**Crowdedness-Aware Recommender System.** To keep things simple, we avoid exploring the effect of personalisation and focus on non personalised RSs. This experiment design serves two purposes. First, users often prefer not to register or disclose their preferences, making a non personalised model the only viable option. Second, in this case study we are not comparing different recommendation models. Instead, by using just one RS, we simulate the impact of recommendation salience on the user estimation of the decision utility and therefore on the choices. Then, choices are supposed to be visited and to produce experienced user utilities. For a better recommendation impact, obviously, personalised models could be considered in a future work.

To be aligned with the original problem aiming to improve experienced user utility, we consider "the next crowdedness-aware POI" recommendation scenario.

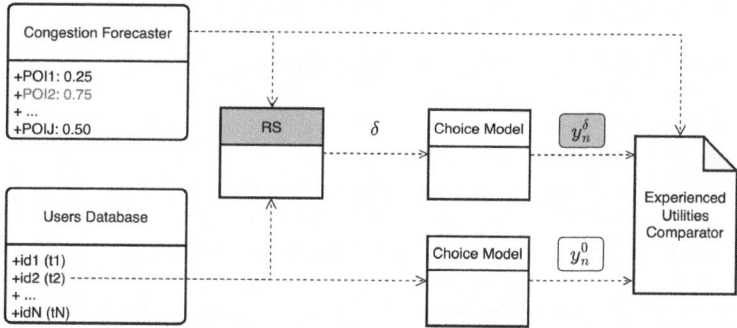

**Fig. 2.** User choices generation and simulation protocol, with and without the users' exposure to recommendations.

The next POI recommendations comprise items, here we recommend $k$ POIs, that are worth to be visited soon by the user: the user is supposed to have already started his/her itinerary and is currently at POI $i$ location. Crowdedness-aware means that we only recommend not overcrowded places for a visit. For identifying popular next POI recommendations, we estimate state transition matrix $T$, where $T[i, j]$ is the probability (estimated based on data) that randomly selected user from the population will make a transition from currently visited POI $i$ to the next POI $j$. We use this global popularity-based model as a proxy for user preferences. Moreover, we query the level of crowdedness for the next 1 h with a crowdedness forecaster. Finally, we recommend to a user at POI $i$ the set of POIs $R_i$ which are the top-k POIs visited after POI $i$ filtered with crowdedness forecaster POIs:

$$R_i = \arg_j \text{top}_k \{T[i, j] \mid T[i, j] \text{ is not overcrowded in the next 1 h}\}. \quad (4)$$

Crowdedness forecaster is an important part of this RS. Ideally, one should use an online forecaster with a horizon of 1 h (typical time required to visit a POI) for each POI. Most modern cities may collect this information. In our experiment, this information is not available. Therefore, we have estimated it based on Google Popular Times feature.

**Google Popular Times Feature.** This serves as a proxy model for crowding. However, with this model, we cannot accurately estimate neither the number of tourists at a particular POI nor how its popularity relates to its maximum carrying capacity. To calculate popular times, Google uses aggregated and anonymous data from users who have opted in to Google Location History[2]. Google Popular Times graph, available in Google Maps, shows how busy the POI location typically is during different times of the day. Popular times are based on average popularity over the last few months. Popularity for any given hour is shown

---

[2] https://support.google.com/business/answer/6263531?hl=en.

relative to the typical peak popularity for the business for the week. Figure 3 shows POI profiles of congestion in Verona city extracted from Google Maps. We assume this information is available to the RS and will be exploited to filter out congested places.

For each POI and hour, we manually classify its crowding level into 4 quartiles: $(0, 0.25)$, $(0.25, 0.5)$, $(0.5, 0.75)$, and $(0.75, 1.0)$, from less crowded condition to more crowded condition. We set the 4th quartile, $(0.75, 1.0)$, as the one when the POI should not be recommended. That is, if POI in the next 1 h is estimated to be in the 4th quartile level of congestion, it will be filtered-out from the recommendations in our non personalised context-aware RS. In practice we are using a post filtering context-aware RS approach [2].

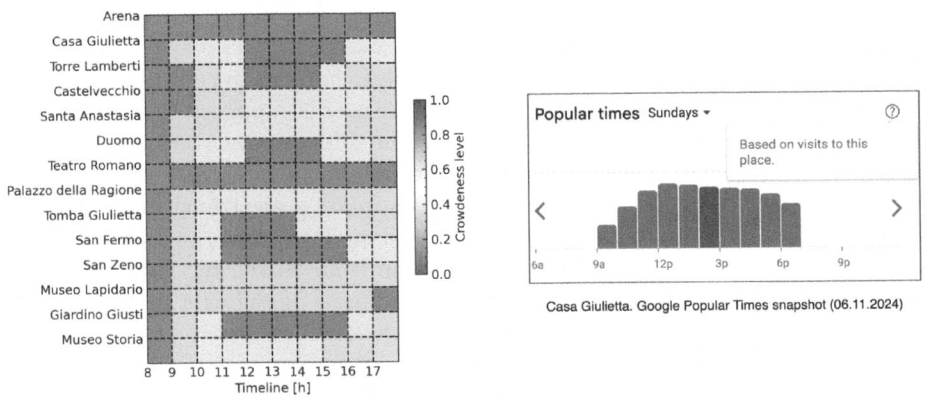

**Fig. 3.** The city crowdedness profile during the day. Only q4 (red colour) incurs a penalty on user's experienced utility. In Verona, q4 happens mostly during peak hours. (Color figure online)

**Protocol.** We use Google Popular Times information to query the level of congestion. Before visiting a POI (immediately after leaving the previous one), we assume that each user consults the RS. This RS is designed to suggest the next crowdedness-aware POI. That is, the system predicts the expected congestion at each location for the next hour, and recommends the top 2 POIs which are also not under the threat (4th quartile) to be overcrowded. Note that these recommendations are supposed to receive, because they are recommended, a $\delta$ salience, which in turn increases the decision utility for these POIs. Each user makes a choice according to the PL model and visits the chosen POI in the next hour. Finally, we evaluate the impact of the RS with salience $\delta$ by calculating the resulting experienced utility for each user. Below we define the exact formula for experienced utility (Eq. 5).

## 3.5   Decision Utility Vs. Experienced Utility

As we mentioned earlier, we distinguish between decision utilities $\{u_j\}$ and experienced utilities $\{s_j\}$. Decision utility reflects the user's expectation (beliefs) of the quality of a POI, and it can be influenced by the RS. Experienced utility, on the other hand, is the actual satisfaction experienced during/after visiting a POI. In urban environments, there is a discrepancy $h$ between the two utilities and the value of this discrepancy is greater at higher levels of crowding. In this paper, we assume that POI crowding is the only source of the mismatch between decision utility and experienced utility:

$$s_j(h) = u_j \cdot \left[1 - 1_{\left\{\text{load}_j \geq 0.75\right\}} \cdot h\right]. \tag{5}$$

Two key points are important here. First, the penalty $h \in [0,1]$ is a step function and is only applied if the chosen POI is in the 4th quartile of load (75% capacity or more). This assumption simplifies modelling in the absence of detailed knowledge of how congestion levels affect experience. Second, we assume that recommendation salience $\delta$—increase in decision utility $u_j$ when item $j$ is recommended—does not change experienced utility $s_j$. Finally, only crowding can change experienced utility; value $h$ is a free parameter that depends very much on external and internal factors. In our experiments, we test different values of $h$ on a progressive grid.

# 4   Experimental Results

The goal of our experiments is to simulate how the RS can impact on tourist experienced utility. In this section, we first describe the evaluation setup and the success metric. In the second part, we report the results of our simulation experiments.

## 4.1   Setup

We split data 67/33% chronologically for train/test parts. The choice model calibration is performed on the train part. All simulations in this section will be conducted using the test part. Simulation protocol is shown in Fig. 2. We use the test part to sample users one by one. For each user $n = 1, \ldots, N$, two pipelines are applied. One uses the proposed non personalised RS, while the other does not, i.e., in the second case the users make choices according to the calibrated choice model but without any salience modification produced by the RS, hence without simulating the exposure of the users to the RS. Hence, we have two sets of simulated choices: $\{y_n^\delta : n = 1, \ldots, N\}$ and $\{y_n^0 : n = 1, \ldots, N\}$. The vector $y_n^x$ has $J$ components $y_{nj}^x$ that are either 1 if POI $j$ is chosen and visited by user $n$, or 0 otherwise, from both pipelines are collected.

By design, only the pipeline where the RS is employed may affect user behaviour due to the assumed recommendation salience ($\delta$). Finally, we compare the simulated choices, and estimate the incremental effect on experienced user utility caused by the RS.

## 4.2   Metric

Uplift metrics are a gold standard in uplift [28] and causal research [27] literature. Uplift metrics measure the incremental effect of an action or intervention—in our case, the impact of the RS and the recommendation salience. Here we evaluate uplift metrics by comparing the simulated outcomes obtained with the proposed RS policy (with salience $\delta$) and without (also known as a control policy). Note that the control policy runs in the same simulation environment, but does not provide any recommendations; it therefore mimics the observed user behaviour in the data. Given the fact, that users are aware of all the 14 POIs, in reality the control policy has the same effect of an RS policy with salience equal to 0. We are interested in measuring the uplift in total experienced utility across the population of $N$ users:

$$\tau^{\delta h} = \frac{1}{N} \sum_{n=1}^{N} \sum_{j=1}^{J} s_{nj}(h) \cdot (y_{nj}^{\delta} - y_{nj}^{0}). \tag{6}$$

Metric $\tau^{\delta h}$ captures the incremental effect for a given level of salience $\delta$ and penalty $h$ for crowding. A positive value indicates that the RS is doing its job correctly; higher values correspond to a greater improvement in experienced utility. In our experiments, we will test different levels of $\delta$ and $h$ to capture the relationship between salience and the outcome.

## 4.3   Recommendation Salience to Conversion Rate

Recommendation salience, which is measured by the non-negative constant $\delta$, is difficult to interpret on its own. It is much clearer to look at how it increases the conversion rate (CVR). Here, CVR is the ratio (a positive surplus) of users who are converted to one of the recommended POIs, compared to user behaviour without recommendations. By design, salience and CVR are positively correlated: higher salience values lead directly to higher CVR values. There is a one-to-one correspondence between salience $\delta$ and conversion rate. Therefore, when we report our simulated results, we replace the salience $\delta$ with the corresponding CVR value, which we calculated beforehand for our non personalised RS policy. For our case study, we expect real values of CVR to be in the range 0–10%. Higher values seem unrealistic, as a simple non personalised RS policy cannot generate such a strong effect, so we have excluded them from the experiments and discussion.

## 4.4   Results

The results of our experiments are summarised in Fig. 4 and selected findings are also highlighted in Table 3. For each CVR value in the range (0, 10%), corresponding to a particular recommendation salience $\delta$, and for each value of the experienced utility penalty for crowding $h$ in the range (0, 1), we have computed the uplift $\tau^{\delta h}$ of the experienced utility.

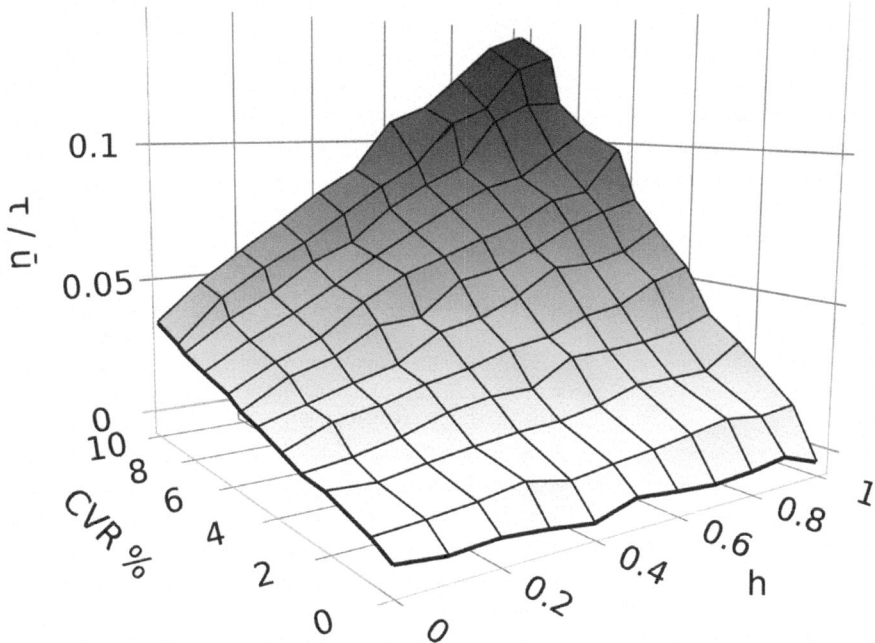

**Fig. 4.** Simulated uplift surface. CVR and utility penalty $h$ are free parameters. Uplift $\tau^{\delta h}$ is normalised by the population-level average decision utility, $\bar{u}$, estimated by the PL model in the VeronaCard data.

Results show, that salience indeed changes users' choice behaviour and ultimately their experienced utility. Positive values indicate that the RS can improve experienced utility. Two observations are worth noting. First, there is no impact (apart from the simulation error) of a 0 CVR on the simulated uplift. This is to be expected, since in this case the recommendations do not generate any salience. Second, even when $h = 0$ there is a slight improvement in uplift, for moderate to large CVR values. This effect can be explained by the fact that a typical tourist follows the PL model, which is a stochastic model. As a result, users sometimes make sub-optimal choices in terms of utility, and even a non personalised RS can help improve these choices, if it is able to produce some salience and convert users.

Apart from these marginal cases, the impact of the crowdedness-aware RS on VeronaCard tourists grows steadily with higher values of CVR and $h$: larger values generate a greater uplift. Selected uplift values as a function of CVR and penalty for crowding are summarised in Table 3. For example, considering a particular scenario where CVR = 10% and $h = 0.2$, here the crowdedness-aware RS converts an additional 10% of tourists to choose a recommended POI as their next stop, and tourists are assumed to experience a 20% penalty if they visit a crowded POI, regardless of whether it was recommended or not. In this case, our simulated crowdedness-aware RS can save on average $\tau^{\delta h} = 0.059\,\bar{u}$ of experienced utility for each tourist trajectory, where $\bar{u}$ is the average decision utility estimated by the PL model for Verona tourists.

It is worth commenting that interpreting accurate values realistically is a task for the policy makers. This simulated surface provides an initial information for them to grasp the potential impact of a recommendation policy (a non personalised context aware RS in our case study) on a population of tourists.

**Table 3.** Simulated uplift surface.

| CVR(%) | h | | | | | |
|---|---|---|---|---|---|---|
| | 0.0 | 0.2 | 0.4 | 0.6 | 0.8 | 1.0 |
| 0.0 | 0.000 | 0.000 | 0.000 | 0.000 | 0.000 | 0.000 |
| 2.5 | 0.010 | 0.015 | 0.022 | 0.031 | 0.032 | 0.039 |
| 5.0 | 0.018 | 0.031 | 0.040 | 0.056 | 0.069 | 0.078 |
| 10.0 | 0.034 | 0.059 | 0.080 | 0.108 | 0.126 | 0.144 |

## 5   Conclusion and Future Works

This paper proposes an offline simulation protocol to estimate the impact of an RS, i.e., its recommendation salience relation with decision utility and choice behaviour. The simulated choice behaviour can then show the impact of the RS on the experienced utility of tourists in an urban environments. The importance of this research stems from the fact that tourists often experience less satisfaction than they expect at the trip planning stage (when deciding what to visit). While recommendations could help solve this problem, it is often unclear—or very costly to determine through A/B testing and user studies—what the actual impact of these recommendations might be.

Our protocol is based on the Plackett-Luce choice model with a structural decision utility function that accounts for popularity bias, topic preferences, and spatial distribution of POIs. We have explained a mechanism for how recommendation salience changes user behaviour. In our case study, we simulate how salience, by changing the decision utility and the user's choice behaviour, may impact on user experienced utility in Verona. Our results suggest that even an non personalised RS that recommends popular but not crowded POIs may be beneficial.

We acknowledge that this approach may have lower accuracy than real online tests. This is mainly due to the accuracy of the choice model in simulating the true user behaviour. In a future work we will analyse the impact of the choice model accuracy on the precise estimation of the target metrics (uplift), and how diverse RSs may be influenced. Policy makers should consider this protocol as a first step, low-risk baseline check for their RS models, rather than as the final determinant of the suitability of their models. For future research, we also plan to conduct online user studies to address the limitations of this work. A key limitation to explore is the empirical effect of recommendation salience on user choice. In our simulations, salience affects popularity component of all items equally; however, in reality, this effect may vary depending on the initial popularity of POIs, affecting niche items more than popular ones. Understanding this difference could significantly improve the accuracy of future simulations in urban scenarios.

**Disclosure of Interests.** The authors have no competing interests to declare that are relevant to the content of this article.

# References

1. Abbeel, P., Ng, A.Y.: Apprenticeship learning via inverse reinforcement learning. In: Proceedings of the Twenty-First International Conference on Machine Learning. p. 1. ICML 2004, Association for Computing Machinery, New York, NY, USA (2004). https://doi.org/10.1145/1015330.1015430
2. Adomavicius, G., Bauman, K., Tuzhilin, A., Unger, M.: Context-aware recommender systems: From foundations to recent developments. In: Recommender Systems Handbook, pp. 211–250. Springer US (2022)
3. Barto, A.G., Sutton, R.S., Watkins, C.: Learning and sequential decision making, vol. 89. University of Massachusetts Amherst, MA (1989)
4. Blei, D.M.: Probabilistic topic models. Commun. ACM **55**(4), 77–84 (2012). https://doi.org/10.1145/2133806.2133826
5. Bountouridis, D., Harambam, J., Makhortykh, M., Marrero, M., Tintarev, N., Hauff, C.: Siren: a simulation framework for understanding the effects of recommender systems in online news environments. In: Proceedings of the Conference on Fairness, Accountability, and Transparency, pp. 150–159. FAT* 2019, Association for Computing Machinery (2019). https://doi.org/10.1145/3287560.3287583
6. Cairns, P.E., Cox, A.L.: Research Methods for Human-Computer Interaction. Cambridge University Press (2008)
7. Carter, S., McBride, M.: Experienced utility versus decision utility: Putting the 's' in satisfaction. J. Socio-Econ. **42**, 13–23 (2013)
8. Chaney, A.J.B., Stewart, B.M., Engelhardt, B.E.: How algorithmic confounding in recommendation systems increases homogeneity and decreases utility. In: Proceedings of the 12th ACM Conference on Recommender Systems (2017)
9. Figini, P., Leoni, V., Vici, L.: And suddenly, the rain! how surprises shape experienced utility. Working Papers wp1185, Dipartimento Scienze Economiche, Universita' di Bologna, April 2023
10. Fleder, D., Hosanagar, K.: Blockbuster culture's next rise or fall: the impact of recommender systems on sales diversity. Manage. Sci. **55**(5), 697–712 (2009)
11. Ghanem, N., Leitner, S., Jannach, D.: Balancing consumer and business value of recommender systems: a simulation-based analysis. Electron. Commer. Res. Appl. **55**, 101195 (2022)
12. Gunawardana, A., Shani, G., Yogev, S.: Evaluating recommender systems. In: Recommender Systems Handbook, pp. 547–601. Springer US (2022)
13. Hazrati, N., Ricci, F.: Recommender systems effect on the evolution of users' choices distribution. Inf. Process. Manage. (2022)
14. Hinz, O., Eckert, J.: The impact of search and recommendation systems on sales in electronic commerce. Bus. Inf. Syst. Eng. **2**, 67–77 (2010)

15. Hofschen, K., Massimo, D., Ricci, F.: Expected and experienced utility of points of interest in tourism recommender systems. In: Adjunct Proceedings of the 31st ACM Conference on User Modeling, Adaptation and Personalization, pp. 50–55. UMAP 2023 Adjunct, Association for Computing Machinery, New York, NY, USA (2023). https://doi.org/10.1145/3563359.3597405

16. Kahneman, D., Thaler, R.H.: Anomalies: utility maximization and experienced utility. J. Econ. Perspect. **20**(1), 221–234 (2006)

17. Kohavi, R., Tang, D., Xu, Y.: Trustworthy Online Controlled Experiments: A Practical Guide to a/b Testing. Cambridge University Press (2020)

18. Luce, R.D.: Individual Choice Behavior: A Theoretical analysis. Wiley, New York, NY, USA (1959)

19. Massimo, D., Ricci, F.: Combining reinforcement learning and spatial proximity exploration for new user and new POI recommendations. In: UMAP, pp. 164–174. ACM (2023)

20. McFadden, D.: Conditional logit analysis of qualitative choice behavior (1972)

21. Migliorini, S., Carra, D., Belussi, A.: Distributing tourists among pois with an adaptive trip recommendation system. IEEE Trans. Emerg. Top. Comput. **9**(4), 1765–1779 (2021). https://doi.org/10.1109/TETC.2019.2920484

22. Ng, A.Y., Russell, S.J.: Algorithms for inverse reinforcement learning. In: Proceedings of the Seventeenth International Conference on Machine Learning. pp. 663–670. ICML 2000, Morgan Kaufmann Publishers Inc., San Francisco, CA, USA (2000)

23. Oliver, R.L.: A cognitive model of the antecedents and consequences of satisfaction decisions. J. Mark. Res. **17**(4), 460–469 (1980)

24. Piliponyte, G., Massimo, D., Ricci, F.: Simulation of recommender systems driven tourism promotion campaigns. Inf. Technol. Tourism **26**(3), 407–448 (2024)

25. Plackett, R.L.: The analysis of permutations. J. Royal Stat. Soc. Ser. C (Appl. Stat.) **24**(2), 193–202 (1975). http://www.jstor.org/stable/2346567

26. Ricci, F., Rokach, L., Shapira, B.: recommender systems: techniques, applications, and challenges, pp. 1–35. Springer US, New York, NY (2022). https://doi.org/10.1007/978-1-0716-2197-4_1

27. Rubin, D.B.: Estimating causal effects of treatments in randomized and nonrandomized studies. J. Educ. Psychol. **66**, 688–701 (1974)

28. Rzepakowski, P., Jaroszewicz, S.: Uplift modeling in direct marketing. J. Telecommun. Inf. Technol. (2), 43–50 (2012). https://doi.org/10.26636/jtit.2012.2.1263, https://jtit.pl/jtit/article/view/1263

29. Sutton, R.S., Barto, A.G.: Reinforcement Learning: An Introduction. The MIT Press, 2nd edn. (2018)

30. Tkachenko, M., Lauw, H.W.: Plackett-luce regression mixture model for heterogeneous rankings. In: Proceedings of the 25th ACM International on Conference on Information and Knowledge Management, CIKM 2016, pp. 237–246. Association for Computing Machinery, New York, NY, USA (2016). https://doi.org/10.1145/2983323.2983763

31. Train, K.E.: Discrete Choice Methods with Simulation. Cambridge University Press (2009)

32. Umeda, T., Ichikawa, M., Koyama, Y., Deguchi, H.: Evaluation of collaborative filtering by agent-based simulation considering market environment. In: Developments in Business Simulation and Experiential Learning: Proceedings of the Annual ABSEL Conference, vol. 36 (2009)

33. Yao, S., et al.: Measuring recommender system effects with simulated users. ArXiv **abs/2101.04526** (2021)
34. Yu, J., Egger, R.: Tourist experiences at overcrowded attractions: A text analytics approach. In: Wörndl, W., Koo, C., Stienmetz, J.L. (eds.) Information and Communication Technologies in Tourism 2021, pp. 231–243. Springer International Publishing, Cham (2021)

# Knowledge Data Modeling in Food Recommendation: A Case Study on Nutritional Values

Giacomo Balloccu⬭, Ludovico Boratto⬭, Gianni Fenu⬭, Mirko Marras⬭,
Giacomo Medda(✉)⬭, and Giovanni Murgia

University of Cagliari, Cagliari, Italy
{giacomo.balloccu,fenu,giacomo.medda}@unica.it,
{ludovico.boratto,mirko.marras}@acm.org, g.murgia68@studenti.unica.it

**Abstract.** Domains such as movie or music, typically addressed in recommendation studies, focus on suggesting items that do not need thorough analysis to estimate their social impact, with the main goal often being to increase sales. Conversely, recommending items with higher social involvement, such as insurances and food, requires the introduction of specific constraints, including socioeconomic, sustainability, and healthiness considerations. In this paper, we address the intricate domain of food recommendation, focusing on analyzing the nutritional intake of food recipes suggested by automatic systems. We base our investigation on a public user-recipe knowledge graph, which embeds information about ingredients, nutrients, and healthiness scores of food recipes. Our experiments highlight the importance of assessing factors beyond accuracy in food recommendation and opens discussions about the complexity in interpreting nutritional intake based solely on raw values.

**Keywords:** Recommender Systems · Knowledge Graphs · Food Recommendation · Healthiness · Nutrition

## 1 Introduction

Recommender systems are notably widespread among entertainment industries, such as music and movie streaming platforms, and e-commerce. These applications support content discovery and sales increment by suggesting items that capture users' preferences and encourage them to interact with new items.

Nonetheless, these objectives cannot be seamlessly shared across different domains, but other criteria might be addressed in the recommendation process. For instance, recommender systems adopted in the health [10] and food [12] sector need to consider critical users' features, such as diseases, to provide well-informed suggestions. These aspects are especially relevant in the food sector, due to the pressing need to encourage healthier food habits [7, 8, 15, 18]. Supporting healthy lifestyles and nutrition is also central to the Sustainable Development

L. Boratto et al. (Eds.): RecSoGood 2024, CCIS 2470, pp. 52–62, 2025.
https://doi.org/10.1007/978-3-031-87654-7_5

Goals (SDGs) [11], specifically the objective of promoting *good health and well-being.*

This objective becomes crucial in food recommendation, as typical recommender systems do not naturally steer toward healthy choices. Instead, they are influenced by the popularity of items and patterns in users' interaction histories [19], often overlooking personal factors essential for promoting healthier eating habits. To this end, researchers have been focusing on instilling healthiness knowledge into the recommendation process [4,6,17,21,23]. For instance, [4] proposed a connected dataset including rich nutrient information and explored three healthiness-aware post-processing techniques, while [17] used Graph Neural Networks (GNNs) to generate within-category food substitutions and ranked food options according to their healthiness. Despite numerous works on healthy food recommendations, researchers have predominantly focused on developing novel datasets [4,15] or methods [6,17,22,23] for generating healthier recommendations. However, this focus often neglects a critical evaluation of the actual recommendation and healthiness performance [9,25] of state-of-the-art systems. This gap is evident in a recent study [4] that proposed a healthiness-aware knowledge graph (KG). The KG relations, linking recipes and features (e.g., ingredients), could enable specialized methods, such as knowledge-aware models, to refine the recommendation process. Nonetheless, the study relied solely on old-fashioned recommender systems for testing, thereby limiting the insights that could be gained about the effectiveness of the latest approaches.

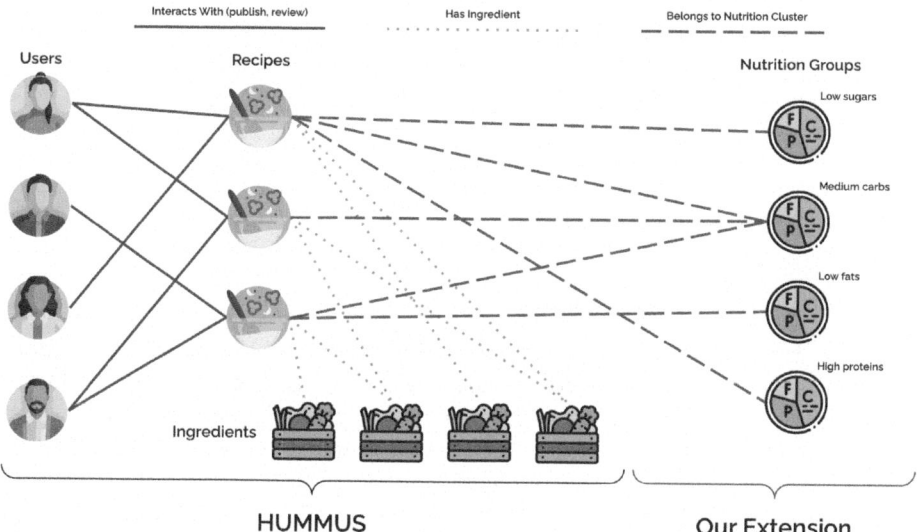

**Fig. 1.** A simplified version of HUMMUS alongside our extension, which incorporates relations between recipes and nutrient clusters in the KG.

In this paper, we address this gap by comprehensively assessing the performance of a wide set of models in recommending relevant and healthy recipes. We consider 10 recommender systems covering diverse architectural families, including matrix factorization, autoencoders, graph-based, and knowledge-aware methods. Our experimental evaluation is driven by HUMMUS [4], a KG that connects users, reviews, recipes, and ingredients into an unified structure. To address the SDG objective of healthy nutrition, we particularly focus our investigation on the nutrient intake of recommended recipes. Specifically, we identify clusters of recipes based on the distribution of their nutritional values and leverage these clusters to accomplish two goals. First, we aim to simplify the analysis of the nutritional intake distribution in models' recommendations, as interpreting nutritional values, e.g., sodium amount, in their common continuous form can be challenging without expert knowledge. Second, we integrate nutrient clusters as KG entities to enable knowledge-aware recommender systems to extract insightful patterns from the newly established relationships between recipes and nutritional groups. Figure 1 depicts a simplified version of HUMMUS and the described extension. Our results highlight the inability of recommender systems to properly capture users' distinct preferences and underscore the urgent need to concretely assess the potential damage of unhealthy food recommendations.

## 2   Methodology

### 2.1   Recommendation Task

In a food recommendation scenario, systems aim to encode users' preferences towards recipes by learning from past interactions. Implicit interactions between users $\mathcal{U}$ and recipes $\mathcal{I}$ are typically represented as a matrix $S \in \{0,1\}^{|\mathcal{U}| \times |\mathcal{I}|}$, where $s_{u,i} = 1$ denotes user $u$ interacted with recipe $i$, e.g., by writing a review for it. A model $f$ predicts a score $\hat{s}_{u,i}$, i.e. the predicted relevance of recipe $i$ for user $u$. Recommendation lists are generated for each user by suggesting the $k$ recipes with the highest predicted scores in the corresponding row vector $\hat{s}_u$.

### 2.2   Food Knowledge Graph

A food knowledge graph encodes contextually interconnected information about food in a graph $\mathcal{G} = \{(e_h, r, e_t) \mid e_h, e_t \in \mathcal{E}, r \in \mathcal{R}\}$, where $\mathcal{E}$ represents the set of entities, e.g., recipes, ingredients, and $\mathcal{R}$ the set of relations. Each triplet $(e_h, r, e_t)$ in $\mathcal{G}$ describes a concept, e.g., recipe A has ingredient B, as a relation $r$ (has) between a head entity $e_h$ (recipe A) and a tail entity $e_t$ (ingredient B). Our investigation focused on HUMMUS [4], a food knowledge graph connecting users, reviews, recipes, and ingredients. HUMMUS includes 1,409,914 reviews of 271,240 recipes by 276,377 users. We retain a simplified section of the KG item features, which includes only the relevant connections between recipes and corresponding ingredients, for a total of 524,649 entities and 3,827,549 relations.

**Table 1.** Amount of recipes clustered across three groups for each nutritional value.

|        | PRT | CAL | CFF | TTF | STF | CHL | SDM | CRB | DTF | SGR |
|--------|-----|-----|-----|-----|-----|-----|-----|-----|-----|-----|
| LOW    | 339k | 389k | 416k | 416k | 410k | 360k | 411k | 405k | 362k | 449k |
| MEDIUM | 136k | 101k | 79k | 79k | 86k | 123k | 85k | 87k | 115k | 46k |
| HIGH   | 28k | 13k | 10k | 10k | 8k | 20k | 8k | 11k | 25k | 9k |

## 2.3  Nutritional Features Modeling

HUMMUS represents an essential knowledge base for research into food recommendation. Nonetheless, the lack of nutrient entities in the food KG represents a significant limitation for several tasks. For instance, i) it prevents KG-based models from learning recipe-nutrient associations, ii) it hinders analytical assessments of model outputs in terms of nutrition and healthiness, e.g., model M mostly recommends low-carb food, and iii) it limits the extraction of KG paths between recipes and nutrient groups, which are used to generate informative explanations for end-users alongside recommended recipes [1–3].

In light of these issues, we extend HUMMUS by representing nutritional values as additional KG entities. We consider *proteins* (PRT), *calories* (CAL), *calories from fat* (CFF), *total fat* (TTF), *saturated fat* (STF), *cholesterol* (CHL), *sodium* (SDM), *carbohydrate* (CRB), *dietary fiber* (DTF), *sugars* (SGR). HUMMUS provides nutritional food composition as continuous values, which prevents recipes from sharing common nutrient entities as neighbors in the graph. Hence, to create meaningful associations as paths in the KG nutritional values need to be transformed in discrete nutritional categories. Due to the multifaceted nature of nutrition, nutrient requirements vary widely based on factors such as age, activity level, and health status. It follows that defining clear thresholds to categorize recipes into specific nutritional groups, such as low-, medium-, or high-protein food, is challenging and requires expert consultation.

Since existing categorizations are primarily limited to binary partitions [23] and aggregated healthiness scores, such as the WHO and FSA scores [4], might be confusing to non-experts, we employ clustering algorithms to generate fine-grained nutritional groups. In detail, we used the popular k-means algorithm to identify distinct intervals from the continuous nutritional features. Beforehand, we conducted an outlier detection analysis, which revealed some recipes reporting ambiguous nutrient amounts. For each nutrient amount $x$, we computed the Z-score $Z = (x - \mu)/\sigma$, where $\mu$ and $\sigma$ are the nutrient amount mean and standard deviation, respectively. Then, we removed recipes' nutrients reporting a Z-score greater than 3 [14]. To provide clear interpretations of nutrient distributions in food recommendations, we used k-means to discretize nutrient amounts into 3 intuitive clusters, namely *LOW, MEDIUM, HIGH*. We measured the clustering goodness with the silhouette score, which positively reported values greater than 0.6 for [24] each run. Table 1 reports the resulting distributions of the 3 clusters across each nutrient.

# 3   Experiments

## 3.1   Experimental Setup

**Data Preprocessing.** We employ k-core filtering to retain users and recipes with at least 5 interactions, repeating the process until no further nodes can be removed and discarding the corresponding KG entities. The dataset is split into train, validation, and test sets with a 6:2:2 ratio by sorting each user's interactions by recency, such that the test set includes the most recent interactions.

**Models.** Motivated by the goal of comprehensively assessing food recommendation in terms of utility and nutritional intake, we selected a wide range of diverse models. We considered traditional methods (Pop, ItemKNN), methods based on the Matrix Factorization (MF) architecture (BPR), Autoencoders (AE)-based methods (RaCT [16], DiffRec [27]), GNN-based methods (LightGCN [13], SGL [29]), KG-based methods (KGCN [26], KGAT [28], MCCLK [30]).

**Performance and Beyond-accuracy Assessment.** Following [4], we do not consider metrics that address personal users' features, e.g., medical properties, to score the personalization power of the tested models, due to the lack of such information in the dataset. We used common metrics to measure recommendation utility on top-$k$, $k \in \{10, 20\}$, such as Recall@$k$ and NDCG@$k$. To estimate nutritional intake of the recommendations we analyzed the distribution of different nutrients across the suggested lists and across the predicted clusters. We plan on implementing specific metrics that capture healthiness signals from the recommendations in future, such as nutrition-aware NDCG extensions.

## 3.2   Benchmark in Food Recommendation

We first evaluate the ability of the selected models to recommend relevant recipes according to personal users' preferences. As emphasized in previous sections, such an analysis was not addressed in prior studies and it still unclear how state-of-the-art systems perform in food recommendation.

Table 2 reports the recommendation utility in terms of Recall@$k$ and NDCG@$k$, highlighting the specific family each recommendation model belongs to. Except for ItemKNN and RaCT, the other models reported similar recommendation utility with respect to the traditional methods. Nonetheless, MCCLK exhibited as the model performing the best, followed by LightGCN. The latent representations learnt from the (knowledge) graph by such models led to higher recommendation utility compared with old-fashioned models, e.g., BPR, but such an observation is not consistent across models' families. Indeed, the other knowledge-aware systems, namely KGCN and KGAT, were outperformed by the common Pop baseline. The relevant performance of Pop implicitly reveals that the popularity bias issue affecting recommender systems employed in entertainment may also affect the food sector. This issue can cause various negative effects depending on the context in which recommender systems are used. While recommending only popular items in entertainment scenarios may damage providers' experience, suggesting a limited set of recipes in a food recommendation platform may significantly impact users' eating habits and expose them to potential health risks.

**Table 2.** Performance in food recommendation utility of the employed models. Bold and underlined values denote the best and second-best results, respectively.

|  |  | Recall@10 | Recall@20 | NDCG@10 | NDCG@20 |
|---|---|---|---|---|---|
| Traditional | Pop | 0.0210 | 0.0346 | 0.0159 | 0.0197 |
|  | ItemKNN | 0.0040 | 0.0060 | 0.0034 | 0.0038 |
| MF-based | BPR | 0.0209 | 0.0341 | 0.0159 | 0.0196 |
| AE-Based | RaCT | 0.0102 | 0.0173 | 0.0074 | 0.0094 |
|  | DiffRec | 0.0207 | 0.0314 | 0.0156 | 0.0186 |
| GNN-Based | SGL | 0.0202 | 0.0328 | 0.0156 | 0.0192 |
|  | LightGCN | 0.0220 | **0.0355** | 0.0163 | 0.0202 |
| KG-based | KGCN | 0.0188 | 0.0318 | 0.0142 | 0.0179 |
|  | KGAT | 0.0188 | 0.0301 | 0.0142 | 0.0173 |
|  | MCCLK | **0.0231** | 0.0352 | **0.0172** | **0.0206** |

**Table 3.** Models comparison in terms of utility (NDCG) and popularity bias (APLT). Bold and underlined values denote the best and second-best results, respectively.

|  |  | NDCG@10 | APLT@10 |
|---|---|---|---|
| Traditional | Pop | 0.0159 | 0.00% |
|  | ItemKNN | 0.0034 | **92.45%** |
| MF-based | BPR | 0.0159 | 3.15% |
| AE-Based | RaCT | 0.0074 | 9.18% |
|  | DiffRec | 0.0156 | 1.16% |
| GNN-Based | SGL | 0.0156 | 4.29% |
|  | LightGCN | 0.0163 | 4.66% |
| KG-based | KGCN | 0.0142 | 5.05% |
|  | KGAT | 0.0142 | 3.10% |
|  | MCCLK | **0.0172** | 2.17% |

In light of this, we briefly examine the impact of popularity bias on the tested models. In detail, we compare the utility of the top-10 recommendations in terms of NDCG with the average representation of less popular recipes. Following [5, 20], we categorize the 20% most popular items as the *short-head* and the remaining 80% items as the *long-tail*. To estimate the popularity bias, we use the average percentage of long-tail recipes (APLT) [5,20] as a proxy metric.

Table 3 compares side by side the NDCG and APLT values for the recommendations generated by the employed models. Results reveal that recommending recipes of varying popularity levels tends to decrease recommendation utility. Most of the models remained close to the 5% threshold for long-tail representation, while ItemKNN and RaCT managed to include at least 9% long-tail recipes. The higher APLT observed for these models may be attributed to the recipe-side viewpoint adopted by ItemKNN and to the RaCT's stochastic exploration within its reinforcement learning process. Despite achieving the highest utility, MCCLK exhibits a severe sensitivity to popularity bias, excelling primarily at selecting the most relevant recipes within the restricted short-head set. These findings highlight the importance of beyond-accuracy analyses in food recommendation.

Overall, although this experiment focused on a single dataset given its refined and interconnected knowledge, it opens up several research questions, such as whether recommender systems can suggest relevant food options without user-side knowledge.

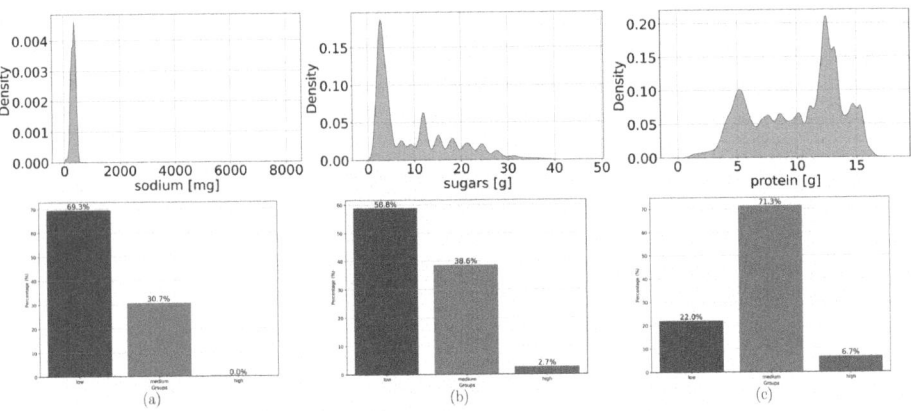

**Fig. 2.** First row: nutrient distribution across top-10 recommendations as continuous amount per 100g. Second row: nutrient distribution across top-10 recommendations across predicted clusters. (a) Sodium (SDM), (b) Sugars (SGR), (c) Protein (PRT).

### 3.3   Nutritional Intake Assessment

Our final experiment addresses the nutritional intake of the recommended recipes. We limit this analysis to MCCLK, given its higher utility on top-10 recommendation lists against all the other models. To highlight the benefits offered by the proposed nutritional clusters in terms of interpretability, we compare the distribution of nutrients across recommended recipes according to their standard continuous nature and according to their corresponding clusters.

Figure 2 depicts the described distributions across three nutrients, namely SDM, SGR, PRT, among the ten embedded as entities in the HUMMUS KG. The first two nutrients (from left to right) present a left-skewed distribution on the continuous space, while PRT is more uniform. However, it is straightforward to notice that additional expertise is needed to interpret such graphs. While individuals prone to physical activity, e.g., bodybuilders, may be used to recognize a high-protein recipe, sugars and sodium intake typically require expert monitoring and guidelines [18, 23]. Conversely, the distributions over the clusters are more easily interpretable due to their simplified three-fold nature. MCCLK recommended quite equally LOW- and MEDIUM-SDM recipes, mostly LOW-SGR and MEDIUM-PRT food options. Following related works' guidelines [18, 23], the most impactful nutrients SGR and SDM reflect healthy recipes when their representation is assigned to the LOW cluster. It can then be stated that MCCLK satisfies the SGR healthiness requirement and partially the SDM one.

Despite the limited assessment across models and nutrients, such an analysis exemplifies the potential benefits in encoding nutritional values in distinct groups and instilling recipe-nutrient information in knowledge bases.

## 4    Conclusions and Future Works

We addressed significant gaps in the literature that highlighted improper evaluation protocols in food recommendation. Specifically, we underlined the lack of prior studies comprehensively addressing performance of recent models at suggesting useful and healthy recipes. First, we extended a recent interconnected user-recipe-ingredient KG with novel entities representing nutrient categories identified by means of the k-means clustering algorithm. Second, we analyzed the distribution of nutrition values across recommendations by considering both their standard continuous nature and grouping them according to the corresponding nutrient cluster. Our analysis of popularity bias emphasizes the need for more balanced recommendation strategies in food recommendation systems. While most of the models achieve high utility, their reliance on popular recipes may limit the diversity and personalization of recommendations, potentially restricting users' exposure to nutritionally beneficial options from the long tail. This work aims to raise attention on healthiness concerns in line with the SDGs and promote healthier living habits. In future works, we plan to i) extend the HUMMUS KG by properly handling the aggregated nature of healthiness scores, ii) embeds sustainability ingredients estimates, and iii) adopt explainability tools based on KG path traversal.

## References

1. Afreen, N., et al.: Learner-centered ontology for explainable educational recommendation. In: Adjunct Proceedings of the 32nd ACM Conference on User Modeling, Adaptation and Personalization, UMAP Adjunct 2024, Cagliari, Italy, 1-4 July 2024, ACM (2024). https://doi.org/10.1145/3631700.3665226

2. Balloccu, G., Boratto, L., Cancedda, C., Fenu, G., Marras, M.: Knowledge is power, understanding is impact: Utility and beyond goals, explanation quality, and fairness in path reasoning recommendation. In: Kamps, J., (eds.) Advances in Information Retrieval - 45th European Conference on Information Retrieval, ECIR 2023, Dublin, Ireland, 2–6 April 2023, Proceedings, Part III, LNCS, vol. 13982, pp. 3–19. Springer (2023). https://doi.org/10.1007/978-3-031-28241-6_1

3. Balloccu, G., Boratto, L., Fenu, G., Marras, M.: Post processing recommender systems with knowledge graphs for recency, popularity, and diversity of explanations. In: Amigó, E., Castells, P., Gonzalo, J., Carterette, B., Culpepper, J.S., Kazai, G. (eds.) SIGIR 2022: The 45th International ACM SIGIR Conference on Research and Development in Information Retrieval, Madrid, Spain, 11–15 July 2022, pp. 646–656. ACM (2022). https://doi.org/10.1145/3477495.3532041

4. Bölz, F., Nurbakova, D., Calabretto, S., Gerl, A., Brunie, L., Kosch, H.: HUMMUS: a linked, healthiness-aware, user-centered and argument-enabling recipe data set for recommendation. In: Zhang, J., (eds.) Proceedings of the 17th ACM Conference on Recommender Systems, RecSys 2023, Singapore, Singapore, 18–22 September 2023. pp. 1–11. ACM (2023). https://doi.org/10.1145/3604915.3609491

5. Boratto, L., Fabbri, F., Fenu, G., Marras, M., Medda, G.: Robustness in fairness against edge-level perturbations in gnn-based recommendation. In: Goharian, N. (eds.) ECIR (3), LNCS, vol. 14610, pp. 38–55. Springer (2024)

6. Chavan, P., Thoms, B., Isaacs, J.T.: A recommender system for healthy food choices: building a hybrid model for recipe recommendations using big data sets. In: 54th Hawaii International Conference on System Sciences, HICSS 2021, Kauai, Hawaii, USA, 5 January 2021, pp. 1–10. ScholarSpace (2021). https://hdl.handle.net/10125/71074

7. Chelmis, C., Gergin, B.: Recipe networks and the principles of healthy food on the web. In: Lin, Y., Cha, M., Quercia, D. (eds.) Proceedings of the Seventeenth International AAAI Conference on Web and Social Media, ICWSM 2023, Limassol, Cyprus, 5–8 June 2023, pp. 95–102. AAAI Press (2023). https://doi.org/10.1609/ICWSM.V17I1.22129

8. Djojosoeparto, S.K., et al.: PEN consortium: strength of EU-level food environment policies and priority recommendations to create healthy food environments. Eur. J. Public Health **32**(3), 504–511 (2022)

9. Elsweiler, D., Trattner, C., Harvey, M.: Exploiting food choice biases for healthier recipe recommendation. In: Kando, N., Sakai, T., Joho, H., Li, H., de Vries, A.P., White, R.W. (eds.) Proceedings of the 40th International ACM SIGIR Conference on Research and Development in Information Retrieval, Shinjuku, Tokyo, Japan, 7–11 August 2017, pp. 575–584. ACM (2017). https://doi.org/10.1145/3077136.3080826

10. Etemadi, M., et al.: A systematic review of healthcare recommender systems: open issues, challenges, and techniques. Expert Syst. Appl. **213**(Part), 118823 (2023). https://doi.org/10.1016/J.ESWA.2022.118823

11. Felfernig, A., et al.: Recommender systems for sustainability: overview and research issues. Front. Big Data **6** (2024). https://doi.org/10.3389/FDATA.2023.1284511

12. Ge, M., Ricci, F., Massimo, D.: Health-aware food recommender system. In: Werthner, H., Zanker, M., Golbeck, J., Semeraro, G. (eds.) Proceedings of the 9th ACM Conference on Recommender Systems, RecSys 2015, Vienna, Austria, 16–20 September 2015, pp. 333–334. ACM (2015). https://dl.acm.org/citation.cfm?id=2796554

13. He, X., Deng, K., Wang, X., Li, Y., Zhang, Y., Wang, M.: Lightgcn: simplifying and powering graph convolution network for recommendation. In: Huang, J.X. (eds.) Proceedings of the 43rd International ACM SIGIR conference on research and development in Information Retrieval, SIGIR 2020, Virtual Event, China, 25–30 July 2020, pp. 639–648. ACM (2020). https://doi.org/10.1145/3397271.3401063

14. Ilyas, I.F., Chu, X.: Data cleaning, ACM Books, vol. 28. ACM (2019). https://doi.org/10.1145/3310205

15. Li, M., Li, L., Tao, X., Huang, J.X.: Mealrec$^+$: A meal recommendation dataset with meal-course affiliation for personalization and healthiness. In: Yang, G.H., Wang, H., Han, S., Hauff, C., Zuccon, G., Zhang, Y. (eds.) Proceedings of the 47th International ACM SIGIR Conference on Research and Development in Information Retrieval, SIGIR 2024, Washington DC, USA, 14–18 July 2024, pp. 564–574. ACM (2024). https://doi.org/10.1145/3626772.3657857

16. Lobel, S., Li, C., Gao, J., Carin, L.: Towards amortized ranking-critical training for collaborative filtering. CoRR **abs/1906.04281** (2019), http://arxiv.org/abs/1906.04281

17. Loesch, J., van Lier, I., de Boer, A., Scholtes, J., Dumontier, M., Celebi, R.: Automated identification of healthier food substitutions through a combination of graph neural networks and nutri-scores. J. Food Compos. Anal. **125**, 105829 (2024)

18. Martínez-Milán, M.A., Davó-Blanes, M.C., Comino, I., Caballero, P., Soares, P.: Sustainable and nutritional recommendations for the development of menus by school food services in Spain. Foods **11**(24) (2022). https://doi.org/10.3390/foods11244081, https://www.mdpi.com/2304-8158/11/24/4081

19. Musto, C., Trattner, C., Starke, A., Semeraro, G.: Towards a knowledge-aware food recommender system exploiting holistic user models. In: Kuflik, T., Torre, I., Burke, R., Gena, C. (eds.) Proceedings of the 28th ACM Conference on User Modeling, Adaptation and Personalization, UMAP 2020, Genoa, Italy, 12–18 July 2020, pp. 333–337. ACM (2020). https://doi.org/10.1145/3340631.3394880

20. Naghiaei, M., Rahmani, H.A., Deldjoo, Y.: Cpfair: Personalized consumer and producer fairness re-ranking for recommender systems. In: Amigó, E., Castells, P., Gonzalo, J., Carterette, B., Culpepper, J.S., Kazai, G. (eds.) SIGIR, pp. 770–779. ACM (2022)

21. Pecune, F., Callebert, L., Marsella, S.: A recommender system for healthy and personalized recipes recommendations. In: Said, A., Schäfer, H., Torkamaan, H., Trattner, C. (eds.) Proceedings of the 5th International Workshop on Health Recommender Systems co-located with the 14th ACM Conference on Recommender Systems 2020 (RecSys 2020), Worldwide, 26 September 2020, CEUR Workshop Proceedings, vol. 2684, pp. 15–20. CEUR-WS.org (2020). https://ceur-ws.org/Vol-2684/3-paginated.pdf

22. Rostami, M., Berahmand, K., Forouzandeh, S., Ahmadian, S., Farrahi, V., Oussalah, M.: A novel healthy food recommendation to user groups based on a deep social community detection approach. Neurocomputing **576**, 127326 (2024). https://doi.org/10.1016/J.NEUCOM.2024.127326

23. Rostami, M., Farahi, V., Berahmand, K., Forouzandeh, S., Ahmadian, S., Oussalah, M.: A novel explainable and health-aware food recommender system. In: Bernardino, J., Masciari, E., Rolland, C., Filipe, J. (eds.) Proceedings of the 14th International Joint Conference on Knowledge Discovery, Knowledge Engineering and Knowledge Management, IC3K 2022, Volume 3: KMIS, Valletta, Malta, 24–26 October 2022, pp. 208–215. SCITEPRESS (2022). https://doi.org/10.5220/0011561700003335

24. Shahapure, K.R., Nicholas, C.: Cluster quality analysis using silhouette score. In: Webb, G.I., Zhang, Z., Tseng, V.S., Williams, G., Vlachos, M., Cao, L. (eds.) 7th IEEE International Conference on Data Science and Advanced Analytics, DSAA 2020, Sydney, Australia, 6–9 October 2020, pp. 747–748. IEEE (2020). https://doi.org/10.1109/DSAA49011.2020.00096

25. Trattner, C., Elsweiler, D.: Investigating the healthiness of internet-sourced recipes: implications for meal planning and recommender systems. In: Barrett, R., Cummings, R., Agichtein, E., Gabrilovich, E. (eds.) Proceedings of the 26th International Conference on World Wide Web, WWW 2017, Perth, Australia, 3–7 April 2017. pp. 489–498. ACM (2017). https://doi.org/10.1145/3038912.3052573

26. Wang, H., Zhao, M., Xie, X., Li, W., Guo, M.: Knowledge graph convolutional networks for recommender systems. In: Liu, L. (eds.) The World Wide Web Conference, WWW 2019, San Francisco, CA, USA, 13–17 May 2019, pp. 3307–3313. ACM (2019). https://doi.org/10.1145/3308558.3313417

27. Wang, W., Xu, Y., Feng, F., Lin, X., He, X., Chua, T.: Diffusion recommender model. In: Chen, H., Duh, W.E., Huang, H., Kato, M.P., Mothe, J., Poblete, B. (eds.) Proceedings of the 46th International ACM SIGIR Conference on Research and Development in Information Retrieval, SIGIR 2023, Taipei, Taiwan, 23–27 July 2023, pp. 832–841. ACM (2023). https://doi.org/10.1145/3539618.3591663

28. Wang, X., He, X., Cao, Y., Liu, M., Chua, T.: KGAT: knowledge graph attention network for recommendation. In: Teredesai, A., Kumar, V., Li, Y., Rosales, R., Terzi, E., Karypis, G. (eds.) Proceedings of the 25th ACM SIGKDD International Conference on Knowledge Discovery & Data Mining, KDD 2019, Anchorage, AK, USA, 4–8 August 2019, pp. 950–958. ACM (2019). https://doi.org/10.1145/3292500.3330989

29. Wu, J., Wang, X., Feng, F., He, X., Chen, L., Lian, J., Xie, X.: Self-supervised graph learning for recommendation. In: Diaz, F., Shah, C., Suel, T., Castells, P., Jones, R., Sakai, T. (eds.) SIGIR 2021: The 44th International ACM SIGIR Conference on Research and Development in Information Retrieval, Virtual Event, Canada, 11–15 July 2021, pp. 726–735. ACM (2021). https://doi.org/10.1145/3404835.3462862

30. Zou, D., et al.: Multi-level cross-view contrastive learning for knowledge-aware recommender system. In: Amigó, E., Castells, P., Gonzalo, J., Carterette, B., Culpepper, J.S., Kazai, G. (eds.) SIGIR 2022: The 45th International ACM SIGIR Conference on Research and Development in Information Retrieval, Madrid, Spain, 11–15 July 2022, pp. 1358–1368. ACM (2022). https://doi.org/10.1145/3477495.3532025

# Modeling Social Media Recommendation Impacts Using Academic Networks: A Graph Neural Network Approach

Sabrina Guidotti[1], Gregor Donabauer[2], Simone Somazzi[1], Udo Kruschwitz[2], Davide Taibi[3], and Dimitri Ognibene[1(✉)]

[1] Università degli Studi di Milano-Bicocca, Milan, Italy
`dimitri.ognibene@unimib.it`
[2] University of Regensburg, Regensburg, Germany
[3] National Research Council of Italy, Palermo, Italy

**Abstract.** The widespread use of social media has highlighted potential negative impacts on society and individuals, largely driven by recommendation algorithms that shape user behavior and social dynamics. Understanding these algorithms' impact is essential but challenging due to the complex, distributed nature of social media networks as well as limited access to real-world data and in particular recommendations, usually not reported. This study proposes to use academic social networks as a proxy for investigating recommendation systems in social media. By employing Graph Neural Networks (GNNs), we develop a model that separates the prediction of academic infosphere (in which a recommender can play a main role) from user behavior prediction, allowing us to simulate recommender-generated infospheres and assess different recommenders' impact on the model's performance in predicting future co-authorships. Our approach aims to improve our understanding of recommendation systems' roles and social networks modeling. To support the reproducibility of our work we publicly make available our implementations: https://github.com/DimNeuroLab/academic_network_project

**Keywords:** Social Networks · Societal Well-Being · GNNs

## 1 Introduction

The widespread use of social media has revealed various aspects that may negatively affect both society and individuals using such platforms [2,11,19]. Social networks are complex systems where user interactions are heavily influenced by recommendation algorithms, which shape user behavior and, in turn, the broader social impact [22,23]. Examples for algorithmic threats on social media include filter bubbles [21] and echo chambers [11,18]. To achieve a more *sustainable* social media landscape, it has been argued that platforms should as a first step open their personalization algorithms [25]. However, this has not happened so far, which highlights the importance of understanding the underlying mechanisms to mitigate negative effects and promote societal well-being [23]. Studying these mechanisms is challenging [4,6] due to the distributed, heterogeneous, and large-scale nature of social media networks [5,7] as well as a lack of access to real-world data and in particular recommendations, usually not available, making it difficult to align theoretical models with real-world dynamics.

As a solution, academic social networks, which share similarities with social media networks [15,16], could serve as a proxy for research in the field [10]. While they still miss recommendations, they provide easier access to data [33] and allow to study connectivity dynamics when recommendation systems are introduced.

However, modeling academic behavior is complex due to the non-local nature of academic activities, which involve diverse topics, venues, and collaborations [16]. Such activities are likely determined by an academic being exposed to non-local information presented to them by recommenders (infosphere) [3]. Characterizing the recommenders' contribution could therefore lead to more realistic academic models and improve computational efficiency. Yet this requires analyzing a large set of potential interactions, often overlooking computational efficiencies that could be achieved through network structures.

In this work, we aim to better understand the role of recommendation systems in social media by using academic networks as a proxy. We employ Graph Neural Networks (GNNs) to develop a model that separates predicting an academic infosphere from predicting its behavior. This allows us to simulate different potential infospheres generated by different recommender systems and parametrizations. We study if under the same data conditions different assumptions on the recommender model lead to a different model performance in link prediction of future co-authorships.

## 2   Related Work

Much research in recommender systems focuses on the broader social and behavioral impact. Studies for example showed that recommendations can influence user satisfaction [20] or that social explanations can affect user interactions but do not always improve satisfaction with the content [29]. Recommenders are also known to influence user preferences through mechanisms like the anchoring effect [1]. Similarly, in context of social media, recommenders can influence users through effects like filter bubbles [21] or echo chambers [11].

Simulations of recommenders can help to reveal such effects. Studies have for example investigated how repeated interactions can amplify biases, such as popularity bias and filter bubbles, impacting long-term user behavior [34] or how personalized recommendations can increase commonality among users [9,13]. Our research follows along these lines of work with an explicit focus on how simulated recommenders influence can support prediction of user behavior in social networks.

While datasets from real social media platforms (such as Facebook [17,26,27], Twitter [8,17], and Twitch [26,28]) do exist, most of them are either outdated or contain only a limited number of interacting agents (typically tens of thousands of nodes). In contrast, academic social network datasets are released on a regular basis and contain significantly higher numbers of agents and interactions (millions of nodes)[1].

Building on work that has used academic networks in tasks like web user profiling [30], topic expertise search [32] or social network extraction of academics [31], we want to use such data to improve understanding how different simulated infospheres influence learning of user behaviour.

# 3   Methodology

Our approach involves three key components: **(1)** characterizing the **history** of the agents' behavior within the social network, **(2)** simulating a recommender system by integrating **infosphere** into the network, and **(3)** learning models on these networks to evaluate how different infospheres influence the model's prediction performance of the agents' future behavior.

## 3.1   Agent History and Infosphere Simulation

For modelling the authors' **History** we track the papers they have written, the co-authors they have collaborated with, and the topics they have worked on. This history is represented as a time-dependent graph $G_y$, containing all observable information up to year $y$. Each graph $G_y$ includes three types of nodes: *author*, *paper*, and *topic*, as well as three types of edges: (*author, writes, paper*), (*paper, deals_with, topic*), and (*paper, cites, paper*). Paper nodes are characterized by the year of publication. All other nodes in the graph are initialized with random embeddings which are jointly learnt during model training.

We then introduce the concept of **Infosphere**, representing the information an author might encounter through a recommender system or other algorithmic components (e.g. search engines). Such systems access content and authors beyond the author's direct and local experience, with suggestions guided by the author's prior interactions rather than random selection. Our concept of infosphere is related to the idea of *impressions*, which are defined as the recommendations presented to the user along with their corresponding interactions [24]. Although difficult to model due to limited knowledge of the underlying algorithms, we simulate the infosphere with minimal assumptions, ensuring that it includes both information the author has definitely encountered and what they might have encountered through similar processes. Adopting an hindsight approach, we use information from subsequent years' graphs to derive a set of paths that represent the author's connections with nodes in their history as they appear in the following year within the current year's graph. By adding noise based on a set of probabilities which determine whether to follow existing paths or switch directions we aim to make the simulation more realistic. This approach

---

[1] https://www.aminer.cn/citation.

allows us to develop models that keep user and recommender modeling separate, so that the recommenders can pursue different objectives. By creating a minimal infosphere, we develop a more robust and general model of authors, which can be used to refine recommender systems based on principles such as content similarity. For comparison, we also generated alternative infospheres: one consisting of the $n$ most popular papers in a given year $y$, and another focusing on the $n$ most popular papers within the $m$ most-used topics by an author $x$ in that year.

## 3.2   Seedgraph and Expansion

Our infosphere calculation is based on a seedgraph, a directed graph composed of paths associated with each author. Each path traces the shortest connection from an element in the author's history in year $y + 1$ back to the graph in year $y$.

We first initialize a "frontier-seeds" dictionary with the author's publications and related information, then iteratively expand both the author node and the "frontier-seeds" by 1-hop. A "compare-frontiers" function identifies paths when overlaps occur. The process continues until all paths are identified, allowing efficient seedgraph construction by merging node lists when common nodes are found.

To achieve realistic expansion, the seedgraph is extended with plausible alternative paths. For better understanding, nodes can be interpreted as colored as white, orange, or green, where orange nodes belong to the seed graph, green nodes are added during expansion, and white nodes belong to neither. The algorithm requires several inputs: the author-node, the full-graph, the seed graph, and parameters (p1, p2, p3, f):

**p1:** Probability of following a path of orange nodes (seedgraph). Higher values extend the original infosphere.
**p2:** Probability of following a path of green nodes (expanded graph). Higher values create paths similar to the seedgraph.
**p3:** Probability of returning to the author node. Higher values concentrate noise near the author node.
**f:** Number of new nodes added per seedgraph path (2, 4, or 6).

## 3.3   Behaviour Prediction

To assess the impact of the simulated recommender via infosphere on the prediction of future actions of agents (authors) within the social network, we evaluate how the configurations described previously affect a model's ability to forecast future co-authorship collaborations.

We model the task of co-authorship prediction as a link prediction problem and learn a GNN that predicts future co-authorships that do not yet exist as edges in the current graph. To do this, we add co-author edges derived by multi-hop walks from author nodes across the existing heterogeneous graph. In both scenarios - predicting links within a specific year or forecasting future connections - we also add and sample negative examples of edges at a ratio of 1:1.

# 4 Experiments

## 4.1 Dataset

We use the *DBLP-Citation-network v14* dataset [33] from AMiner, which includes data from sources like DBLP, ACM, and MAG to provide a comprehensive overview of academic publications and their citation relationships. We selected this dataset as it is the most up-to-date dataset available (released in 2023) and offers a reasonable number of nodes and edges making it a good fit for our experiments. Specifically, it contains 5,259,858 paper nodes and 36,630,661 citation edges. Additionally, each paper is associated with related information, such as authors, venues, and topics, which can be modeled as additional nodes in a heterogeneous network.

## 4.2 Infosphere Parameters

We evaluate different parameters for creating the infosphere as described previously. When reporting results based on these combinations we refer to the run ids assigned here.

- *trial0* Random Infosphere
- *trial1* (p1=0.5; p2=0.5; p3=0.5; f=2)
- *trial2* (p1=0.75; p2=0.5; p3=0.5; f=2)
- *trial3* (p1=0.5; p2=0.75; p3=0.5; f=2)
- *trial4* (p1=0.5; p2=0.5; p3=0.75; f=2)
- *trial5* (p1=0.25; p2=0.75; p3=0.25; f=2)

## 4.3 Model and Training

For the learning process, we use an encoder-decoder network. The encoder consists of a heterogeneous Graph Neural Network with two consecutive graph convolution layers to encode the input graphs and generate expressive node representations. In our experiments we evaluated GraphSAGE [12] and Heterogeneous Graph Transformer (HGT) [14] as encoder layers. While HGT uses Transformer blocks for neighborhood aggregation we vary the aggregation strategies for GraphSAGE. The decoder is a simple two-layer feed-forward neural network that classifies node pairs as either connected (existing edge/link) or not, making the task as a binary classification problem. The model is trained end-to-end using binary cross-entropy loss and the Adam optimizer. We run training for 500 epochs with early stopping and a patience of 10, the batch-size is set to 1024 and the the learning rate to 0.00001.

**Table 1.** Accuracy scores for prediction of next year's co-authors without and with different infospheres as well as various model setups. *Infosphere dropped* refers to the number of infosphere edges that were removed in the respective setup. *Infosphere Params* refers to the trials introduced in Sect. 4.2 for infosphere type author, note that some (2–4) are omitted due to similar results.

| Inf. Type | Inf. Params | Inf. Dropped | Accuracy | Aggregation | GNN Type |
|---|---|---|---|---|---|
| - | - | - | 0.788 | max | SAGE |
| - | - | - | 0.780 | mean | SAGE |
| - | - | - | 0.796 | min | SAGE |
| - | - | - | 0.802 | sum | SAGE |
| - | - | - | 0.798 | N/A | HGT |
| author | 0 | - | 0.892 | max | SAGE |
| author | 0 | - | 0.892 | mean | SAGE |
| author | 0 | - | 0.893 | min | SAGE |
| author | 0 | - | 0.886 | sum | SAGE |
| author | 0 | - | 0.893 | N/A | HGT |
| author | 5 | - | 0.889 | max | SAGE |
| author | 5 | - | 0.891 | mean | SAGE |
| author | 5 | - | 0.890 | min | SAGE |
| author | 5 | - | 0.888 | sum | SAGE |
| author | 0 | 10% | 0.888 | sum | SAGE |
| author | 0 | 25% | 0.881 | sum | SAGE |
| author | 0 | 50% | 0.883 | sum | SAGE |
| author | 0 | 75% | 0.862 | sum | SAGE |
| author | 0 | 90% | 0.834 | sum | SAGE |
| author | 0 | 100% | 0.789 | sum | SAGE |
| top-paper | 10 | - | 0.501 | sum | SAGE |
| top-paper | 10 | - | 0.585 | max | SAGE |
| top-paper | 10 | - | 0.772 | mean | SAGE |
| top-paper | 10 | - | 0.750 | min | SAGE |
| top-paper | 10 | - | 0.508 | sum | SAGE |
| top-paper | 10 | - | 0.662 | N/A | HGT |
| top-paper | 50 | - | 0.649 | sum | SAGE |
| top-paper | 50 | - | 0.741 | max | SAGE |
| top-paper | 50 | - | 0.745 | mean | SAGE |
| top-paper | 50 | - | 0.793 | min | SAGE |
| top-paper | 50 | - | 0.704 | sum | SAGE |
| top-paper | 50 | - | 0.770 | N/A | HGT |
| top-paper-per-topic | [1,10] | - | 0.678 | sum | SAGE |
| top-paper-per-topic | [1,10] | - | 0.754 | max | SAGE |

continued

**Table 1.** continued

| Inf. Type | Inf. Params | Inf. Dropped | Accuracy | Aggregation | GNN Type |
|-----------|-------------|--------------|----------|-------------|----------|
| top-paper-per-topic | [1,10] | - | 0.690 | mean | SAGE |
| top-paper-per-topic | [1,10] | - | 0.748 | min | SAGE |
| top-paper-per-topic | [1,10] | - | 0.643 | sum | SAGE |
| top-paper-per-topic | [1,10] | - | 0.728 | N/A | HGT |
| top-paper-per-topic | [1,50] | - | 0.667 | sum | SAGE |
| top-paper-per-topic | [1,50] | - | 0.745 | max | SAGE |
| top-paper-per-topic | [1,50] | - | 0.676 | mean | SAGE |
| top-paper-per-topic | [1,50] | - | 0.789 | min | SAGE |
| top-paper-per-topic | [1,50] | - | 0.621 | sum | SAGE |
| top-paper-per-topic | [1,50] | - | 0.778 | N/A | HGT |
| top-paper-per-topic | [2,5] | - | 0.723 | sum | SAGE |
| top-paper-per-topic | [2,5] | - | 0.755 | N/A | HGT |
| top-paper-per-topic | [5,10] | - | 0.709 | sum | SAGE |
| top-paper-per-topic | [5,10] | - | 0.784 | N/A | HGT |
| top-paper-per-topic | [10,1] | - | 0.562 | sum | SAGE |
| top-paper-per-topic | [10,1] | - | 0.734 | N/A | HGT |
| top-paper-per-topic | [10,5] | - | 0.721 | sum | SAGE |
| top-paper-per-topic | [10,5] | - | 0.787 | N/A | HGT |
| top-paper-per-topic | [50,1] | - | 0.753 | sum | SAGE |
| top-paper-per-topic | [50,1] | - | 0.781 | N/A | HGT |

## 5  Results

Table 1 summarizes the results from our experiments on predicting co-authors using various model setups and infosphere configurations. We achieved an accuracy of 78–80% when predicting co-authors without any infosphere. When incorporating the infosphere generated by our methods, performance improved, with accuracy reaching around 88%, particularly in setups without seedgraph expansions. Testing different aggregation functions (sum, min, mean, max) yielded minimal differences in outcomes.

We also evaluated an alternative infosphere based on the most popular papers (10 and 50). This approach performed worse than using the future infosphere and was comparable to or worse than having no infosphere, likely due to the noise introduced by less relevant papers. The min aggregation function slightly improved results but remained close to those without an infosphere.

Finally, we evaluated an infosphere configuration that connects authors to the most popular papers within their frequently used topics. Various combinations of topics and papers were evaluated and the results are again much lower than with author-based infosphere, sometimes even falling below the scores we get when using no infosphere at all.

## 6     Conclusion

In this study, we successfully demonstrated how simulating recommenders through infospheres helps understanding user behavior when based on academic network data. Our analysis showed that the training process does not cancel out recommender assumptions when splitting the network prediction model in user model and recommender based infosphere. On the contrary, integrating correct or incorrect recommender systems throughout the learning process can have a substantial impact on the accuracy of the user model. In addition, not integrating an explicit recommender model was still better than integrating some reasonable but inaccurate recommender model. Moreover, our analysis shows that the infosphere most benefits predictions of new edges that are not present in the history. These findings can help to improve the understanding of how recommender mechanisms influence communities, especially those currently exposed to negative impacts in social networks.

**Acknowledgments.** We want to thank the anonymous reviewers for their insightful comments which have helped us to improve the paper.

This work was supported by the project COURAGE funded by the Volkswagen Foundation, grant number 95564.

## References

1. Adomavicius, G., Bockstedt, J.C., Curley, S.P., Zhang, J.: Do recommender systems manipulate consumer preferences? A study of anchoring effects. Inf. Syst. Res. **24**(4), 956–975 (2013)
2. Almourad, M.B., McAlaney, J., Skinner, T., Pleya, M., Ali, R.: Defining digital addiction: key features from the literature. Psihologija **53**(3), 237–253 (2020)
3. Chen, J., Dong, H., Wang, X., Feng, F., Wang, M., He, X.: Bias and debias in recommender system: a survey and future directions. ACM Trans. Inf. Syst. **41**(3), 1–39 (2023)
4. Chen, R., Hua, Q., Chang, Y.S., Wang, B., Zhang, L., Kong, X.: A survey of collaborative filtering-based recommender systems: From traditional methods to hybrid methods based on social networks. IEEE Access **6**, 64301–64320 (2018)
5. Covington, P., Adams, J., Sargin, E.: Deep neural networks for YouTube recommendations. In: Proceedings of the 10th ACM Conference on Recommender Systems, pp. 191–198 (2016)
6. Eirinaki, M., Gao, J., Varlamis, I., Tserpes, K.: Recommender systems for large-scale social networks: a review of challenges and solutions (2018)
7. Eksombatchai, C., et al.: Pixie: A system for recommending 3+ billion items to 200+ million users in real-time. In: Proceedings of the 2018 World Wide Web Conference, pp. 1775–1784 (2018)

8. Fink, C.G., Omodt, N., Zinnecker, S., Sprint, G.: A congressional twitter network dataset quantifying pairwise probability of influence. Data in Brief (2023)
9. Fleder, D., Hosanagar, K., Buja, A.: Recommender systems and their effects on consumers: the fragmentation debate. In: Proceedings of the 11th ACM Conference on Electronic Commerce, pp. 229–230 (2010)
10. Fortunato, S., et al.: Science of science. Science **359**(6379), eaao0185 (2018)
11. Gillani, N., Yuan, A., Saveski, M., Vosoughi, S., Roy, D.: Me, my echo chamber, and I: introspection on social media polarization. In: Proceedings of the 2018 World Wide Web Conference, pp. 823–831 (2018)
12. Hamilton, W., Ying, Z., Leskovec, J.: Inductive representation learning on large graphs. In: Advances in Neural Information Processing Systems, vol. 30 (2017)
13. Hosanagar, K., Fleder, D., Lee, D., Buja, A.: Will the global village fracture into tribes? Recommender systems and their effects on consumer fragmentation. Manage. Sci. **60**(4), 805–823 (2014)
14. Hu, Z., Dong, Y., Wang, K., Sun, Y.: Heterogeneous graph transformer. In: Proceedings of the Web Conference 2020, pp. 2704–2710 (2020)
15. Jordan, K.: From social networks to publishing platforms: a review of the history and scholarship of academic social network sites. Front. Digit. Humanit. **6**, 5 (2019)
16. Kong, X., Shi, Y., Yu, S., Liu, J., Xia, F.: Academic social networks: modeling, analysis, mining and applications. J. Netw. Comput. Appl. **132**, 86–103 (2019)
17. Leskovec, J., Mcauley, J.: Learning to discover social circles in ego networks. In: Advances in Neural Information Processing Systems, vol. 25 (2012)
18. Lomonaco, F., Taibi, D., Trianni, V., Buršić, S., Donabauer, G., Ognibene, D.: Yes, echo-chambers mislead you too: A game-based educational experience to reveal the impact of social media personalization algorithms. In: Fulantelli, G., Burgos, D., Casalino, G., Cimitile, M., Lo Bosco, G., Taibi, D. (eds.) Higher Education Learning Methodologies and Technologies Online, pp. 330–344. Springer Nature Switzerland, Cham (2023). https://doi.org/10.1007/978-3-031-29800-4_26
19. Marengo, D., Longobardi, C., Fabris, M.A., Settanni, M.: Highly-visual social media and internalizing symptoms in adolescence: the mediating role of body image concerns. Comput. Hum. Behav. **82**, 63–69 (2018)
20. Nanou, T., Lekakos, G., Fouskas, K.: The effects of recommendations' presentation on persuasion and satisfaction in a movie recommender system. Multimedia Syst. **16**, 219–230 (2010)
21. Nikolov, D., Oliveira, D.F., Flammini, A., Menczer, F.: Measuring online social bubbles. PeerJ Comput. Sci. **1**, e38 (2015)
22. Ognibene, D., et al.: Moving beyond benchmarks and competitions: towards addressing social media challenges in an educational context. Datenbank-Spektrum **23**(1), 27–39 (2023)
23. Ognibene, D., et al.: Challenging social media threats using collective well-being-aware recommendation algorithms and an educational virtual companion. Front. Artif. Intell. **5**, 654930 (2023)
24. Pérez Maurera, F.B., Ferrari Dacrema, M., Saule, L., Scriminaci, M., Cremonesi, P.: Contentwise impressions: an industrial dataset with impressions included. In: Proceedings of the 29th ACM International Conference on Information & Knowledge Management, pp. 3093–3100. CIKM 2020, Association for Computing Machinery, New York, NY, USA (2020). https://doi.org/10.1145/3340531.3412774
25. Reviglio, U., Agosti, C.: Thinking outside the black-box: The case for "algorithmic sovereignty" in social media. Social Media + Society **6**(2), 2056305120915613 (2020). https://doi.org/10.1177/2056305120915613

26. Rozemberczki, B., Allen, C., Sarkar, R.: Multi-scale attributed node embedding (2019)
27. Rozemberczki, B., Davies, R., Sarkar, R., Sutton, C.: GEMSEC: graph embedding with self clustering. In: Proceedings of the 2019 IEEE/ACM International Conference on Advances in Social Networks Analysis and Mining 2019, pp. 65–72. ACM (2019)
28. Rozemberczki, B., Sarkar, R.: Twitch gamers: a dataset for evaluating proximity preserving and structural role-based node embeddings (2021)
29. Sharma, A., Cosley, D.: Do social explanations work? Studying and modeling the effects of social explanations in recommender systems. In: Proceedings of the 22nd International Conference on World Wide Web, pp. 1133–1144 (2013)
30. Tang, J., Yao, L., Zhang, D., Zhang, J.: A combination approach to web user profiling. ACM TKDD **5**(1), 1–44 (2010)
31. Tang, J., Zhang, D., Yao, L.: Social network extraction of academic researchers. In: ICDM 2007, pp. 292–301 (2007)
32. Tang, J., et al.: Topic level expertise search over heterogeneous networks. Mach. Learn. J. **82**(2), 211–237 (2011)
33. Tang, J., Zhang, J., Yao, L., Li, J., Zhang, L., Su, Z.: ArnetMiner: extraction and mining of academic social networks. In: Proceedings of the 14th ACM SIGKDD International Conference on Knowledge Discovery and Data Mining, pp. 990–998 (2008)
34. Yao, S., et al.: Measuring recommender system effects with simulated users. arXiv preprint arXiv:2101.04526 (2021)

# Green Recommender Systems: Optimizing Dataset Size for Energy-Efficient Algorithm Performance

Ardalan Arabzadeh[1(✉)], Tobias Vente[1], and Joeran Beel[1,2]

[1] Department of Electrical Engineering and Computer Science, University of Siegen,
Siegen, Germany
`ardalan.arabzadeh@student.uni-siegen.de, joeran.beel@uni-siegen.de`
[2] Recommender-Systems.com, Siegen, Germany
`https://www.recommender-systems.com`

**Abstract.** As recommender systems become increasingly prevalent, the environmental impact and energy efficiency of training these large-scale models have come under scrutiny. This paper investigates the potential for energy-efficient algorithm performance by optimizing dataset sizes through downsampling techniques. We conducted experiments on the MovieLens 100K, 1M, 10M and Amazon Toys and Games datasets, analyzing the performance of various recommender algorithms under different portions of dataset size. Our results indicate that while more training data generally leads to higher performance in algorithms, certain algorithms, such as FunkSVD and BiasedMF, particularly in cases involving more unbalanced and sparse dataset like Amazon Toys and Games, maintain high-quality recommendations with up to 50% reduction in training data, achieving nDCG@10 scores within ∼13% of their full dataset performance. These findings suggest that strategic dataset reduction can decrease computational and environmental costs without substantially compromising recommendation quality. This study advances sustainable and green recommender systems by providing actionable insights for reducing energy consumption while maintaining effectiveness.

**Keywords:** Sustainability · Green RecSys · Dataset Downsampling · Energy Efficiency · Environmental Impact

## 1 Introduction

Advancements in recommender systems have enhanced user experience. However, these advancements came at a substantial computational and energy cost [26,30]. Large datasets do not only increase operational expenses but also result in higher energy consumption and carbon emissions, contributing to a more significant environmental impact [1,13,26,27,30]. In extreme cases, energy consumption between datasets differs by factor 1,444, such as between LastFM vs. Yelp with the DGCF algorithm [30].

L. Boratto et al. (Eds.): RecSoGood 2024, CCIS 2470, pp. 73–82, 2025.
https://doi.org/10.1007/978-3-031-87654-7_7

Given the environmental and computational challenges associated with large datasets, it's important to question whether using the entire datasets is always necessary. For instance, datasets like MovieLens 10M are frequently employed in training recommender systems. But is it necessary to use 10 million instances, especially with simple baseline algorithms? Or would downsampling the dataset to e.g. 10% suffices, which, in turn, might save 90% of energy?

In our work, we investigate whether downsampling the dataset can lead to an acceptable trade-off between energy efficiency and the performance of recommender algorithms. We see our work in the context of "Green Recommender Systems" as defined by Beel et al. as follows [8].

*"Green Recommender Systems" are recommender systems designed to minimize their environmental impact throughout their life cycle - from research and design to implementation and operation. Green Recommender Systems typically aim to match the performance of traditional systems but may also accept trade-offs in accuracy or other metrics to prioritize sustainability. Minimizing environmental impact typically but not necessarily means minimizing energy consumption and $CO_2$ emissions. [8]*

For our current work, we hypothesize that by downsampling recommender system datasets, we can save time, energy, and CO2 emissions, while obtaining nearly the same performance as with the full datasets.

## 2    Related Work

The field of green recommender systems has only started evolving recently [26,30]. We also recently proposed "e-fold cross-validation", an energy-efficient alternative to k-fold cross-validation [4,19]. Wegmeth et al. introduced EMERS, a tool to measure the electricity consumption of recommender system experiments [31]. Also, judging based on the "accepted papers" list of the RecSoGood workshop, more related work is to be published very soon [22,28].

While the "green" concept in recommender systems is new, other disciplines, like Automated Machine Learning, explore options to save energy for a longer time [2,10,11,16,23,25,29].

In the domain of recommender systems, several studies have explored the impact of dataset size on the efficiency of algorithmic performance, which aligns the key focus of this study. Notably, Bentzer and Thulin explore the trade-off between accuracy and computational efficiency in collaborative filtering algorithms under limited data conditions [9]. They found that IBCF algorithm performs better in terms of accuracy with smaller datasets compared to SVD algorithm, while SVD outperforms IBCF in terms of speed and scalability with larger datasets. Their study highlights the performance differences between these two algorithms but does not address how other algorithms perform under similar constraints. This gap is relevant to our research, which seeks to evaluate a wider range of algorithms for optimizing both energy efficiency and performance.

Additionally, Jain and Jindal's review emphasizes that strategic sampling and filtering can enhance recommendation efficiency by improving computational speed and accuracy [17]. However, their review lacks experimental validation of how these techniques impact algorithm performance with varying dataset sizes. Our study addresses this gap by empirically evaluating these effects on recommender systems. Judging based on the paper's title and abstract, Spillo et al. appear to have conducted research similar to ours [27]. However, at the time of conducting our research and writing our manuscript, the work of Spillo et al. was not yet publicly available but only announced on the ACM Recommender Systems conference website as an accepted paper.

It is worth mentioning that most papers and experiments focusing on downsampling and data efficiency are predominantly conducted in domains like (automated) machine learning, AI and computer vision [2,10,11,16,23,29], with more extensive research compared to the recommender systems domain. Moreover, studies within this broader field also corroborate the potential benefits of downsampling. Research by Zogaj et al. demonstrates that reducing dataset sizes can enhance both computational efficiency and predictive accuracy in genetic programming-based AutoML systems [32]. Their experiments show that downsampling large datasets can even in some cases result in better performance than using the full dataset, with shorter search times.

These studies underscore and evaluate the potential benefits of downsampling and its impact on model performance, but are not directly applicable to traditional recommender system algorithms, where such effects remain underexplored.

## 3   Methodology

### 3.1   Datasets and Preprocessing

We used four datasets for our experiment: **MovieLens 100K**, **MovieLens 1M**, **MovieLens 10M**, and **Amazon Toys and Games**. The MovieLens datasets feature relatively balanced ratings across a scale from 1 to 5. In contrast, the Amazon Toys and Games dataset exhibits a skewed distribution, with ∼90% of ratings concentrated in the 4 and 5 ranges. The following preprocessing steps were applied to the datasets: removal of duplicate rows, averaging duplicate ratings, and applying 10-core pruning to retain users and items with at least 10 interactions.

The dataset details before and after preprocessing are in Table 1.

### 3.2   Data Splitting and Downsampling

We applied a User-Based Split [20], with 10% of each user's interactions randomly selected for the test set, 10% for validation, and 80% for training. The validation set was used for hyperparameter tuning, maintaining a comparable size between the validation and test sets to account for the impact of the training-to-validation/test ratio on results, as highlighted in prior research [12]. The training

**Table 1.** Basic information of datasets before and after preprocessing

| Dataset | Before Preprocessing | | | | | After Preprocessing | | | | |
|---|---|---|---|---|---|---|---|---|---|---|
| | #Users | #Items | #Interactions | Avg. #Int. per user | Avg. #Int. per item | #Users | #Items | #Interactions | Avg. #Int. per user | Avg. #Int. per item |
| MovieLens 100K | 943 | 1,682 | 100,000 | 106 | 59 | 943 | 1,152 | 97,953 | 103 | 85 |
| MovieLens 1M | 6,040 | 3,706 | 1,000,209 | 165 | 269 | 6,040 | 3,260 | 998,539 | 165 | 306 |
| MovieLens 10M | 69,878 | 10,677 | 10,000,054 | 143 | 936 | 69,878 | 9708 | 9,995,471 | 143 | 1029 |
| Amazon Toys and Games | 208,180 | 78,772 | 1,828,971 | 8 | 23 | 11,609 | 8,443 | 202,721 | 17 | 24 |

set was downsampled to various proportions (10%, 20%, 30%, up to 100%) by randomly selecting different portions of each user's interactions. This approach ensures consistency in user representation across all sets while varying the number of interactions in the training set.

### 3.3   Algorithms and Evaluation

We trained the following algorithms on the downsampled training sets using the LensKit [14] and RecPack [21] libraries (Table 2):

**Table 2.** Information of algorithms used in our experiment

| Algorithms | Bias | Popular | Random | UserKNN | ItemKNN | BiasedMF | FunkSVD | Popularity | ItemKNN | SVD | NMF |
|---|---|---|---|---|---|---|---|---|---|---|---|
| **Library** | LensKit | LensKit | LensKit | LensKit | LensKit | LensKit | LensKit | RecPack | RecPack | RecPack | RecPack |

Performance was evaluated using the nDCG@10 metric, ensuring that all libraries adhered to an identical standard calculation logic to facilitate a fair comparison of results across algorithms [24].

## 4   Results and Conclusion

Our research investigated the impact of downsampling on the efficiency of recommender system algorithms by analyzing performance metrics and dataset characteristics. Variations in user/item interaction densities and rating distributions, as discussed in Subsect. 3.1, impact algorithm performance. Preprocessing facilitated consistent evaluations across varying dataset sizes. Before presenting the experimental results (Fig. 1), it is useful to estimate the potential environmental benefits of the downsampling strategy proposed in this work, specifically in terms of reducing carbon footprint and $CO_2e$ emissions, with a calculation example where the training set is downsampled to 50% of its original size.

Based on our observations and calculations, downsampling the training data to 50% reduces the runtime for training and evaluation phases to $\sim$72% of the runtime required for the full dataset, on average. Furthermore, the energy consumption for a single run of a recommender algorithm on one dataset is estimated at 0.51 kWh [30]. Assuming 10 hyperparameter configurations per algorithm and using the global average conversion factor of 481 gCO2e per kWh [15], and accounting for a potential increase by a factor of 40 to consider preliminary tasks such as algorithm prototyping, initial tests, debugging, and re-runs [30], we estimate the potential carbon equivalent emissions savings from downsampling the training set to 50% compared to the full set per algorithm per dataset as follows:

$$(100\% - 72\%) \times 0.51\,\mathrm{kWh} \times 10 \times 481\,\mathrm{gCO2e/kWh} \times 40 \approx 27.4\,\mathrm{KgCO2e}.$$

This estimation roughly quantifies the reduction in CO2e emissions resulting from the training of a single algorithm on a single dataset, based solely on the reduction in runtime following downsampling. It assumes that the hardware used for the full dataset will also be employed for the downsampled dataset and that a nearly linear relationship exists between runtime, energy consumption, and carbon emissions, as supported by the ML CO2 Impact calculator tool [18]. In the upcoming sections, we detail the principal observations derived from our results and delve into how they inform the objectives of our research. For simplicity in discussing the algorithms examined in this study, we have categorized the algorithms into two groups. This division reflects the observed similarities in performance and results within each group, with distinct behaviors compared to the other group as shown in Fig. 1, facilitating clearer analysis of their comparative effectiveness. The Random algorithm serves as a baseline for comparison but is not included in the statistics of either group. Table 3 provides an overview of these categorizations.

**Table 3.** Categorization of Examined Algorithms

| Group | Algorithms included |
|---|---|
| Group 1 | UserKNN, SVD, ItemKNN (both LensKit and RecPack version), NMF |
| Group 2 | Bias, Popularity, FunkSVD, BiasedMF, Popular |

**Observations.** Several key observations can be outlined from our analysis of recommender system algorithms across different datasets, each numbered for easy reference. (1) larger datasets consistently resulted in improved performance across all algorithms, with Group 1 algorithms benefiting significantly from increased data availability. (2) In examining the performance metrics, we observed that Group 1 algorithms displayed significant improvements when the dataset used for training exceeded ~30% of the total data. Specifically, downsampling the MovieLens 100K dataset to ~50% resulted in a ~50% decrease in average nDCG@10 values of this group's algorithms, while reducing to ~30% led to a ~65% decrease, highlighting a near-linear relationship between dataset size and performance. (3) Conversely, Group 2 algorithms demonstrated more gradual performance improvements, with nDCG@10 values decreasing by ~23% and

~29% in average when the dataset was downsampled to ~50% and ~30%, respectively. (4) The sparse Amazon Toys and Games dataset particularly illustrated a more pronounced performance gap between these two groups of algorithms. When downsampling to ~50% and ~30%, Group 2 algorithms experienced only ~13% and ~17% average drops in performance, respectively, which is less severe compared to the denser MovieLens datasets.

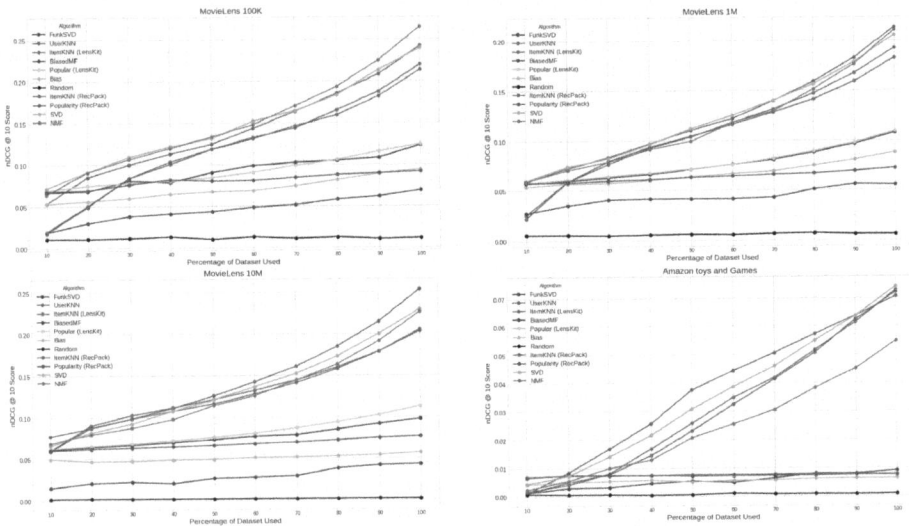

**Fig. 1.** nDCG@10 scores for each algorithm trained on varying portions of the datasets. The horizontal axis shows the percentage of the full training set, where 100% equals 80% of the total dataset, with other percentages relative to this.

**Interpretation.** From these observations, it appears that the size and sparsity of datasets significantly influence the performance of recommender system algorithms. Observation (1) highlights that contrary to our expectations, larger data volumes, including those from extensive datasets like MovieLens 10M, generally lead to better algorithm performance. However, the extent of improvement depends on the specific algorithm and the characteristics of the dataset. Observations (2) and (3) highlight that Group 1 algorithms are highly dependent on larger datasets to perform optimally. In contrast, Group 2 algorithms maintain relatively stable performance even with reduced data, striking a balance between performance and computational efficiency. This observation is evident from the narrower gap in the nDCG@10 scores distribution box plot between 50% and 100% dataset utilization for algorithms in Group 2, compared to the larger gap seen in Group 1, as shown in Fig. 2. The detailed analysis in observation (4) shows that in sparse environments, such as the Amazon Toys and Games dataset, downsampling effectively reduces computational demands with

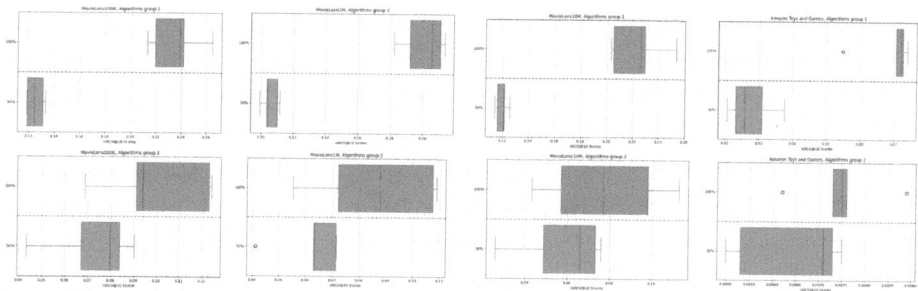

**Fig. 2.** Distribution of nDCG@10 Scores Across Four examined Datasets for Two Distinct Algorithm Groups at 50% and 100% Dataset Utilization.

only minimal performance loss. This indicates that strategic downsampling can be a viable method especially in contexts where energy optimization is crucial without significantly compromising accuracy.

**Conclusion.** This study underscores the potential for optimizing recommender systems through dataset size reduction. Although most algorithms demonstrate enhanced performance with larger training datasets, our analysis has pinpointed specific scenarios where the trade-off between energy efficiency and accuracy favors efficiency. In these cases, significant savings are achieved with minimal detriment to accuracy. Some algorithms consistently maintain high performance even with reduced data volumes, highlighting their potential for energy-efficient AI development.

Therefore, we answer our research question by affirming that it can be possible to identify an optimal trade-off between maintaining algorithmic performance and reducing dataset size. Specifically, our analysis shows that strategic downsampling may improve energy efficiency while maintaining performance comparable to the original dataset size, thereby supporting the optimization of AI systems and recommenders. However, more research is necessary to find out when exactly downsampling is a sensible approach, as sometimes, performance varies notably. We hope that in the long term, downsampling datasets becomes an accepted best-practice [6,7], for the recommender-system community that helps to contribute to green and sustainable recommender systems.

**Acknowledgment.** This paper benefited from ChatGPT for grammar and wording improvements [5]. The code used for conducting the experiments is publicly available on GitHub [3].

# References

1. Al-Jarrah, O., Yoob, P., Muhaidat, S., Karagiannidis, G., Taha, K.: Efficient machine learning for big data: a review. Big Data Res. **2**(3), 87–99 (2015). https://doi.org/10.1016/j.bdr.2015.04.002
2. Alzoubi, Y.I., Mishra, A.: Green artificial intelligence initiatives: potentials and challenges. J. Clean. Prod. **468**, 143090 (2024)
3. Arabzadeh, A.: Green RecSys github repository (2024). https://github.com/Ardalan224/RecSoGood2024/
4. Baumgart, M., Wegmeth, L., Vente, T., Beel, J.: e-fold cross-validation for recommender-system evaluation. In: International Workshop on Recommender Systems for Sustainability and Social Good (RecSoGood) at the 18th ACM Conference on Recommender Systems (ACM RecSys) (2024)
5. Beel, J.: Our use of AI-tools for writing research papers (2024). https://isg.beel.org/blog/2024/08/19/our-use-of-ai-tools-for-writing-research-papers/, in: Intelligent Systems Group, Blog
6. Beel, J.: A call for evidence-based best-practices for recommender systems evaluations. In: Bauer, C., Said, A., Zangerle, E. (eds.) Report from Dagstuhl Seminar 24211: Evaluation Perspectives of Recommender Systems: Driving Research and Education (2024). https://doi.org/10.31219/osf.io/djuac, https://isg.beel.org/pubs/2024_Call_for_Evidence_Based_RecSys_Evaluation__Pre_Print_.pdf
7. Beel, J., Jannach, D., Said, A., Shani, G., Vente, T., Wegmeth, L.: Best-practices for offline evaluations of recommender systems. In: Bauer, C., Said, A., Zangerle, E. (eds.) Report from Dagstuhl Seminar 24211 – Evaluation Perspectives of Recommender Systems: Driving Research and Education (2024)
8. Beel, J., Said, A., Vente, T., Wegmeth, L.: Green recommender systems - A call for attention. Recommender-Systems.com Blog (2024). https://doi.org/10.31219/osf.io/5ru2g, https://isg.beel.org/pubs/2024_Green_Recommender_Systems-A_Call_for_Attention.pdf
9. Bentzer, C., Thulin, H.: Recommender systems using limited dataset sizes (2023). degree Project in Computer Science and Engineering, First cycle, 15 credits, KTH Royal Institute of Technology
10. Castellanos-Nieves, D., García-Forte, L.: Strategies of automated machine learning for energy sustainability in green artificial intelligence. Appl. Sci. **14**(14), 2076–3417 (2024)
11. Castellanos-Nieves, D., García-Forte, L.: Improving automated machine-learning systems through green AI. Appl. Sci. **13**(20) (2023). https://doi.org/10.3390/app132011583, https://www.mdpi.com/2076-3417/13/20/11583
12. Cañamares, R., Castells, P., Moffat, A.: Offline evaluation options for recommender systems. Inf. Retrieval J. **23**(4), 387–410 (2020). https://doi.org/10.1007/s10791-020-09371-3
13. Chen, C., et al.: Deep learning on computational-resource-limited platforms: a survey. Advances in Artificial Intelligence (2020). https://doi.org/10.1155/2020/8454327. first published: 01 March 2020
14. Ekstrand, M.: Lenskit for python: next-generation software for recommender systems experiments. In: Proceedings of the 29th ACM International Conference on Information & Knowledge Management, pp. 2999–3006. Virtual Event, Ireland (2020). https://doi.org/10.1145/3340531.3412778

15. Ember: Carbon intensity of electricity generation - Ember and energy institute (2024). https://ourworldindata.org/grapher/carbon-intensity-electricity, yearly Electricity Data by Ember; Statistical Review of World Energy by Energy Institute. Dataset processed by Our World in Data

16. Hennig, L., Tornede, T., Lindauer, M.: Towards leveraging AutoML for sustainable deep learning: a multi-objective HPO approach on deep shift neural networks. In: arXiv (2024). https://arxiv.org/abs/2404.01965

17. Jain, K., Jindal, R.: Sampling and noise filtering methods for recommender systems: a literature review. Eng. Appl. Artif. Intell. **122**, 106129 (2023)

18. Lacoste, A., Luccioni, A., Schmidt, V., Dandres, T.: Quantifying the carbon emissions of machine learning. arXiv preprint (2019). https://mlco2.github.io/impact/, arXiv:1910.09700

19. Mahlich, C., Vente, T., Beel, J.: From theory to practice: implementing and evaluating e-fold cross-validation. In: International Conference on Artificial Intelligence and Machine Learning Research (CAIMLR) (2024). https://isg.beel.org/blog/2024/09/16/e-fold-cross-validation/

20. Meng, Z., McCreadie, R., Macdonald, C., Ounis, I.: Exploring data splitting strategies for the evaluation of recommendation models. In: Proceedings of RecSys 2020: The 14th ACM Recommender Systems Conference (RecSys 2020), pp. 8. ACM, New York, NY, USA (2020). https://doi.org/10.1145/1122445.1122456

21. Michiels, L., Verachtert, R., Goethals, B.: RecPack: An(other) experimentation toolkit for top-n recommendation using implicit feedback data. In: Proceedings of the 16th ACM Conference on Recommender Systems, pp. 648–651. RecSys 2022, Association for Computing Machinery, New York, NY, USA (2022). https://doi.org/10.1145/3523227.3551472, https://doi.org/10.1145/3523227.3551472

22. Plaza, A., Gil, J., Parra Santander, D.: 14 kg of CO2: analyzing the carbon footprint and performance of session-based recommendation algorithms. In: RecSoGood Workshop (2024)

23. Santos, S.O.S., et al.: Green machine learning: analysing the energy efficiency of machine learning models. In: 2024 35th Irish Signals and Systems Conference (ISSC), pp. 1–6 (2024). https://doi.org/10.1109/ISSC61953.2024.10603302

24. Schmidt, M., Prinz, T., Nitschke, J.: Evaluating the performance-deviation of itemKNN in RecBole and LensKit. arXiv preprint (2024). https://arxiv.org/abs/2407.13531, arXiv:2407.13531v1

25. Schwartz, R., Dodge, J., Smith, N.A., Etzioni, O.: Green AI. Commun. ACM **63**(12), 54–63 (Nov2020)

26. Spillo, G., De Filippo, A., Milano, M., Musto, C., Semeraro, G.: Towards sustainability-aware recommender systems: Analyzing the trade-off between algorithms performance and carbon footprint. In: Proceedings of the ACM Conference, p. 7. Singapore, Singapore (2023). https://doi.org/10.1145/3604915.3608840

27. Spillo, G., De Filippo, A., Musto, C., Milano, M., Semeraro, G.: Towards green recommender systems: investigating the impact of data reduction on carbon footprint and algorithm performances. In: 18th ACM Conference on Recommender Systems (2024)

28. Spillo, G., et al.: RecSys carbonator: predicting carbon footprint of recommendation system models. In: RecSoGood Workshop (2024)

29. Tornede, T., Tornede, A., Hanselle, J., Mohr, F., Wever, M., Hüllermeier, E.: Towards green automated machine learning: status quo and future directions. J. Artif. Intell. Res. **77**, 427–457 (2021/2023)

30. Vente, T., Wegmeth, L., Said, A., Beel, J.: From clicks to carbon: the environmental toll of recommender systems. In: Proceedings of the 18th ACM Conference on Recommender Systems, pp. 580–590. RecSys 2024, Association for Computing Machinery, New York, NY, USA (2024). https://doi.org/10.1145/3640457.3688074, https://arxiv.org/abs/2408.08203
31. Wegmeth, L., Vente, T., Said, A., Beel, J.: EMERS: energy meter for recommender systems. In: International Workshop on Recommender Systems for Sustainability and Social Good (RecSoGood) at the 18th ACM Conference on Recommender Systems (ACM RecSys) (2024). https://arxiv.org/pdf/2409.15060
32. Zogaj, F., Cambronero, J., Rinard, M., Cito, J.: Doing more with less: characterizing dataset downsampling for automl. Proc. VLDB Endowment (PVLDB) **14**(11), 2059–2072 (2021). https://doi.org/10.14778/3476249.3476262

# EMERS: Energy Meter for Recommender Systems

Lukas Wegmeth[1]([⊠]) [ID], Tobias Vente[1] [ID], Alan Said[2] [ID], and Joeran Beel[1] [ID]

[1] University of Siegen, Siegen, Germany
`lukas.wegmeth@uni-siegen.de`
[2] University of Gothenburg, Gothenburg, Sweden

**Abstract.** Due to recent advancements in machine learning, recommender systems use increasingly more energy for training, evaluation, and deployment. However, the recommender systems community often does not report the energy consumption of their experiments. In today's research landscape, no tools exist to easily measure the energy consumption of recommender systems experiments. To bridge this gap, we introduce EMERS, the first software library that simplifies measuring, monitoring, recording, and sharing the energy consumption of recommender systems experiments. EMERS measures energy consumption with smart power plugs and offers a user interface to monitor and compare the energy consumption of recommender systems experiments. Thereby, EMERS improves sustainability awareness and simplifies self-reporting energy consumption for recommender systems practitioners and researchers.

**Keywords:** Recommender Systems · Sustainability · Green Computing · GreenRecSys · Carbon Footprint · Energy Consumption

## 1 Introduction

Recommender systems research seldom discusses and reports energy consumption for executing experiments [7,8]. This is exacerbated by missing author guidelines[1] and tools [7,8] for measuring and reporting energy consumption. We identify two significant reasons why measuring and reporting the energy consumption of recommender systems experiments is necessary.

The first reason is to understand the environmental impact of recommender systems experiments to facilitate decision-making toward green solutions. Scientists agree that climate change is man-made [1,6]. Electricity generation creates greenhouse gases that accelerate climate change[2]. According to optimistic forecasting, computing will contribute to global energy usage by more than 7% in 2030 [3]. However, the recommender systems community rarely gauges the energy

---

[1] https://recsys.acm.org/recsys24/call/.
[2] https://www.iea.org/reports/co2-emissions-in-2023.

L. Boratto et al. (Eds.): RecSoGood 2024, CCIS 2470, pp. 83–89, 2025.
https://doi.org/10.1007/978-3-031-87654-7_8

consumption of experiments, making it difficult to estimate their environmental impact. Consequently, this impedes the recommender systems community in making evidence-based decisions to reduce their environmental impact.

The second reason for measuring and reporting the energy consumption of recommender systems experiments is the ability to compare the energy consumption of running recommender systems. Like run time and accuracy, energy consumption could be a significant factor in deciding which recommender systems algorithm is best for a given task. The ability to compare the energy consumption of related approaches would add a precise metric to gauge the efficiency of recommender systems.

To our knowledge, no straightforward solution enables recommender systems practitioners to measure the energy consumption of their experiments easily. Modifying existing software-based power consumption estimation solutions to work for recommender systems experiments is possible with additional engineering and development effort. However, as outlined in the following paragraphs, these solutions would still lack accuracy or usability.

Software packages exist to measure energy consumption for general computing [2,4]. However, they have inherent shortcomings [5], e.g., the inability to support all hardware configurations and operating systems. For example, some hardware, e.g., memory and cooling, often do not have sensors, meaning energy consumption must be estimated, making software energy meters inaccurate and infeasible for scientific reproducibility. Furthermore, system settings may restrict software from reading sensors, and some software is only available for specific operating systems or CPU architectures. Finally, the energy consumption estimation software may not support infrequently used, modified, and new hardware due to missing interfaces.

Hardware energy meters are often found in commercially available off-the-shelf smart plugs sold for usage in smart home systems. These enable measuring the energy draw at high frequency, e.g., at least once a second, providing accurate measurements of the energy use of connected devices. They are also independent of the hardware and software configuration of the computing resource. While plenty of open software for reading smart plug sensors exists, we cannot find software that can integrate smart plugs from different manufacturers with recommender systems experiments and provide monitoring capabilities.

To fill this gap, we present EMERS, a software library that simplifies measuring, monitoring, recording, and sharing the energy consumption of recommender systems experiments. EMERS is open-source and available on GitHub[3].

## 2    EMERS

EMERS is an open-source and platform-independent Python library that simplifies measuring, monitoring, recording, and sharing the energy consumption of recommender systems experiments. EMERS reads and logs energy measurements

---

[3] https://code.isg.beel.org/emers.

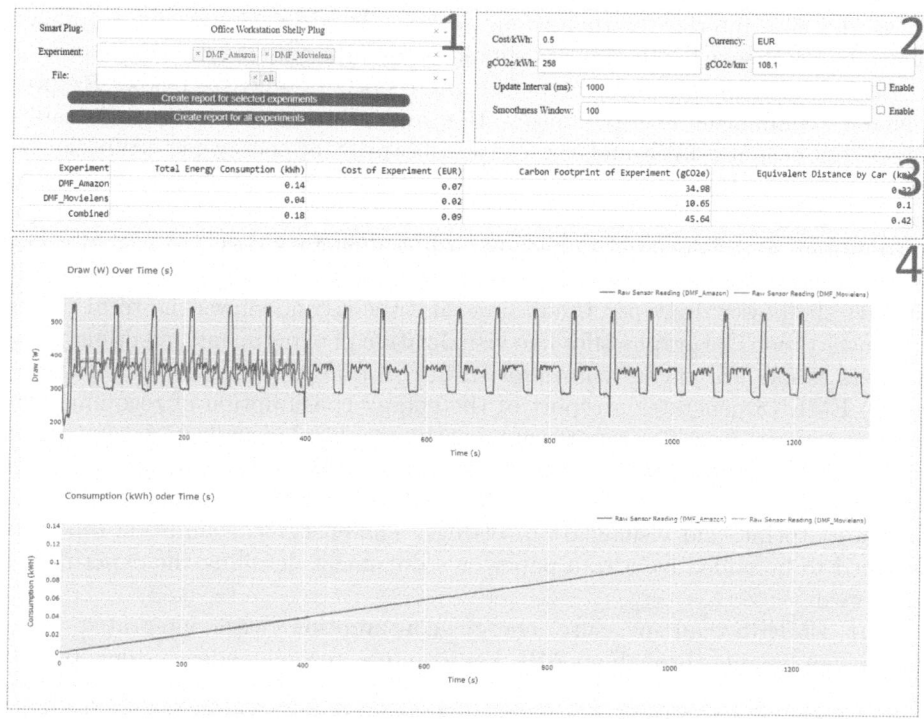

**Fig. 1.** The user interface for EMERS is divided into four regions. We mark each region with a red number. (1) Experiment Selection and Report Generation. (2) Energy Cost, Carbon Footprint, and Graph Settings. (3) Experiment Information. (4) Energy Consumption Graph. (Color figure online)

from smart plugs, organizes them based on the associated experiment, provides a user interface to monitor and analyze measurements, and creates a standardized, automated report to share with the community. While smart plugs, or energy meters, come with a small cost in terms of hardware, we believe the accuracy of measurements and compatibility with all hardware systems compensate for it.

## 2.1  Features

EMERS has four features: (i) a user interface for monitoring and analyzing the energy consumption of recommender systems experiments, (ii) standardized energy consumption report generation, (iii) integrated, per-experiment energy consumption logging through our API, and (iv) standalone energy consumption logging with a Python script. We provide a detailed description of these features below.

(i) EMERS offers a user interface to interactively monitor, visualize, and analyze the energy consumption of recommender systems experiments. Figure 1 shows the user interface with its four regions. **Region 1** contains dropdown menus to select which experiments should be monitored.

It also contains buttons to generate the reports detailed in below. **Region 2** enables configuring energy consumption and visualization settings. Notably, the energy cost per kWh and the carbon footprint of energy per kWh can be configured here. **Region 3** contains a table that displays energy consumption statistics per experiment and of all selected experiments. An experiment's energy consumption and associated impact regarding monetary cost and carbon footprint is immediately tangible. **Region 4** consists of two graphs, where the first displays the power draw per timestamp, and the second shows the total power draw over time. The graphs offer live visualization of experiments, enabling practitioners to monitor energy consumption in real time.

(ii) EMERS generates a report of the energy consumption of recommender systems experiments. The report contains the graphical visualizations and tabular energy consumption data shown in the user interface. It uses the configuration made in the user interface, e.g., the selected experiments, as well as the cost, carbon footprint, and visualization settings. The energy consumption report is designed to be added to, e.g., a paper or a document detailing the experiments performed.

(iii) EMERS can measure energy consumption with integrated, per-experiment logging through an API. For example, recommender systems practitioners can import EMERS into their code to measure the energy consumption of the training process of their deep neural network recommender system with a single API call. This feature enables targeted energy consumption measurement in experiments and organizing energy consumption logs. Hereby, practitioners may define the scope of an experiment and decide the granularity by which they would like to measure energy consumption. For example, an experiment could be defined as a training process of one algorithm or the entire evaluation pipeline of multiple algorithms.

(iv) EMERS offers standalone energy consumption logging. For example, EMERS can run independently of an experiment or other software to continuously measure and log energy consumption. Thereby, EMERS runs as a lightweight background process that polls the smart plug with the desired frequency and organizes the measurements in a log file. Standalone logging with EMERS helps gauge energy consumption for a broader range of use cases over an unspecified time without being tied to specific execution blocks.

## 2.2   Requirements

Measuring energy consumption with EMERS requires a computer connected to the same network as the smart plug. Besides that, EMERS is lightweight and can be run on the computing resource that executes the experiments without noticeable performance impact. EMERS can also run on a small, single-board computer, e.g., a Raspberry Pi.

The EMERS monitoring user interface runs on a Flask server and can be configured to be accessible only from the host, the local network, or the internet if desired. It only requires access to the energy consumption logs and no network access to the smart plug.

Smart power plugs can generally be accessed remotely, e.g., through WiFi or Bluetooth. EMERS supports two types of WiFi-based smart plugs out of the box: the Shelly Plug Plus S[4], and the TP-Link Tapo P115[5]. Both plugs fit the CEE Type 7 socket in continental European countries and are available in variations for other electrical sockets, such as NEMA sockets in the USA. EMERS energy consumption logging can be used from any computer within the plug's network and is independent of the computing resource that runs the experiments. Therefore, physical access to the measured computing resource is required only once to install the smart plug. Furthermore, support for measuring energy consumption with other remotely accessible smart plugs can be easily implemented through a simple interface in EMERS.

**Table 1.** The idle energy consumption of different hardware configurations.

| System Type | CPU | GPU | RAM in GB | Storage in TB | Idle Energy Consumption in Watts |
|---|---|---|---|---|---|
| Windows 11 Workstation | Intel Xeon W-2255 @ 3.70 GHz | NVIDIA GeForce RTX 3090 | 256 | 2 | $69.15 \pm 2.45$ |
| Windows 10 Workstation | Intel Core i7-6700K @ 4.00 GHz | NVIDIA GeForce GTX 980 Ti | 128 | 1 | $80.45 \pm 3.45$ |
| 2022 Mac Studio | M1 Ultra | M1 Ultra | 64 | 1 | $18.55 \pm 1.55$ |
| 2020 MacBook Pro | M1 | M1 | 16 | 1 | $12.20 \pm 1.3$ |

## 2.3 Measurement Considerations

Using a smart plug, EMERS implicitly measures the energy consumption of the complete system to which the smart plug is connected. Therefore, measurements may be affected by factors other than a recommender systems experiment, e.g., other software running on the system and the system's energy consumption without load. In Table 1, we show our measurements of the idle energy consumption of four different hardware configurations. Here, idling means the system only runs necessary, repetitive background tasks with low computing demands. We observe that the idle energy consumption has a consistent baseline value with minor deviations.

If the system does not run a recommender systems experiment, EMERS can effectively measure this noise with its standalone energy consumption logging mode. However, other computationally demanding software, especially with

---

[4] https://kb.shelly.cloud/knowledge-base/shelly-plus-plug-s-1.
[5] https://www.tp-link.com/se/home-networking/smart-plug/tapo-p115/.

varying energy consumption, may significantly impact the measured energy consumption. Ideally, a system that runs computationally demanding tasks besides the recommender systems experiments should not be used when the goal is measuring energy consumption. This is not a limitation of EMERS in particular but of energy measurement methods in general. To illustrate, in theory, even more sophisticated energy measurement methods are challenged by the confounding effects of running multiple software packages on a system, e.g., on cooling and memory, but precisely measuring only the impact of one of them. Therefore, we recommend running EMERS on an otherwise idling system and measuring the idle energy consumption with EMERS, if desired.

### 2.4   Measurement Reliability

The reliability of measurements with EMERS largely depends on the chosen smart plug. For example, considering the two smart plugs that EMERS supports out-of-the-box, we find that the Shelly Plug Plus S allows more frequent measurements than the TP-Link Tapo P115, providing a higher resolution. However, comparing the measurements of both smart plugs with different measurement intervals but on the same hardware configuration and recommender systems experiment, we find differences of $< 0.1\%$ over whole experiments. Therefore, we conclude that the measurements from at least the two aforementioned smart plugs are comparable and reliable due to their similarity.

EMERS receives the measurements from a smart plug's sensors, for example, via HTTP API, and writes them to a text file. In this sense, EMERS trusts the smart plug and guarantees reliable measurements as long as it retains access to its log file and has a stable connection with the smart plug.

Finally, EMERS notifies the user if any unexpected error or connection issue arises. The user may then decide whether the measurements are still reliable based on the error. Furthermore, the EMERS user interface allows visual inspection of measurements, providing an additional layer for auditing measurements.

## 3   Demo

In the demo video[6], we show the setup of EMERS and present its features.

*Setup*: We demonstrate how to install a smart plug that is required by EMERS and then how to get EMERS and register the smart plug.

*Features*: We provide an overview of the monitoring user interface of EMERS, with its four regions. Then, we show how EMERS is integrated with recommender systems pipelines to measure energy consumption. We demonstrate how the EMERS monitoring user interface enables recommender systems practitioners to monitor the energy consumption of their experiments actively. Finally, we present the energy consumption report that EMERS generates.

---

[6] https://youtu.be/vmXOcrVpRDg.

# References

1. Cook, J., et al.: Consensus on consensus: a synthesis of consensus estimates on human-caused global warming. Environ. Res. Lett. **11**(4), 048002 (2016)
2. Courty, B., et al.: MinervaBooks: mlco2/codecarbon: v2.4.1 (2024). https://doi.org/10.5281/zenodo.11171501
3. Gupta, U., et al.: Chasing carbon: the elusive environmental footprint of computing. In: 2021 IEEE International Symposium on High-Performance Computer Architecture (HPCA), pp. 854–867 (2021). https://doi.org/10.1109/HPCA51647.2021.00076
4. Henderson, P., Hu, J., Romoff, J., Brunskill, E., Jurafsky, D., Pineau, J.: Towards the systematic reporting of the energy and carbon footprints of machine learning. J. Mach. Learn. Res. **21**(248), 1–43 (2020). http://jmlr.org/papers/v21/20-312.html
5. Jay, M., Ostapenco, V., Lefevre, L., Trystram, D., Orgerie, A.C., Fichel, B.: An experimental comparison of software-based power meters: focus on CPU and GPU, pp. 106–118 (2023). https://doi.org/10.1109/CCGrid57682.2023.00020
6. Lynas, M., Houlton, B.Z., Perry, S.: Greater than 99% consensus on human caused climate change in the peer-reviewed scientific literature. Environ. Res. Lett. **16**(11), 114005 (2021)
7. Spillo, G., De Filippo, A., Musto, C., Milano, M., Semeraro, G.: Towards sustainability-aware recommender systems: Analyzing the trade-off between algorithms performance and carbon footprint. In: Proceedings of the 17th ACM Conference on Recommender Systems, pp. 856–862. RecSys 2023, Association for Computing Machinery, New York, NY, USA (2023). https://doi.org/10.1145/3604915.3608840
8. Vente, T., Wegmeth, L., Said, A., Beel, J.: From clicks to carbon: the environmental toll of recommender systems. In: Proceedings of the 18th ACM Conference on Recommender Systems. RecSys 2024, Association for Computing Machinery, New York, NY, USA (2024). https://doi.org/10.1145/3640457.3688074

# e-Fold Cross-Validation
# for Recommender-System Evaluation

Moritz Baumgart[1]([⊠])(iD), Lukas Wegmeth[1](iD), Tobias Vente[1](iD),
and Joeran Beel[1,2](iD)

[1] Department of Electrical Engineering and Computer Science, University of Siegen,
Siegen, Germany
moritz.baumgart@student.uni-siegen.de ,
joeran.beel@uni-siegen.de
[2] Recommender-Systems.com, Siegen, Germany
https://www.recommender-systems.com

**Abstract.** To combat the rising energy consumption of recommender systems we implement a novel alternative for k-fold cross-validation. This alternative, named e-fold cross-validation, aims to minimize the number of folds to achieve a reduction in power usage while keeping the reliability and robustness of the test results high. We tested our method on 5 recommender system algorithms across 6 datasets and compared it with 10-fold cross-validation. On average e-fold cross-validation only needed 41.5% of the energy that 10-fold cross-validation would need, while its results only differed by 1.81%. We conclude that e-fold cross-validation is a promising approach that has the potential to be an energy efficient but still reliable alternative to k-fold cross-validation.

**Keywords:** Energy efficiency · Cross-validation · Sustainability

## 1 Introduction

As the recommender systems community moves towards more deep learning based models [23,31], it also faces the problem that a higher energy consumption can be observed [12,30]. Recent research even suggests that a paper on recommender systems, which uses deep learning algorithms, needs around 42 times more energy than a paper that uses traditional algorithms [27]. A higher energy consumption leads to more carbon emissions, which are one of the main causes for climate change and all the negative consequences that come with it [9]. Therefore, we should strive towards sustainable development of recommender systems and make model learning more energy efficient and low-carbon emitting.

To ensure the robustness of test results, k-Fold cross-validation ($k$-CV) is a favored approach often used in practice today [8,18,34]. $k$-CV splits the dataset into $k$ folds and conducts tests on each one of them, while the other $k - 1$ folds are used for training [24,29,32]. The issue with this technique is, that it increases

© The Author(s), under exclusive license to Springer Nature Switzerland AG 2025
L. Boratto et al. (Eds.): RecSoGood 2024, CCIS 2470, pp. 90–97, 2025.
https://doi.org/10.1007/978-3-031-87654-7_9

the power consumption roughly by the factor $k$. This is especially problematic when the $k$ is chosen arbitrarily, which often seems to be the case [1].

Recently, the recommender system community started to investigate "Green Recommender Systems" [4], i.e. methods to minimize environmental impact. Also, we proposed tools to measure energy consumption [28] and save energy through downsampling datasets [2]. The machine learning community started already some years ago to explore "Green" (Automated) Machine Learning [26], and explored an early-stopping approach that is similar to ours [6].

While there is lots of research that tries to find an optimal $k$, there seems to be no one who chooses $k$ from an energy saving perspective. Marcot and Hanea [22] try out different values for $k$. They support the common use of $k = 10$, but they also notice that in some cases $k = 5$ is sufficient. This indicates a potential to save energy by determining when a smaller $k$ is enough. Arlot and Celisse [3] support such a range for $k$ and conclude that a value between 5 and 10 is optimal with no statistical improvement for larger values. Similarly, Kohavi and John [17] recommend choosing $k = 10$. Anguita et al. [1] consider $k$ as a tunable hyperparameter. While this approach produces a statistically robust value for $k$, it only further increases the power consumption needed to tune the value.

To address the relatively high energy consumption of $k$-CV, we recently proposed the idea of "e-fold cross-validation" ($e$-CV), which replaces the often arbitrarily chosen $k$ with an intelligently chosen parameter $e$ [5]. Our intension was that $e$ is chosen as small as possible to maximize energy savings, but large enough to provide robust results. The first results in the general machine learning domain were promising [21].

Our proposal [5] sets the goal of this paper and was the namesake of the algorithm described in the following sections. We want to create and evaluate a first possible implementation of $e$-CV with a focus on recommender systems. Our key idea is, that we halt the folding process early, once a certain confidence in the test results is reached.

## 2  Methodology

To gather data for evaluating our $e$-CV implementation we trained 5 algorithms on 6 datasets using 10-CV and tested them using a top-n prediction task with NDCG@10 as a metric. Afterwards we then incrementally provide $e$-CV with the obtained scores, similar to how the scores of the individual folds would appear in a real cross-validation scenario. Since the order in which the folds happen is arbitrary, we evaluated $e$-CV on 5000 permutations of the folds. Considering all possible permutations was unfeasible.

Our proposed $e$-CV implementation calculates the mean of all scores it has so far, as well as the confidence interval (CI) of that mean. It then uses a criterion on the CI width to determine at which fold to stop. We consider the index of that fold as the value of $e$. Let $C = \{c_1, ..., c_n\}$ be the set of CI widths then we stop folding if $|c_{n-1} - c_n| \leq \frac{\alpha}{c_n}$ holds, with $\alpha$ being a user-selectable parameter which can be used to prioritize energy-saving (large $\alpha$) or accuracy (small $\alpha$). In Fig. 1 an example of the algorithm working can be seen.

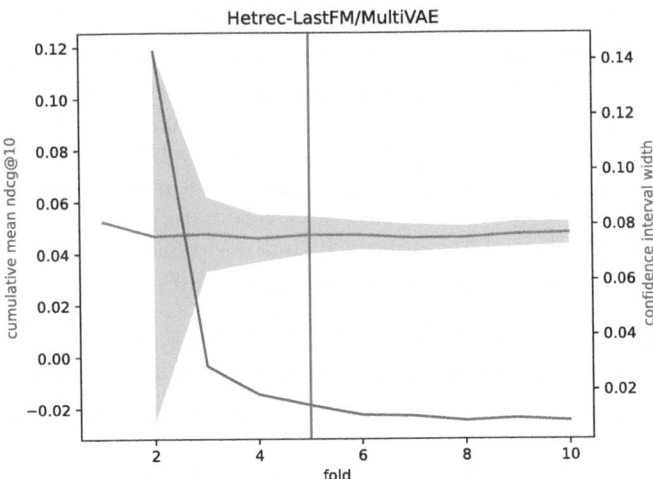

**Fig. 1.** Exemplary $e$-CV run. Mean of all scores up to the current fold and the confidence interval in blue on the left axis. The right axis shows the width of the confidence interval in green. The red vertical line is the fold at which the stopping criterion was first met, i.e. the value of $e$.

As discussed before, a value of $k$ between 5 and 10 is typical, so we compared our $e$-CV implementation with 10-CV as ground truth. We calculated the percentage difference $d(x,y) = \frac{|x-y|}{(x+y)\div 2} \cdot 100$ between the final $e$-CV score and the 10-CV score and we record the stopping point calculated by $e$-CV. This enables us to compare how much the results differ for how much energy saving. Lastly, we also ranked the algorithms using the $e$-CV scores and using the 10-CV scores to verify ranking consistency between both methods. To cover a wide variety of algorithm types, the following algorithms were chosen: From LensKit [11] we chose *ImplicitMF* as a matrix-factorization method, and from RecBole [33] we chose *ItemKNN* [10] as a traditional algorithm, *MultiVAE* [19] as an autoencoder, *NeuMF* [15] as a deep learning model and *Popularity based (Pop)* as a simple baseline. We chose the following datasets: Three subsets from the Amazon2014 dataset [14] and two differently sized MovieLens [13] datasets, which contain product reviews from Amazon and movie ratings from the MovieLens website respectively, as well as the Hetrec 2011 Last.FM dataset [7], which contains artist listening records from users of the Last.fm online music system. For preprocessing we orientate ourselves on other papers and apply 5-core pruning [16,25,27] and convert explicit feedback to implicit feedback by counting the presence of a rating as positive feedback [8,20,27]. An overview of the datasets after this preprocessing is shown in Table 1. To prepare the datasets for 10-CV they were each split into 10 partitions, for each one it was ensured that each user is equally represented. If a user had less than 10 interactions, these were assigned to partitions randomly.

**Table 1.** Overview of used dataset after preprocessing

| Dataset Name | #Users | #Items | #Interactions | Density |
|---|---|---|---|---|
| Amazon2014 Cell-Phones-And-Accessories [14] | 27879 | 10429 | 194439 | 0,0669 |
| Amazon2014 Apps-For-Android [14] | 87271 | 13209 | 752937 | 0,0653 |
| Amazon2014 Amazon-Instant-Video [14] | 5130 | 1685 | 37126 | 0,4295 |
| Hetrec-LastFM [7] | 1090 | 3646 | 52551 | 1,3223 |
| MovieLens-100K [13] | 943 | 1349 | 99287 | 7,8049 |
| MovieLens-1M [13] | 6040 | 3416 | 999611 | 4,8448 |

## 3    Results and Discussion

On average, across all datasets/algorithms, e-CV differs only by 1.81% from 10-CV (Fig. 2), while it stops already after 4.15 folds (Fig. 3), which means that e-CV uses only 41.5% of 10-CV the energy while generally providing similar results.

In Fig. 2 we can see that e-CV seems to work well for the ItemKNN algorithm on most of the datasets, with percentage differences of 0.7% and 0.63% on the MovieLens datasets and between 1.04% and 1.26% on the Amazon datasets. For some algorithms like MultiVAE and Pop it performs slightly worse with percentage differences of 2.41%, 4.98% and 2.87% for MultiVAE on Amazon2014-Amazon-Instant-Video, Amazon2014-Apps-For-Android and Hetrec-LastFM respectively and 2.66%, 2.11%, 2.26% and 5.6% for Pop on Amazon2014-Amazon-Instant-Video, Amazon2014-Apps-For-Android, Amazon2024-Cell-Phones-And-Accessories and Hetrec-LastFM respectively. We can also see that it works well on the two MovieLens datasets, with the percentage difference being between 0.63% and 1.35% across all algorithms on both datasets.

Looking at Fig. 3, we can see at which fold e-CV decided to stop the folding process on average. For the MovieLens datasets it stopped at later folds, for

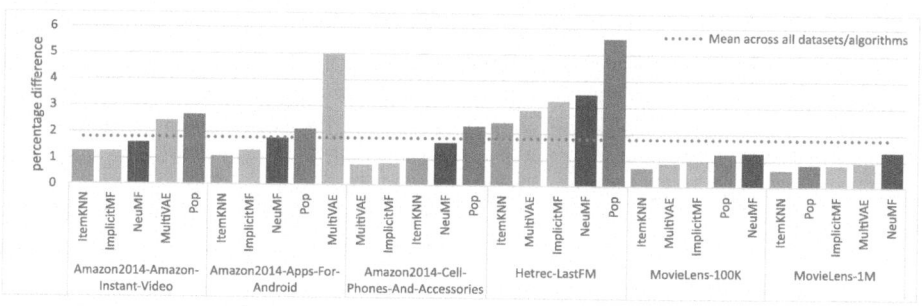

**Fig. 2.** Percentage difference, as described in Sect. 2, between final e-CV score and 10-CV score for each dataset/algorithm, averaged across tested permutations.

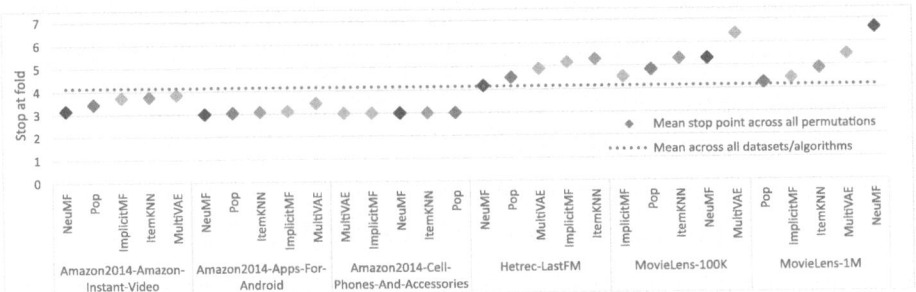

**Fig. 3.** Stopping point determined by *e*-CV for each dataset/algorithm, averaged across tested permutations.

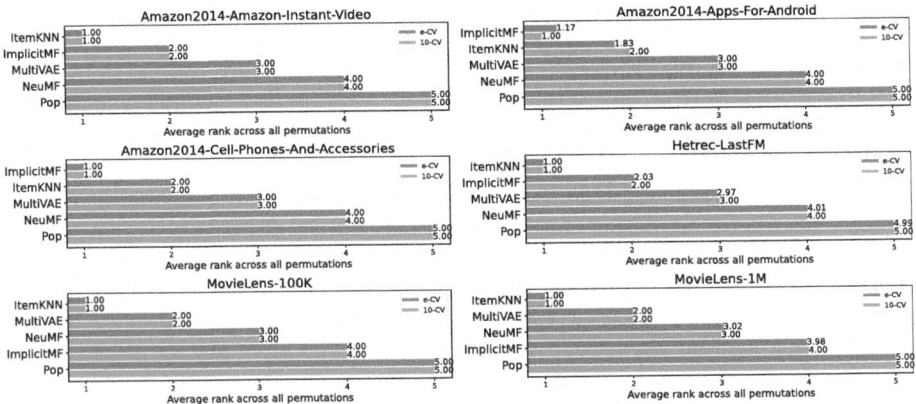

**Fig. 4.** Ranking of the algorithms, averaged across tested permutations.

some algorithms up to fold 6.62. For the three Amazon datasets the folding was halted earlier between fold 3 and 3.83. The Hetrec-LastFM dataset was somewhere in between with stopping points between fold 4.16 to 5.29 for the different algorithms.

In Fig. 4, we can see that the average ranking of the algorithms for a dataset stayed consistent with *e*-CV. A slight deviation can be observed only for ItemKNN vs. ImplicitMF on the Amazon2014-Apps-For-Android dataset and for ImplicitMF vs. MultiVAE as well as NeuMF vs. Pop on the Hetrec-LastFM.

The results suggest that for some algorithm/datasets combinations, especially MultiVAE on Amazon2014-Apps-For-Android and Pop on Hetrec-LastFM stopping at a later fold would probably have been better. On the MovieLens datasets the percentage difference was rather small, which matches the higher stopping points on these datasets. Perhaps more energy could have been saved by stopping earlier on these datasets. Apart from these exception *e*-CV seems to be able to correctly determine when to stop folding and to find a balance between energy savings and reliability in the results.

All in all, we can say that the idea of $e$-CV seems to have a lot of potential. Especially, since we could achieve these promising results with a rather simple implementation. We think that more sophisticated implementations that consider more factors are likely to perform even better and fix the weaknesses of our current implementation.

# References

1. Anguita, D., Ghelardoni, L., Ghio, A., Oneto, L., Ridella, S.: The 'k' in k-fold cross validation. In: 20th European Symposium on Artificial Neural Networks, ESANN 2012, Bruges, Belgium, 25-27 April, 2012 (2012). https://www.esann.org/sites/default/files/proceedings/legacy/es2012-62.pdf
2. Arabzadeh, A., Vente, T., Beel, J.: Green recommender systems: optimizing dataset size for energy-efficient algorithm performance. In: International Workshop on Recommender Systems for Sustainability and Social Good (RecSoGood) at the 18th ACM Conference on Recommender Systems (ACM RecSys) (2024). https://isg.beel.org/pubs/2024-Green-RecSys-Dataset-Sampling-Ardalan.pdf
3. Arlot, S., Celisse, A.: A survey of cross-validation procedures for model selection. Stat. Surv. **4**, 1–50 (2016). https://doi.org/10.1214/09-ss054
4. Beel, J., Said, A., Vente, T., Wegmeth, L.: Green recommender systems - A call for attention. Recommender-Systems.com Blog (2024). https://doi.org/10.31219/osf.io/5ru2g, https://isg.beel.org/pubs/2024_Green_Recommender_Systems-A_Call_for_Attention.pdf
5. Beel, J., Wegmeth, L., Vente, T.: e-fold cross-validation: a computing and energy-efficient alternative to k-fold cross-validation with adaptive folds (2024). https://doi.org/10.31219/osf.io/exw3j
6. Bergman, E., Purucker, L., Hutter, F.: Don't waste your time: early stopping cross-validation (2024). https://arxiv.org/abs/2405.03389
7. Cantador, I., Brusilovsky, P., Kuflik, T.: Second workshop on information heterogeneity and fusion in recommender systems (hetrec2011). In: Proceedings of the Fifth ACM Conference on Recommender Systems. RecSys 2011, ACM (2011). https://doi.org/10.1145/2043932.2044016
8. Chen, H., et al.: Adversarial collaborative filtering for free. In: Proceedings of the 17th ACM Conference on Recommender Systems. RecSys 2023, ACM (2023). https://doi.org/10.1145/3604915.3608771
9. Crimmins, A., et al.: The impacts of climate change on human health in the united states: a scientific. Assessment (2016). https://doi.org/10.7930/j0r49nqx
10. Deshpande, M., Karypis, G.: Item-based top-nrecommendation algorithms. ACM Trans. Inf. Syst. **22**(1), 143–177 (2004). https://doi.org/10.1145/963770.963776
11. Ekstrand, M.D.: Lenskit for python: next-generation software for recommender systems experiments. In: Proceedings of the 29th ACM International Conference on Information & Knowledge Management. CIKM 2020, ACM (2020). https://doi.org/10.1145/3340531.3412778
12. Gupta, U., et al.: Chasing carbon: the elusive environmental footprint of computing. In: 2021 IEEE International Symposium on High-Performance Computer Architecture (HPCA). IEEE (2021). https://doi.org/10.1109/hpca51647.2021.00076
13. Harper, F.M., Konstan, J.A.: The MovieLens datasets: history and context. ACM Trans. Interact. Intell. Syst. **5**(4), 1–19 (2015). https://doi.org/10.1145/2827872

14. He, R., McAuley, J.: Ups and downs: modeling the visual evolution of fashion trends with one-class collaborative filtering (2016). https://doi.org/10.1145/2872427.2883037
15. He, X., Liao, L., Zhang, H., Nie, L., Hu, X., Chua, T.S.: Neural collaborative filtering. In: Proceedings of the 26th International Conference on World Wide Web. WWW 2017, International World Wide Web Conferences Steering Committee (2017). https://doi.org/10.1145/3038912.3052569
16. Kang, W.C., McAuley, J.: Self-attentive sequential recommendation (2018). https://doi.org/10.48550/ARXIV.1808.09781
17. Kohavi, R., John, G.: The Wrapper Approach, vol. 14, pp. 33–50. Springer US (2001). https://doi.org/10.1007/978-1-4615-5725-8_3, https://www.researchgate.net/publication/2352264_A_Study_of_Cross-Validation_and_Bootstrap_for_Accuracy_Estimation_and_Model_Selection
18. Li, Y., Tang, X., Chen, B., Huang, Y., Tang, R., Li, Z.: AutoOpt: automatic hyperparameter scheduling and optimization for deep click-through rate prediction. In: Proceedings of the 17th ACM Conference on Recommender Systems. RecSys 2023, ACM (2023). https://doi.org/10.1145/3604915.3608800
19. Liang, D., Krishnan, R.G., Hoffman, M.D., Jebara, T.: Variational autoencoders for collaborative filtering. In: Proceedings of the 2018 World Wide Web Conference on World Wide Web - WWW 2018, pp. 689–698. WWW 2018, ACM Press (2018). https://doi.org/10.1145/3178876.3186150
20. Ma, H., et al.: Exploring false hard negative sample in cross-domain recommendation. In: Proceedings of the 17th ACM Conference on Recommender Systems. RecSys 2023, ACM (2023). https://doi.org/10.1145/3604915.3608791
21. Mahlich, C., Vente, T., Beel, J.: From theory to practice: implementing and evaluating e-fold cross-validation. In: International Conference on Artificial Intelligence and Machine Learning Research (CAIMLR) (2024). https://isg.beel.org/blog/2024/09/16/e-fold-cross-validation/
22. Marcot, B.G., Hanea, A.M.: What is an optimal value of k in k-fold cross-validation in discrete bayesian network analysis? Comput. Stat. **36**(3), 2009–2031 (2021). https://doi.org/10.1007/S00180-020-00999-9
23. Mu, R.: A survey of recommender systems based on deep learning. IEEE Access **6**, 69009–69022 (2018). https://doi.org/10.1109/access.2018.2880197
24. Refaeilzadeh, P., Tang, L., Liu, H.: Cross-Validation, pp. 1–7. Springer New York (2009). https://doi.org/10.1007/978-1-4899-7993-3_565-2
25. Sun, F., et al.: BERT4REC: sequential recommendation with bidirectional encoder representations from transformer. In: Proceedings of the 28th ACM International Conference on Information and Knowledge Management. CIKM 2019, ACM (2019). https://doi.org/10.1145/3357384.3357895
26. Tornede, T., Tornede, A., Hanselle, J., Mohr, F., Wever, M., Hüllermeier, E.: Towards green automated machine learning: Status quo and future directions. J. Artif. Intell. Res. **77**, 427–457 (2021/2023)
27. Vente, T., Wegmeth, L., Said, A., Beel, J.: From clicks to carbon: the environmental toll of recommender systems. In: Proceedings of the 18th ACM Conference on Recommender Systems, pp. 580–590. RecSys 2024, Association for Computing Machinery, New York, NY, USA (2024). https://doi.org/10.1145/3640457.3688074, https://arxiv.org/abs/2408.08203
28. Wegmeth, L., Vente, T., Said, A., Beel, J.: EMERS: energy meter for recommender systems. In: International Workshop on Recommender Systems for Sustainability and Social Good (RecSoGood) at the 18th ACM Conference on Recommender Systems (ACM RecSys) (2024). https://arxiv.org/pdf/2409.15060

29. Yadav, S., Shukla, S.: Analysis of k-fold cross-validation over hold-out validation on colossal datasets for quality classification. In: 2016 IEEE 6th International Conference on Advanced Computing (IACC). IEEE (2016). https://doi.org/10.1109/iacc.2016.25

30. Yang, T.J., Chen, Y.H., Emer, J., Sze, V.: A method to estimate the energy consumption of deep neural networks. In: 2017 51st Asilomar Conference on Signals, Systems, and Computers. IEEE (2017). https://doi.org/10.1109/acssc.2017.8335698

31. Zhang, S., Yao, L., Sun, A., Tay, Y.: Deep learning based recommender system: a survey and new perspectives. ACM Comput. Surv. **52**(1), 1–38 (2019). https://doi.org/10.1145/3285029

32. Zhang, Y., Yang, Y.: Cross-validation for selecting a model selection procedure. J. Econ. **187**(1), 95–112 (2015). https://doi.org/10.1016/j.jeconom.2015.02.006

33. Zhao, W.X., et al.: Recbole: Towards a unified, comprehensive and efficient framework for recommendation algorithms (2020). https://doi.org/10.48550/ARXIV.2011.01731

34. Zhu, J., Wang, Y., Zhu, F., Sun, Z.: Domain disentanglement with interpolative data augmentation for dual-target cross-domain recommendation. In: Proceedings of the 17th ACM Conference on Recommender Systems. RecSys 2023, ACM (2023). https://doi.org/10.1145/3604915.3608802

# RecSys CarbonAtor: Predicting Carbon Footprint of Recommendation System Models

Giuseppe Spillo[1]([✉])(iD), Alberto Gaetano Valerio[1](iD), Felice Franchini[1](iD),
Allegra De Filippo[2](iD), Cataldo Musto[1](iD), Michela Milano[2](iD),
and Giovanni Semeraro[1](iD)

[1] University of Bari, Bari, Italy
{giuseppe.spillo,cataldo.musto,giovanni.semeraro}@uniba.it,
{a.valerio31,f.franchini9}@phd.uniba.it
[2] University of Bologna, Bologna, Italy
{allegra.defilippo,michela.milano}@unibo.it

**Abstract.** Environmental sustainability of AI, or Green AI, is a topic that is getting more and more crucial in the last few years. However, AI systems continue to improve at the cost of huge resources, neglecting the environmental impact in terms of $CO_2$ emissions from computations. In this context, Recommender Systems (RS) are no exception, and the current literature in the field pays little attention to the concept of Green AI. In this paper, we propose a tool that aims at estimating the $CO_2$ emitted by a recommendation model. Our contributions are twofold: first, we built a regression dataset that can be used to feed a regression model aiming at estimating the emissions or RS models; this dataset can be easily expanded, so it can be considered a relevant resource for the whole community. Second, we compared several state-of-the-art regression models to assess which performs the best and in which settings. Results show that Random Forest is the best performing model to effectively estimate the $CO_2$ emissions produced by recommendation models.

**Keywords:** Green AI · Green RecSys · Regression Models

## 1 Introduction and Related Works

During the last decades, Artificial Intelligence (AI) has evolved and improved in several fields and tasks, such as computer vision, natural language processing (NLP), and many other, including recommendation. These improvements led to better performances at the cost of more complex systems, which require more training time and computational power, making AI a *power-hungry technology* [18]. According to [5], back in 2018, almost 1% of the global energy was used to feed data centers, and due to today's technologies, this statistic is set to increase.

This trait of AI models implies higher $CO_2$ emissions, affecting the concentration of greenhouse gases in the atmosphere [3]. Accordingly, the concept of

L. Boratto et al. (Eds.): RecSoGood 2024, CCIS 2470, pp. 98–110, 2025.
https://doi.org/10.1007/978-3-031-87654-7_10

*Green AI* [9,17] was introduced to foster the *environmental* sustainability of AI systems [15]. In a nutshell, the main goals of this research line are to estimate and reduce $CO_2$ emissions related to AI. Generally speaking, the relevance of this research line is also confirmed by some of the Sustainable Development Goals (SDGs)[1], such as SDG 7 (*affordable and clean energy*) and SDG 13 (*climate action*).

Although the environmental sustainability of AI systems is getting more and more relevance, current AI models go in the opposite direction, due to their higher complexity and higher $CO_2$ emissions [4,7,13]. In this scenario, Recommender Systems (RSs) [2] make no exception: as shown in a recent benchmark [11], in which the authors analyse the trade-off between $CO_2$ emissions and recommendation performance, most recent deep-learning models drastically emit more $CO_2$ than simpler models with very little improvements in terms of performance. Similarly, in [16], the authors have assessed the carbon footprint of all the recommendation models proposed at ACM RecSys between 2013 and 2023, and obtain very similar findings to those reported in [11]. In [12], the authors assess how data reduction strategies affect the trade-off between performance and emissions. The results show that data reduction is not always a suitable solution, and that a case-by-case analysis, which takes into account several factors, is needed.

In such context, it can be useful to know a priori the emissions an RS model will produce, or at least the range of possible values, through a prediction model. We believe the impact of this contribution is relevant for the field. Just to give an example, in this way, a company might choose in advance which RS model should be used, taking into account the amount of emissions it will produce. Based on such result, the company might choose a more (or less, depending on the constraints) energy-efficient RS model.

In this work, we propose the first tool to *estimate* the carbon footprint of a recommendation model, given the characteristics of the models and the characteristics of the datasets; results show that, even if it is hard to precisely prediction the exact amount of $CO_2$ emissions of RSs, it is possible to predict the range of emissions that will be produced by a certain RS model, when trained on a specific dataset.

In addition, we release the first regression dataset for this task, made of all the instances we obtained in our work and that we used to train the regression model. To the best of our knowledge, we are the first proposing a standardized protocol to gather data related to emissions of RS models when trained on different machines and datasets, and use them to train an estimator. This is another strength point of our regression dataset, since anyone can enrich it by following the protocol we propose, and foster the research in this field.

Given the relevance Green AI and the lack of research in the RSs field (with the exception of the above mentioned [11,12]), we believe that this is an important contribution for the RSs community.

The paper is structured as follows: in Sect. 2 we present the methodology we designed to build the dataset and train the regression model, and provide

---

[1] https://sdgs.un.org/2030agenda.

details about carbon footprint tracking; in Sect. 3 we present the experimental design and discuss the results; finally, in Sect. 4, we summarize the results and the contributions of this paper.

## 2     Methodology

In this section, we present the standardized protocol designed to estimate the carbon footprint of RS models; the overall workflow is depicted in Fig. 1. In particular, we first built a regression dataset consisting of several instances related to each RS model (each with its own features) trained on different datasets, and the related carbon footprint; then, we trained a regression model to estimate the emissions, starting from a set of features characterizing each instance.

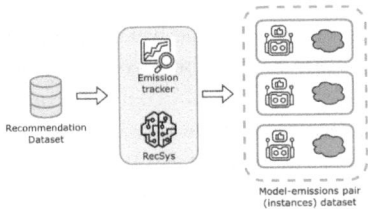

(a) Regression dataset building: RS models are trained on various machines and datasets, while their emissions are tracked. The resulting RS model-emission pairs compose our regression dataset.

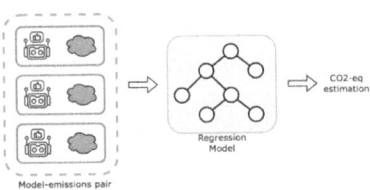

(b) Regression model training: the regression dataset is used to train a regression model so to predict the $CO_2$ of RSs.

**Fig. 1.** Our workflow, which consists of two main phases: 1) Regression dataset building; 2) Regression model training.

### 2.1     Carbon Footprint Tracking

In this section, we will provide details about the methodology we adopted to track and measure the emission of the RS models we trained, in order to build the regression dataset (which will be described more deeply in the next section).

In order to track the emissions of the RS models, we adopted a very common approach to measure the $CO_2$ emissions [6]. In particular, we adopted the $CO_2$-equivalent ($CO_2$-eq) metric, that is a standardized measure used to express the global warming potential of different greenhouse gases in terms of the amount of carbon dioxide ($CO_2$) that would have the same impact on global warming[2].

---

[2] https://ec.europa.eu/eurostat/statistics-explained/index.php?title=Glossary: Carbon_dioxide_equivalent.

In order to obtain the $CO_2$-eq associated to a machine computation, it is possible to compute the product of two factors: the Carbon Intensity (CI) and the Computational Power (PC) [6].

$$CO_2 - eq = CI \cdot PC \qquad (1)$$

$CI$ is calculated as the weighted average of the carbon footprint of each source that makes up the energy mix, as each source has a fixed amount of $CO_2$ emitted per kilowatt-hour. Formally, given an energy source mix $\mathcal{S}$ and each energy source $s \in \mathcal{S}$ with emissions per kilowatt-hour $e_s$, the $CI$ of $\mathcal{S}$ is calculated as $CI = \sum_{s \in \mathcal{S}} e_s \cdot p_s$, where $p_s$ is the percentage of the energy source $s$ in the energy source mix $\mathcal{S}$.

It's also important to point out that different countries use different mixes, so each mix (and therefore each country) has its own $CI$. For example[3], in 2022, Sweden used a mixture consisting of 2% oil, 30% nuclear, 40% hydro-power, 20% wind, 1% solar, and 7% bio-energy, resulting in a $CI$ of 41g/kWh; France used a mixture consisting of 1% coal, 9% gas, 2% oil, 64% nuclear, 10% hydro-power, 8% wind, 4% solar, and 2% bio-energy, leading to a $CI$ of 79 g/kWh.

Next, $PC$ refers to the electrical power needed by the hardware (CPUs, GPUs, RAMs, etc.) to carry out the computation, and it can be measured by accessing low-level primitives provided by the hardware devices themselves. It is expressed in terms kilowatt-hours.

In this paper, we used the Python library CodeCarbon[4] to implement this methodology: first, it takes into account the energy mix of the country where the computation is performed to obtain an accurate $CI$; second, it measures the $PC$ of each hardware component throughout the entire computation. This way, at the end of the computation, it provides a measure of the emitted $CO_2$-eq.

**Table 1.** RS models we have considered to feed the regression models

| Category | Models |
|---|---|
| General | BPR, DGCF, DMF, ItemKNN, LINE, LightGCN, MultiDAE, NGCF, CDAE, DiffRec, ENMF, FISM, GCMC, LDiffRec, MacridVAE, MultiVAE, NCEPLRec, NCL, NeuMF, Pop, Random, RecVAE, SGL, SLIMElastic, SimpleX, SpectralCF, EASE, NAIS, ADMMSLIM, ConvNCF, NNCF |
| KARSs | CFKG, CKE, KGCN, KGNNLS, RippleNet, KGIN, KTUP, MKR |

## 2.2   Regression Dataset Building and Regression Model Training

In this section, we will provide details about the regression dataset we built, the regression models we considered, and how we trained them.

---

[3] We used data available here: https://ourworldindata.org/electricity-mix.

[4] https://mlco2.github.io/codecarbon/.

**Table 2.** Statistics of the recommendation datasets.

| Dataset | Users | Items | Inter. | Sparsity | KG entities | KG relations | KG triples |
|---|---|---|---|---|---|---|---|
| ML1M | 6040 | 3706 | 1000209 | 0.96% | 79347 | 49 | 385923 |
| AmazonBooks | 22155 | 54458 | 1465871 | 0.99% | 26315 | 16 | 96476 |
| Mind | 23679 | 4414 | 1048575 | 0.99% | no KG | | |
| LFM-1b | 19841 | 42457 | 900212 | 0.99% | 50665 | 5 | 46827 |
| ML10M | 50000 | 10000 | 7053774 | 0.96% | 175646 | 31 | 521125 |

**Table 3.** Statistics about the regression dataset we built.

| | |
|---|---|
| Total instances | 254 |
| Max emissions (g) | 89.28 |
| Min emissions (g) | 1.72E-04 |
| AVG emissions (g) | 10.63 |
| Low emissions class threshold (g) | 29.76 |
| High emissions class threshold (g) | 59.52 |
| $\in$ low emission class | 228 |
| $\in$ medium emission class | 17 |
| $\in$ high emission class | 9 |

First, in order to train a regression model, we have built a regression dataset (Fig. 1a); to this end, we run several RS models, reported in Table 1, on different recommendation datasets (which are reported in Table 2), while tracking the related carbon emissions in terms of $CO_2$-eq, through the methodology described in the previous section.

At the end of this process, we obtained several *instances* encoding information related to the characteristics of the recommendation dataset (including information related to the KG, if any), the hardware used for computation, and the considered RS model; these attributes represent the input features, which are used to drive the prediction of the target variable, that is represented by the emissions measured by the emission tracker.

Moreover, we categorized all the instances into three classes: *low emission* class, *medium emission* class, and *high emission* class. To this end, we considered the whole emission spectrum of the instances we obtained; then, we computed two threshold values (low and high emission class thresholds), and used them to divide the spectrum into three ranges, with instances falling into each range labeled accordingly.

Some statistics about our regression dataset are reported in Table 3, while a graphical representation of all the instances, including the three classes, is reported in Fig. 2. In Table 4 we have reported all the input features we considered to drive the prediction of the target variable (emissions), while in Table 5 we report two example instances from the regression dataset we built.

**Table 4.** Regression model input features

| Feature | | Description |
|---|---|---|
| CF data | Users | Number of users in the dataset |
| | Items | Number of items in the dataset |
| | Interactions | Number of interactions encoded in the dataset |
| | Sparsity | Sparsity of the dataset |
| KG data | KG entities | Number of KG entity (if any) |
| | KG relations | Number of KG relations (if any) |
| | KG triples | Number of KG triples (if any) |
| Hardware | CPU cores | Number of CPU cores |
| | RAM size | Size of the RAM used for the computation |
| | GPU used | Flag specifying if a GPU has been used for the computation |
| Model | Model Name | Name of the RS model |
| | Model Type | Type of the RS model (ranges in General, KARS) |

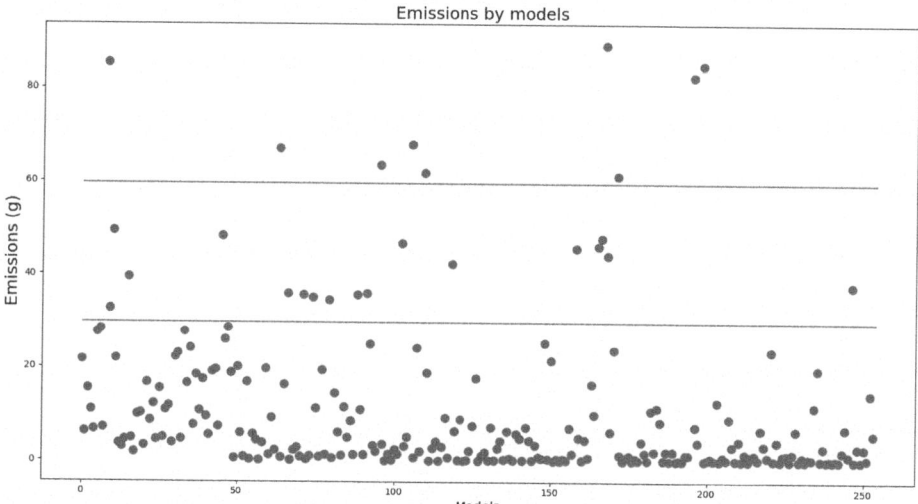

**Fig. 2.** The instances composing the dataset with the related $CO_2$-eq emissions, divided into the three classes (low, medium, high emissions).

**Table 5.** Two example instances from the regression dataset we built

| Input features | | | | | | | | | | | | | Target |
|---|---|---|---|---|---|---|---|---|---|---|---|---|---|
| Users | Items | Inter | Sparsity | KG ents | KG rels | KG triples | KG items | CPU Cores | RAM | GPU | Model name | Model type | Emissions |
| 19841 | 42457 | 900212 | 0.99% | 50665 | 5 | 46827 | 816701 | 4 | 27 | 1 | BPR | general | 0.0213 |
| 6040 | 3706 | 1000209 | 0.96% | 79347 | 49 | 385923 | 3655 | 12 | 64 | 1 | RippleNet | knowledge | 0.007 |

A strength point of our dataset relies in the fact that can be easily expanded by adding new instances obtained following the same methodology; we believe this aspect can foster research in this field.

Once the regression dataset has been built, we can move to the regression model training Fig. 1b. With emissions as the target variable, and all the other features as input features, we trained the regression model so to make it able to predict the emissions of a RS model.

## 3    Experimental Session

We designed our experiments to answer the following Research Questions (RQs):

- **RQ1**: Which is the best Regression Model to estimate the $CO_2$-eq emission of RS models?
- **RQ2**: Which regression model is best at predicting the emission class of RS models?
- **RQ3**: Which is the best splitting strategy between training data and testing data?

**Table 6.** Values of the hyper-parameters of the Regressors we have compared

| Parameter | Value | Description |
|---|---|---|
| *SVR Regressor* | | |
| Kernel | RBF | Type of kernel. RBF measures the similarity between two points |
| Degree | 3 | Degree of the polynomial used |
| Gamma | Scale | Dependent coefficient of the kernel |
| Coef-0 | 0 | Independent coefficient of the kernel |
| Tol | 0.001 | Tolerance |
| C | 1 | Regularizer criterion |
| Epsilon | 0.1 | Tollerance error w.r.t. the prediction |
| Shrinking | True | Reduce or not the support set |
| *Decision Tree Regressor* | | |
| Max depth | 5 | The maximum depth of the tree |
| Random state | 3 | Seed for replicability |
| Criterion | Squared error | Function used to measure the quality of a split |
| *Random Forest Regressor* | | |
| Estimators | 500 | Number of trees in the forest |
| Max depth | 5 | The maximum depth of the tree |
| Random state | 3 | Seed for replicability |
| Criterion | Squared error | Function used to measure the quality of a split |
| *AdaBoost Regressor* | | |
| Estimators | 500 | Number of trees in the forest |
| Random state | 3 | Seed for replicability |
| Estimator type | DecisionTree | The model used for the regression |
| Learning rate | 1 | Learning rate |
| Loss | linear | The loss function |

## 3.1  Experimental Design

**Recommendation Datasets.** As for the datasets we used to train the RS models, we considered well-known state-of-the-art datasets in different domains: we considered MovieLens-1M (ML1M) and MovieLens10M (ML10M) for the movie domain, AmazonBooks for the book domain, Mind for the news domain, and LFM-1b for the music domain; some statistics are reported in Table 2.

Due to the size of the ML10M, AmazonBooks, and LFM-1b datasets, we have performed some pre-processing to them: in particular, for ML10M, we randomly sampled 50000 users and 10000, and considered all the interactions involving them; similarly, for LFM-1b, we sampled 20000 users and 50000 items, keeping all the interactions involving them; finally, for AmazonBooks, we applied the 60-core strategy, so to keep only users and items with at least 60 interactions. These versions of the two datasets are available on our anonymous Github repository (see Footnote 8). The other datasets have not been pre-processed.

**RS Models.** In this section we present the RS models we used together with the emission tracker, in order to build the regression dataset. To guarantee fair comparisons and replaceable results, we used the implementations available in a well-known state-of-the-art Python library, namely RecBole[5] [19,21,22]; in this way, the protocol can easily be replicated. In particular, according to the classification provided by RecBole, we have selected state-of-the-art models falling in two categories: general models, that only use collaborative-filtering (CF) information, and knowledge aware models (KARS), that also exploit external knowledge. We trained all the selected models for 200 epochs, for all the considered datasets. The list of the considered models is reported in Table 1.

All the experiments have been performed on three different machines: in this way, involving different hardware system, we are able to obtain more diverse results, and this enables the regression model to better generalize the results; moreover, this reduces the under-fitting related to the usage of a single machine.

The first machine is based on Ubuntu 20.04.6 LTS, with AMD EPYC 7V12 64-Core as CPU, NVIDIA Tesla T4 16 GB as GPU, and CUDA driver Version 12.2. The second machine is a MacBook Pro with Intel(R) Core(TM) i5-6360, with no GPU. The third machine is a MacBook Pro with Apple M2 Max processor, with 12 cores for the CPU, 38 cores for the GPU, and 64 GB of RAM.

**Measuring the Carbon Footprint.** In order to track and measure the carbon footprint of our RS models, we used the Python library CodeCarbon[6], that implements the measurement introduced in Sect. 2.

**Regression Models.** As regression model, we compared 4 state-of-the-art models: Support Vector Regressor (SVR) [14], Decision Tree Regressor [20], Random Forest Regressor [8], and AdaBoost Regressor [10].

---

[5] https://recbole.io.
[6] https://mlco2.github.io/codecarbon/.

For such models, we have used the implementations available in the Python library Scikit-learn[7]; the source code is available on our Github repository[8].

In Table 6 we report the values for the hyper-parameters we set for the considered regression models. For all the parameters not appearing in the table, we used the default values; further refinements keeping into account these parameters are left as future works.

After the estimation of the emissions, each prediction can be assigned to one of the three emission classes we have defined in the previous paragraph, namely, low emission models, medium emission models, high emission models.

**Evaluation Metrics.** The performance of the regression models have been evaluated in terms of Mean Absolute Error (MAE), Root Mean Squared Error (RMSE), and Mean Squared Logarithmic Error (MLSE).

In addition, as previously described, each instance belongs to a class of emissions (low, medium, high); due to this, the predicted amount of $CO_2$-eq emissions can be assigned to the related emission class, and it is possible to assess the performance of the regression model in the identification of the correct emission class. To this end, we used the classification metrics Accuracy, Precision, Recall, and F1 score.

**Training-Testing Split Ratios.** The regression models have been trained and tested on a different number of train-test split ratios; in particular, we have considered the following ratios: 50–50, 60–40, 70–30, 80–20, 90–10. This has been performed to assess which is the needed amount of training data to be used to feed the regression model.

### 3.2    Discussion of the Results

To answer RQ1, and assess the best performing regression model, we reported the performances obtained by all the regression models in Table 6; it is easy to observe how, according to the error metrics, Random Forest Regressor is the model that behaves better regardless the ratio split between training and test data, followed by Decision Tree, AdaBoost and SVR. This is not a surprising result, since, given the amount of input features (Table 4), the quantity of emitted $CO_2$ is affected by several factors, and simpler models (such as SVR, that is the worst model in all the settings) may not be able to fully capture the complexity of the observations; on the other hand, Random Forest models are designed to minimize overfitting as much as possible, and this is an important issue to be considered in our setting: indeed, it is easy to observe how most of models emit low quantities of $CO_2$ (see Fig. 2).

In this context, there is a risk of overfitting on lower emission values, which can be mitigated by models like Random Forest. Decision Tree models also obtained good performance, but always slightly lower than Random Forest; similar observations can be made for AdaBoost, that has several design similarities

---

[7] https://scikit-learn.org/stable/api/index.html.

[8] https://anonymous.4open.science/r/carbon_recsys_radar-F4C1/README.md.

**Table 7.** Errors of the regression models for each split considered. Best results for each train-test ratio split are in bold, while best overall results are indicated with *.

| Regressor | Error metrics | | | Classification metrics | | | |
|---|---|---|---|---|---|---|---|
| | MAE | RMSE | MLSE | Accuracy | Precision | Recall | F1 |
| *50–50* | | | | | | | |
| SVR | 0.03574 | 0.00142 | 0.00135 | 0.89764 | 0.36745 | **0.62231** | 0.37208 |
| Decision Tree | 0.00711 | 0.00017 | 0.00016 | 0.88189 | 0.49805 | 0.43243 | 0.45593 |
| Random Forest | **0.00679** | **0.00014** | **0.00013** | **0.90551** | 0.37037 | 0.47067 | 0.3786 |
| AdaBoost | 0.00802 | 0.00015 | 0.00014 | 0.88976 | **0.54727*** | 0.59636 | **0.55528*** |
| *60–40* | | | | | | | |
| SVR | 0.03511 | 0.00138 | 0.00132 | 0.89216 | 0.37729 | **0.62121** | 0.38246 |
| Decision Tree | 0.00726 | 0.00015 | 0.00014 | 0.88235 | 0.32967 | 0.3 | 0.31414 |
| Random Forest | **0.00641*** | **0.00010*** | **0.00009*** | **0.90196** | **0.42491** | 0.47279 | **0.43867** |
| AdaBoost | 0.00885 | 0.00016 | 0.00016 | 0.89216 | 0.33333 | 0.30033 | 0.31597 |
| *70–30* | | | | | | | |
| SVR | 0.03517 | 0.00138 | 0.00131 | 0.8961 | 0.39517 | **0.62613** | 0.40035 |
| Decision Tree | 0.00667 | 0.00013 | 0.00012 | 0.85714 | 0.31884 | 0.30137 | 0.30986 |
| Random Forest | **0.00673** | **0.00011** | **0.00011** | **0.90909** | 0.4 | 0.47333 | **0.41468** |
| AdaBoost | 0.00806 | 0.00014 | 0.00013 | 0.80519 | 0.29952 | 0.30392 | 0.3017 |
| *80–20* | | | | | | | |
| SVR | 0.03447 | 0.00134 | 0.00128 | 0.90196 | 0.4372 | **0.63542** | 0.43026 |
| Decision Tree | 0.00741 | 0.00015 | 0.00014 | 0.84314 | 0.31159 | 0.30496 | 0.30824 |
| Random Forest | **0.00698** | **0.00012** | **0.00011** | **0.92157*** | **0.44444** | 0.47959 | **0.45614** |
| AdaBoost | 0.00940 | 0.00016 | 0.00016 | 0.66667 | 0.24638 | 0.30631 | 0.27309 |
| *90–10* | | | | | | | |
| SVR | 0.02969 | 0.00111 | 0.00106 | **0.88462** | **0.48551** | **0.70833*** | **0.47872** |
| Decision Tree | 0.00966 | 0.00021 | 0.00020 | 0.88462 | 0.33333 | 0.30667 | 0.31944 |
| Random Forest | **0.00887** | **0.00017** | **0.00016** | 0.84615 | 0.31884 | 0.30556 | 0.31206 |
| AdaBoost | 0.01159 | 0.00023 | 0.00021 | 0.76923 | 0.28986 | 0.30303 | 0.2963 |

with the Random Forest (see Table 6): both of them use Decision Tree as base models, so this could explain the similarity in their performance.

In summary, to answer RQ1, we can say that **Random Forest Regressor obtained the best results in terms of error metrics, followed by Decision Tree and AdaBoost Regressors (with slight differences). The simplest model, SVR, performed much worse w.r.t. the other models (about 5 times worse when compared to Random Forest), meaning that, in such complex contexts, it is not able to handle overfitting on lower emission values, resulting in a poorly performing model.**

Table 7 presents results related to classification metrics as well, allowing us to answer RQ2. Each estimated emission values has been assigned to a class of emissions (low, medium, high classes), and we computed the classification metrics as explained in the previous section. Also in this case, Random Forest seems to be the best performing models for almost all metrics, but its advantages are not so pronounced as in the case of error metrics. Random Forest models obtained the best results in terms of accuracy, precision, and F1 for the training-testing ratio splits 60–40, 70–30, 80–20; for the split 20–30, AdaBoost obtained the highest precision value. In all these cases, SVR obtained the highest recall value, while for the split 90–10 it performed the best for all the classification metrics. However, note that in the 90–10 split all the models generally performed worse in terms of error metrics, so results related to this split might not be reliable as results for the other split ratios.

Another important aspect to be considered when discussing these results is that here we are only focusing on the classification task, but, as previously observed, this task has been performed on an unbalanced dataset (see Fig. 2). For these reasons, we believe that these results should be discussed together with error metrics to get wider perspective, and from this point of view, Random Forest Regression model is confirmed to be the best performing model. However, we want to stress the lack of data in the high and medium emission classes, that presents a challenge for the community and a call to enrich the dataset, in order to make it more dense and balanced.

In summary, to answer RQ2, we can say that **Random Forest Regression model behaved again as the best performing model, but showed less pronounced enhancements w.r.t. the other regression models, and did obtain the best performance in all metrics and for all the splits. However, the dataset imbalance should be considered as well in this context. Enriching the dataset with new instances falling in the medium and high emission classes would positively affect the overall performance of the models in the classification task.**

Finally, Table 7 allows us to answer RQ3 too. As for the error metrics, it is easy to observe how the train-test ratio splits that allows the model to better estimated the right amount of $CO_2$ emissions are 60–40 and 70–30, with the former outperforming the latter, followed by 50–50 and 80–20; it is worth to observe how the ratio split 90–10 is the one that performs worst with respect to all the others. We believe this behavior depends on the quantity of instances in the datasets: with a relatively low total number of instances, a ratio split closer to 50–50 might increase the overall performance and avoid overfitting; should the dataset be richer, 80–20 or 90–10 splits might perform better than the others. As for the classification metrics, there is no a clear winner (again), but it is likely due to the reasons already discussed related to the unbalanced dataset.

In summary, we can answer RQ3 by stating that, in the context of our dataset, **the 60–40 and 70–30 ratio splits most improve regression model performance based on error metrics, while no clear winner emerges for classification metrics.**

# 4    Conclusions

In this paper, we have presented the first attempt into the direction of *estimating* the quantity of $CO_2$-eq emitted by RS models. To this end, we built a dataset made of recommendation model instances with related emission data; this dataset has been used to train a regression model aiming at estimating the $CO_2$-eq emission of a recommendation model given information about the recommendation dataset, the hardware used for the computation, and the characteristics of the selected recommendation models. To best of our knowledge, this is the first standardized protocol designed to estimate the emissions of RSs.

Results we obtained showed that: *i):* Random Forest regression model outperformed all the other considered models in all the settings; *ii):* simple models, like SVR, are not suitable at handling all the features in an effective way; *iii):* more data is needed, to enrich the dataset and improve the model performance.

The main limitations of our work are related to the size of the dataset, as already discussed; however, we still believe this is a valuable contribution for the community, since it represents the first attempt into the direction of emission estimation, and we released the first regression dataset for this task.

In future works, we will expand the already existing dataset by adding new instances, including ones falling in the medium and high emission groups, in order to balance the dataset; we will also consider other categories of RS models (*e.g..* sequential models), and we will involve new machine, so to allow the model to better generalize hardware features; finally, we will also study approaches and methodologies for automatic dimensioning [1], to improve the environmental sustainability of the recommendation models during their training.

**Acknowledgement.** This research is partially funded by PNRR project FAIR - Future AI Research (PE00000013), Spoke 6 - Symbiotic AI and Spoke 8 - Pervasive AI (CUP H97G22000210007) under the NRRP MUR program funded by the NextGenerationEU, and by the project PHaSE (CUP H53D23003530006) - Promoting Healthy and Sustainable Eating through Interactive and Explainable AI Methods, funded by MUR under the PRIN program; this research has also been partially supported by the Apulia Region under the Program "RIPARTI (assegni di Ricerca per riPARTire con le Imprese)", POC PUGLIA FESR- FSE 2014/2020 - CUP: H93C22000520002, project: "Recommendation systems and Digital Storytelling in Tourism"; this research has also been partially supported by UNIBA-MAML.

# References

1. De Filippo, A., Borghesi, A., Boscarino, A., Milano, M.: Hada: an automated tool for hardware dimensioning of ai applications. Knowl.-Based Syst. **251**, 109199 (2022)
2. Jannach, D., Zanker, M., Felfernig, A., Friedrich, G.: Recommender systems: an introduction. Cambridge University Press (2010)
3. Lannelongue, L., Grealey, J., Inouye, M.: Green algorithms: quantifying the carbon footprint of computation. Adv. Sci. **8**(12), 2100707 (2021)

4. Luccioni, A.S., Viguier, S., Ligozat, A.L.: Estimating the carbon footprint of bloom, a 176b parameter language model. J. Mach. Learn. Res. **24**(253), 1–15 (2023). http://jmlr.org/papers/v24/23-0069.html
5. Masanet, E., Shehabi, A., Lei, N., Smith, S., Koomey, J.: Recalibrating global data center energy-use estimates. Science **367**(6481), 984–986 (2020)
6. Pandey, D., Agrawal, M., Pandey, J.S.: Carbon footprint: current methods of estimation. Environ. Monit. Assess. **178**, 135–160 (2011)
7. Patterson, D.,et al.: Carbon emissions and large neural network training. arXiv preprint arXiv:2104.10350 (2021)
8. Rigatti, S.J.: Random forest. J. Insur. Med. **47**(1), 31–39 (2017)
9. Schwartz, R., Dodge, J., Smith, N.A., Etzioni, O.: Green ai. Commun. ACM **63**(12), 54–63 (2020)
10. Solomatine, D.P., Shrestha, D.L.: Adaboost. rt: a boosting algorithm for regression problems. In: 2004 IEEE International Joint Conference on Neural Networks (IEEE Cat. No. 04CH37541), vol. 2, pp. 1163–1168. IEEE (2004)
11. Spillo, G., De Filippo, A., Musto, C., Milano, M., Semeraro, G.: Towards sustainability-aware recommender systems: analyzing the trade-off between algorithms performance and carbon footprint. In: Proceedings of the 17th ACM Conference on Recommender Systems, pp. 856–862 (2023)
12. Spillo, G., De Filippo, A., Musto, C., Milano, M., Semeraro, G.: Towards green recommender systems: investigating the impact of data reduction on carbon footprint and model performances. In: Proceedings of the 18th ACM Conference on Recommender Systems (2024)
13. Strubell, E., Ganesh, A., McCallum, A.: Energy and policy considerations for deep learning in nlp. arXiv preprint arXiv:1906.02243 (2019)
14. Tong, H., Chen, D.R., Peng, L.: Analysis of support vector machines regression. Found. Comput. Math. **9**(2), 243–257 (2009)
15. Van Wynsberghe, A.: Sustainable ai: Ai for sustainability and the sustainability of ai. AI and Ethics **1**(3), 213–218 (2021)
16. Vente, T., Wegmeth, L., Said, A., Beel, J.: From clicks to carbon: the environmental toll of recommender systems. In: Proceedings of the 18th ACM Conference on Recommender Systems, pp. 580–590. RecSys 2024, Association for Computing Machinery, New York (2024). https://doi.org/10.1145/3640457.3688074, https://doi.org/10.1145/3640457.3688074
17. Verdecchia, R., Sallou, J., Cruz, L.: A systematic review of green ai. Wiley Interdisciplinary Reviews: Data Mining and Knowledge Discovery, p. e1507 (2023)
18. Wu, C.J., et al.: Sustainable ai: environmental implications, challenges and opportunities. Proc. Mach. Learn. Syst. **4**, 795–813 (2022)
19. Xu, L., et al.: Recent advances in recbole: extensions with more practical considerations (2022)
20. Xu, M., Watanachaturaporn, P., Varshney, P.K., Arora, M.K.: Decision tree regression for soft classification of remote sensing data. Remote Sens. Environ. **97**(3), 322–336 (2005)
21. Zhao, W.X., et al.: Recbole 2.0: towards a more up-to-date recommendation library. In: Proceedings of the 31st ACM International Conference on Information & Knowledge Management, pp. 4722–4726 (2022)
22. Zhao, W.X., et al.: Recbole: towards a unified, comprehensive and efficient framework for recommendation algorithms. In: CIKM, pp. 4653–4664. ACM (2021)

# Eco-Aware Graph Neural Networks for Sustainable Recommendations

Antonio Purificato$^{(\boxtimes)}$ ⓘ and Fabrizio Silvestri ⓘ

Sapienza University of Rome, Rome, Italy
{purificato,fsilvestri}@diag.uniroma1.it

**Abstract.** Recommender systems play a crucial role in alleviating information overload by providing personalized recommendations tailored to users' preferences and interests. Recently, Graph Neural Networks (GNNs) have emerged as a promising approach for recommender systems, leveraging their ability to effectively capture complex relationships and dependencies between users and items by representing them as nodes in a graph structure.

In this study, we investigate the environmental impact of GNN-based recommender systems, an aspect that has been largely overlooked in the literature. Specifically, we conduct a comprehensive analysis of the carbon emissions associated with training and deploying GNN models for recommendation tasks. We evaluate the energy consumption and carbon footprint of different GNN architectures and configurations, considering factors such as model complexity, training duration, hardware specifications and embedding size.

By addressing the environmental impact of resource-intensive algorithms in recommender systems, this study contributes to the ongoing efforts towards sustainable and responsible artificial intelligence, promoting the development of eco-friendly recommendation technologies that balance performance and environmental considerations. Code is available at: https://github.com/antoniopurificato/gnn_recommendation_and_environment.

**Keywords:** Graph Neural Networks · Recommendation Systems · Environmental Impact

## 1 Introduction

By offering tailored suggestions, Recommender Systems (RSs) are essential in helping users navigate the overwhelming amount of information available, benefiting users and service providers across various platforms, including e-commerce (e.g., Tmall, Amazon) (Ge et al. 2020) and social networks (e.g., Gowalla, Facebook) (Peng et al. 2020; Zhao et al. 2016). With the recent advances of artificial intelligence and machine learning techniques (Purificato et al. 2023; Bucarelli 2023; Wani et al. 2024), different approaches have been proposed, ranging from

ⓒ The Author(s), under exclusive license to Springer Nature Switzerland AG 2025
L. Boratto et al. (Eds.): RecSoGood 2024, CCIS 2470, pp. 111–122, 2025.
https://doi.org/10.1007/978-3-031-87654-7_11

collaborative filtering techniques that leverage user-item interactions to content-based methods that analyze item features (Chen et al. 2018) to sequential recommendation, aiming to capture the sequential patterns in user behavior and provide recommendations based on the current context or session (Betello et al. 2024; Bacciu et al. 2023).

In addition to sequential recommendation, Graph Neural Networks (GNNs) have emerged as a promising approach for recommender systems (Liu et al. 2024; Mancino et al. 2023). GNNs can effectively capture the complex relationships and dependencies between users and items by representing them as nodes in a graph structure. By propagating and aggregating information along the edges of the graph, GNNs can learn rich representations that encode high-order connectivity patterns, leading to improved recommendation performance (Wu et al. 2022). Furthermore, GNNs can naturally incorporate various types of auxiliary information, such as user profiles, item attributes, and social connections, into the graph structure, enabling the exploitation of heterogeneous data sources for more accurate recommendations (Purificato et al. 2024). Nowadays, resource-intensive algorithms have become prevalent in modern recommender systems, resulting in higher energy consumption for recommendation experiments (Betello et al. 2024a). However, despite some studies having been carried out in regarding the environmental impact of SRSs (Betello et al. 2024a; Spillo et al. 2023), only one work presented an analysis of the computational consumption of GNN-based RSs (Spillo et al. 2023).

In this work, we analyse the environmental impact of GNN-based RSs experiments by faithfully replicating representative experimental pipelines. Through a comprehensive comparative analysis, we shed light on the carbon emissions attributable to the training and deployment of GNN-based RSs. Our study serves as a clarion call for sustainability, underscoring the need to reconcile the pursuit of technological advancements with environmental consciousness within the realm of RSs. This study aims to answer to the following research questions:

- **RQ1**: Which model performs the best, and what are the trade-offs in terms of resource consumption?
- **RQ2**: How does the embedding size of the GNN affect the environmental impact of the results?

## 2   Related Work

In the Glasgow Agreement (Hunter et al. 2021), participating nations committed to reducing $CO_2$ emissions, underscoring the urgent need for environmental action. This commitment is particularly relevant to our field, as the environmental impact of GPU training in machine learning is significant. The energy consumption associated with these computational processes contributes significantly to $CO_2$ emissions, exacerbating climate change (Patterson et al. 2021). It is therefore our responsibility to raise awareness of this issue.

Although the environmental impact of deep learning algorithms has been investigated in certain domains, such as Natural Language Processing (Bender et al., 2021; Wang et al. 2023) and Information Retrieval (Scells et al. 2022), there is a dearth of research examining the environmental footprint of Recommender Systems.

Spillo et al. (2023) benchmark several state-of-the-art recommendation algorithms in terms of both recommendation performance and carbon emissions and analyze the trade-off between energy consumption, carbon emissions and the predictive accuracy of recommendation algorithms. A difference with respect to our approach is that they do not study the impact of some important factors on the performance and on the emissions, such as the embedding size of each model.

Betello et al. (2024a) provide a code resource and a robust framework for developing RSs and establishing a foundation for consistent and reproducible experimentation. They also study how the number of parameters influences the $CO_2$ consumption of the proposed algorithms. Differently from our work, they do not consider GNN-based approaches, but only sequential recommendation algorithms. While their research aims to provide a reproducibility analysis with an associated framework, the objective of our work is to highlight the significance of implementing environmentally sustainable solutions for recommendation tasks.

In the next Section we present our methodological approach to assess the environmental impact of recommender systems.

## 3    Method

### 3.1    Calculating $CO_2$ Emissions

In this study, we use CodeCarbon[1] (Courty et al. 2023), a tool designed to track the power consumption of both CPUs and GPUs. This allows us to measure carbon dioxide equivalent ($CO_2$-eq), a widely accepted standard used by numerous organisations and governments to monitor emissions of various greenhouse gases (Kim and Neff, 2009). $CO_2$-eq facilitates the comparison of greenhouse gas emissions by converting quantities of different gases into an equivalent amount of $CO_2$, based on their respective global warming potentials. By using CodeCarbon, we can accurately assess the environmental impact of our training processes, in line with our commitment to sustainability and responsible research practices in machine learning.

Our decision to focus specifically on $CO_2$-eq emissions is motivated by several factors. First, $CO_2$-eq is a widely recognized and accepted metric for quantifying the combined impact of various greenhouse gases on global warming, allowing us to provide a standardized and comparable measure of the overall environmental impact (Betello et al. 2024a; Spillo et al. 2023). Second, $CO_2$ emissions are particularly relevant in the context of energy-intensive machine learning training processes, which typically rely on electricity generated from fossil fuel sources.

---

[1] https://codecarbon.io.

Tracking $CO_2$-eq emissions allows us to directly assess the carbon footprint associated with the energy consumption of our experiments.

## 3.2   Models

The Neural Graph Collaborative Filtering (NGCF) model (Wang et al. 2019) represents user-item interactions as a bipartite graph and learns user and item embeddings by propagating them on the graph through message passing layers. The key idea is to capture high-order connectivity patterns by recursively propagating embeddings over the graph using graph convolutional layers. NGCF is trained end-to-end to minimize the difference between predicted and actual user-item interactions. It exploits high-order connectivity, learning non-linear relationships, and providing inductive capabilities for new users or items.

LightGCN (He et al. 2020) learns user and item embeddings by propagating them on the user-item interaction graph through a series of graph convolutional layers. Unlike NGCF, LightGCN removes the feature transformation and non-linear activation layers, making it a linear model. The key idea is to simplify the GCN architecture while preserving the ability to capture high-order connectivity patterns between users and items. LightGCN is trained end-to-end to optimize the BCE between the predicted and actual user-item interactions. It has demonstrated competitive performance while being computationally efficient.

SimGCL (Yu et al. 2022) add random uniform noise to hidden representations for augmentations, resulting in more uniform node representations that mitigate the popularity bias. Adjusting the noise magnitude can improve regulation of representation uniformity, leading to advantages on recommendation accuracy and model training efficiency.

In LightGCL (Cai et al. 2023), the graph augmentation is guided by singular value decomposition (SVD) to not only distill the useful information of user-item interactions but also inject the global collaborative context into the representation alignment of contrastive learning. Instead of generating two handcrafted augmented views, important semantic of user-item interactions can be preserved with their paradigm. This enables self-augmented representations to be reflective of both user-specific preferences and cross-user global dependencies.

## 3.3   Experimental Pipeline

To evaluate the impact of different embedding sizes on the model's performance and computational requirements, experiments with embedding sizes of 32, 64, 128, and 256 are conducted. The results of these experiments are presented in Sect. 5. Prior to commencing the training process, we initialize a CodeCarbon tracker to monitor the carbon emissions associated with the training process. Additionally, we utilize the DeepSpeed[2] library to compute the number of floating-point operations (FLOPs) required for each model configuration.

---

[2] https://www.deepspeed.ai.

During the training process, the CodeCarbon library is used to log the power consumption every 30 s, allowing us to track the energy consumption in real-time. Upon completion of the training, we compute the total carbon emissions and various performance metrics, as described in Sect. 4.

In the next Section we will presents the experimental setup and describe the different metrics and datasets used in the experiments.

## 4 Experiments

### 4.1 Datasets

Our analyses encompass a collection of datasets, ensuring comprehensive and robust insights. By incorporating datasets with diverse characteristics, such as varying user and item counts, we aim to unravel the intricate interplay between these factors and our findings. This approach enables us to capture a view of real-world scenarios, thereby fortifying the applicability of our conclusions across a broad spectrum of contexts. All the statistics of these datasets are presented in Table 1.

- MovieLens[3]: The MovieLens dataset (Harper and Konstan, 2015) is widely recognized as a benchmark for evaluating recommendation algorithms. We utilize MovieLens 1M (ML-1M).
- Amazon: These datasets consist of product reviews collected from Amazon.com (McAuley et al. 2015). The data are organized into distinct datasets based on Amazon's primary product categories. For our study, we focus on the "Beauty" category (Beauty).
- DianPing: This dataset contains the user reviews as well as the detailed business meta data information crawled from a famous Chinese online review website[4].

Our data preprocessing pipeline adheres to well-established practices in the field. We adopt an implicit approach, treating all interactions as binary events without considering rating values, as done in (Kang and McAuley, 2018; Sun et al. 2019).

For dataset partitioning, we employ a widely-used strategy in sequential recommendation tasks (Sun et al. 2019; Kang and McAuley, 2018). The most recent interaction for each user is held out for testing, while the second-to-last interaction is reserved for validation. The remaining interactions constitute the training set, providing a chronological sequence of user behavior.

### 4.2 Metrics

To evaluate the performance of sequential recommendation algorithms, we employed four widely adopted metrics commonly used in Information Retrieval

---

[3] https://grouplens.org/datasets/movielens.
[4] DianPing.com.

**Table 1.** Dataset statistics after pre-processing. Density and sparsity are percentage values.

| Dataset name | Users | Items | Interactions | Density | Sparsity |
|---|---|---|---|---|---|
| Amazon Beauty | 1,210,271 | 249,274 | 2,023,070 | 0.001 | 99.999 |
| MovieLens 1M | 6,040 | 3,952 | 999,611 | 4.189 | 95.810 |
| DianPing | 542,706 | 243,247 | 4,422,473 | 0.003 | 99.997 |

(IR) (Kang and McAuley, 2018; Purificato et al. 2024): Precision, Recall, Normalized Discounted Cumulative Gain (NDCG), and Hit Ratio (HIT). These metrics provide a comprehensive assessment of the recommendation system's ability to identify relevant items and rank them effectively. We also present the $CO_2$-eq consumed for training the model, which we denote as Emissions in the results.

- Precision: This metric calculates the proportion of correctly identified relevant items among the recommended items. It measures the system's ability to avoid irrelevant recommendations.
- Recall: It quantifies the fraction of correctly identified relevant items among the recommendations relative to the total number of relevant items in the dataset. This metric evaluates the system's capability to retrieve as many relevant items as possible.
- Normalized Discounted Cumulative Gain (NDCG): This metric evaluates the performance of a ranking system by considering the position of relevant items in the ranked list. It assigns higher scores to relevant items ranked higher, as they are typically where a user's attention is focused. NDCG captures the importance of ranking relevant items at the top of the recommendation list.
- Hit Ratio (HIT): Is a key metric in recommendation systems that measures whether relevant items appear within the top K positions of a model's recommendation list. For each user, if at least one relevant item is included in the top K recommendations, it counts as a "hit." The HIT@K score is then calculated as the proportion of users for whom the model successfully includes at least one relevant item within the top K.
- Emissions: Represents the $CO_2$-eq (measured in Kg) required for training a single model and is the sum of the single $CO_2$-eq emissions over each epoch.

By employing these metrics, we can comprehensively assess the recommendation system's ability to identify relevant items, rank them effectively, and provide high-quality recommendations tailored to the user's preferences and interests while keeping track of the emissions of each model.

### 4.3   Reproducibility

In order to facilitate a rigorous and unbiased comparison, a standardized experimental setup was adopted for all models. The training regime consisted of 400 epochs, with batch sizes of 2048 and 4096 for the training and validation stages, respectively. The optimization was carried out using the Adam algorithm, with a learning rate fixed at 0.001. Furthermore, to mitigate the effects of random initialization and promote reproducibility, an identical seed was employed across all experiments. In order to see how all the experiments evolve over time, no early stopping procedures were applied.

### 4.4   Hardware

All experiments were performed on a single NVIDIA RTX A6000 with 10752 CUDA cores and 48 GB of RAM. The code is written in Python 3 and to train all the models it was used the RecBole library[5] (Xu et al. 2023).

In the next Section we will present the results of the proposed study, in terms of performance metrics and environmental impact.

## 5   Results

### 5.1   RQ1: Which Model Excels, and at What Cost?

As shown in Table 2, LightGCN outperforms all competitors across all datasets, with the most significant lead observed on the Beauty dataset, while the gap narrows on the ML-1M dataset. LightGCN's superior performance can be attributed to two key factors: firstly, it is an advancement over NGCF, with its advantages clearly demonstrated in prior experiments (He et al. 2020). Secondly, both Light-GCL and SimGCL, although promising, involve higher computational complexity, and 400 epochs may not suffice for them to converge to optimal results. In

**Table 2.** Results of the models in terms of Precision@K (P@K), Recall@K (R@K), NDCG@K and HIT@K, with K $\in$ {**10, 100**} ($\uparrow$ is better). Also the emissions in terms of $CO_2$-eq [kg] are shown ($\downarrow$ is better). **Bold** denotes the best model for a dataset by the metric in the main group, underlined the second best.

| Dataset | Model | P@10 | R@10 | NDCG@10 | HIT@10 | P@100 | R@100 | NDCG@100 | HIT@100 | Emissions |
|---|---|---|---|---|---|---|---|---|---|---|
| Beauty | LightGCL | .0019 | .0185 | .0107 | .0187 | .0005 | .0517 | .0190 | .0591 | 12.5521 |
|  | LightGCN | **.0022** | **.0212** | **.0121** | **.0217** | **.0006** | **.0583** | **.0195** | **.0594** | 4.1341 |
|  | NGCF | .0017 | .0160 | .0087 | .0164 | .0005 | .0508 | .0156 | .0519 | **1.1147** |
|  | SimGCL | .0004 | .0039 | .0019 | .0039 | .0002 | .0227 | .0054 | .0230 | 12.9475 |
| DianPing | LightGCL | .0044 | .0239 | .0221 | .0499 | .0018 | .1673 | .0393 | .1734 | 15.0111 |
|  | LightGCN | **.0053** | **.0417** | **.0223** | **.0518** | **.0023** | **.1680** | **.0482** | **.2031** | 13.4835 |
|  | NGCF | .0032 | .0235 | .0123 | .0313 | .0017 | .1205 | .0320 | .1523 | 27.3234 |
|  | SimGCL | .0040 | .0238 | .0101 | .0474 | .0016 | .1435 | .0347 | .1600 | 21.2422 |
| ML-1M | LightGCL | .1986 | .1591 | .2546 | .7341 | .0761 | .5231 | .3366 | .9538 | .0185 |
|  | LightGCN | **.2094** | **.1731** | **.2681** | **.7626** | **.0808** | **.5692** | **.3619** | **.9664** | 0.2146 |
|  | NGCF | .2001 | .1623 | .2549 | .7373 | .0786 | .5492 | .3470 | .9621 | **.1057** |
|  | SimGCL | .1073 | .1188 | .1490 | .6210 | .0438 | .4037 | .2333 | .9386 | 0.1281 |

---

[5] https://recbole.io/.

terms of carbon emissions, NGCF remains the most efficient on two out of the three datasets-a somewhat unexpected outcome, given that LightGCN is touted by its authors as being more lightweight than NGCF. The best trade-off in terms of performance-emission will probably remain LightGCN, which is the second-best model in terms of environmental impact on two of the three datasets.

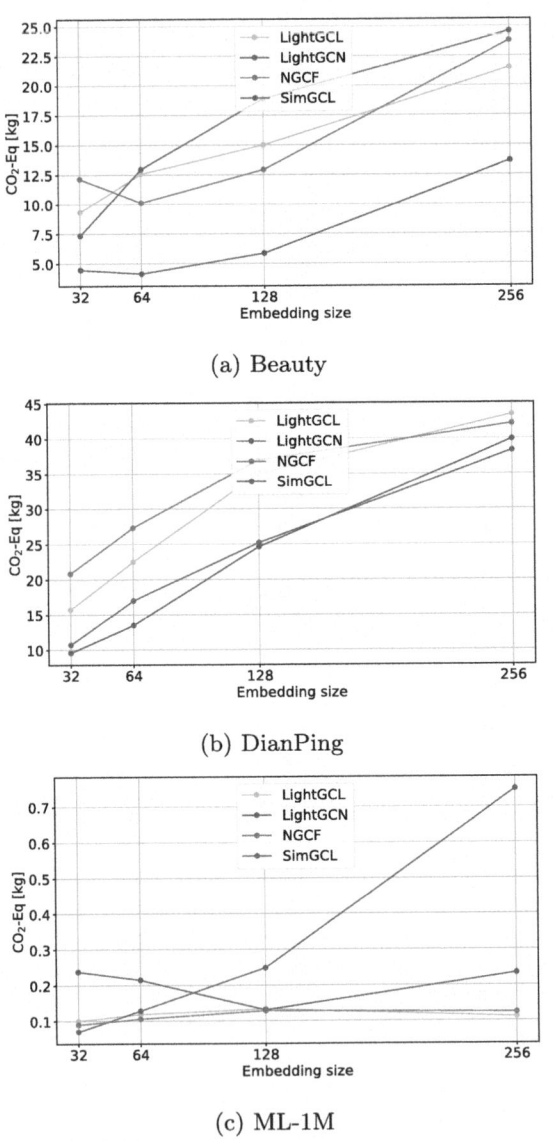

(a) Beauty

(b) DianPing

(c) ML-1M

**Fig. 1.** Difference in terms of environmental impact when changing the embedding size of the GNNs. On the y-axis it can be seen the $CO_2$-eq while on the x-axis the embedding size.

## 5.2   Embedding Size and Environmental Impact

Figure 1 shows that increasing the size of the embeddings generally leads to a higher environmental impact across all models and datasets. This trend is particularly pronounced in the DianPing dataset, which contains a large number of interactions. Interestingly, on the DianPing dataset, NGCF has a higher cost than SimGCL, despite SimGCL being computationally more expensive. However, on the other datasets, SimGCL consistently remains the most computationally demanding model. The same Figure also illustrates how the dataset size affects $CO_2$-eq costs. On the ML-1M dataset, the costs are significantly lower compared to those on the DianPing dataset. This not only depends from the number of users and the number of items, but also from the interactions between users and items. On the DianPing and Beauty datasets, as the embedding size increases, emissions also increase, as expected. It is interesting to note that on the ML-1M dataset, for the NGCF and LightGCL models, emissions related to an embedding size of 256 are higher compared to those with an embedding size of 128. This result requires more detailed investigation in future work, particularly on how each parameter of a model influences the environmental impact of the respective model.

# 6   Conclusions

In this study, we examined the environmental impact of GNN-based recommender systems, an aspect often overlooked in AI research. Our analysis of carbon emissions and energy consumption across different GNN architectures and configurations highlights how model complexity, training duration, hardware specifications, and embedding size affect their environmental footprint.

While GNNs provide significant benefits in capturing complex relationships for recommendation tasks, our findings show that these gains can come with considerable environmental costs, especially when large datasets or extensive embeddings are used. By emphasizing these trade-offs, our study contributes to the discourse on sustainable AI, encouraging the integration of environmental considerations into the development of recommender systems. Future research should focus on optimizing GNN architectures to balance performance with sustainability, exploring new algorithms and energy-efficient methods.

We hope this work inspires further efforts to develop eco-friendly AI technologies that align with global sustainability goals.

**Acknowledgment.** This work was partially supported by projects FAIR (PE0000013) and SERICS (PE00000014) under the MUR National Recovery and Resilience Plan funded by the European Union - NextGenerationEU and by PRIN 2020 project n.2020TA3K9N "LEGO.AI". Supported by the EC H2020RIA project "SoBigData++" (871042), PNRR MUR project IR0000013-SoBigData.it.

# References

Bacciu, A., Siciliano, F., Tonellotto, N., Silvestri, F.: Integrating item relevance in training loss for sequential recommender systems. In: Proceedings of the 17th ACM Conference on Recommender Systems, pp. 1114–1119 (2023)

Bender, E.M., Gebru, T., McMillan-Major, A., Shmitchell, S.: .On the dangers of stochastic parrots: can language models be too big?. In Proceedings of the 2021 ACM Conference on Fairness, Accountability, and Transparency (Virtual Event, Canada) (FAccT 2021), pp. 610–623. Association for Computing Machinery, New York (2021). https://doi.org/10.1145/3442188.3445922

Betello, F., et al.: . A Reproducible Analysis of Sequential Recommender Systems. arXiv preprint arXiv:2408.03873 (2024)

Betello, F., Siciliano, F., Mishra, P., Silvestri, F.: Investigating the robustness of sequential recommender systems against training data perturbations. In: Advances in Information Retrieval, pp. 205–220. Springer Nature Switzerland, Cham (2024). https://doi.org/10.1007/978-3-031-56060-6_14

Bucarelli, M.S., Cassano, L., Siciliano, F., Mantrach, A., Silvestri., F.: Leveraging inter-rater agreement for classification in the presence of noisy labels. In Proceedings of the IEEE/CVF Conference on Computer Vision and Pattern Recognition, pp. 3439–3448 (2023)

Cai, X., Huang, C., Xia, L., Ren, X.: LightGCL: simple yet effective graph contrastive learning for recommendation. In: The Eleventh International Conference on Learning Representations (2023)

Rui Chen, Qingyi Hua, Yan-Shuo Chang, Bo Wang, Lei Zhang, and Xiangjie Kong. 2018. A Survey of Collaborative Filtering-Based Recommender Systems: From Traditional Methods to Hybrid Methods Based on Social Networks. IEEE Access 6 (2018), 64301–64320. https://doi.org/10.1109/ACCESS.2018.2877208

Courty, B., et al.: mlco2/codecarbon: v2.3.2 (2023). https://doi.org/10.5281/zenodo.10213072

Ge, Y., et al.: Understanding echo chambers in E-commerce recommender systems. In Proceedings of the 43rd International ACM SIGIR Conference on Research and Development in Information Retrieval (Virtual Event, China) (SIGIR 2020), pp. 2261–2270. Association for Computing Machinery, New York (2020). https://doi.org/10.1145/3397271.3401431

Harper, M., Konstan, J.A.: The MovieLens datasets: history and context. ACM Trans. Interact. Intell. Syst. 5(4), Article 19 (2015), 19 (2015). https://doi.org/10.1145/2827872

He, X., Deng, K., Wang, X., Li, Y.,Zhang, Y., Wang., M.: LightGCN: simplifying and powering graph convolution network for recommendation. In Proceedings of the 43rd International ACM SIGIR Conference on Research and Development in Information Retrieval (Virtual Event, China) (SIGIR 2020), pp. 639–648. Association for Computing Machinery, New York (2020). https://doi.org/10.1145/3397271.3401063

Hunter, D.B., Salzman, J.E., Zaelke, D.: Glasgow climate summit: Cop26 (2021)

Wang-Cheng Kang and Julian McAuley. . Self-attentive sequential recommendation. In 2018 IEEE International Conference on data Mining (ICDM), pp. 197–206. IEEE (2018)

Kim, B., Neff, R.: Measurement and communication of greenhouse gas emissions from US food consumption via carbon calculators. Ecolog. Econ. 69(1), 186–196 (2009)

Liu, X., Xia, L., Huang, C.: SelfGNN: self-supervised graph neural networks for sequential recommendation. In: Proceedings of the 47th International ACM SIGIR Conference on Research and Development in Information Retrieval (Washington DC,

USA) (SIGIR 2024), pp. 1609–1618. Association for Computing Machinery, New York (2024). https://doi.org/10.1145/3626772.3657716

Mancino, A.C.M., Ferrara, A., Bufi, S., Malitesta, D., Di Noia, T., Di Sciascio, E.: KGTORe: Tailored Recommendations through Knowledge-aware GNN Models. In: Proceedings of the 17th ACM Conference on Recommender Systems (Singapore, Singapore) (RecSys 2023). Association for Computing Machinery, New York (2023). https://doi.org/10.1145/3604915.3608804

McAuley, J., Targett, C., Shi, Q., van den Hengel, A.: Image-Based Recommendations on Styles and Substitutes. In Proceedings of the 38th International ACM SIGIR Conference on Research and Development in Information Retrieval (Santiago, Chile) (SIGIR 2015), pp. 43–52. Association for Computing Machinery, New York (2015). https://doi.org/10.1145/2766462.2767755

Patterson, D., et al.: Carbon emissions and large neural network training (2021)

Peng, Z., et al.: Graph representation learning via graphical mutual information maximization. In: Proceedings of The Web Conference 2020 (Taipei, Taiwan) (WWW 2020), pp. 259–270. Association for Computing Machinery, New York (2020). https://doi.org/10.1145/3366423.3380112

Purificato, A., Cassarà, G., Siciliano, F., Lió, P., Silvestri, F.: Sheaf4Rec: Sheaf Neural Networks for Graph-based Recommender Systems. arXiv:2304.09097 (2024)

Purificato, A., Navigli, R., et al.: Apatt at semeval-2023 task 3: The sapienza nlp system for ensemble-based multilingual propaganda detection. In: Proceedings of the The 17th International Workshop on Semantic Evaluation (SemEval-2023) (2023)

Scells, H., Zhuang, S., Zuccon, G.: Reduce, reuse, recycle: green information retrieval research. In: Proceedings of the 45th International ACM SIGIR Conference on Research and Development in Information Retrieval (Madrid, Spain) (SIGIR 2022), pp. 2825–2837. Association for Computing Machinery, New York (2022). https://doi.org/10.1145/3477495.3531766

Spillo, G., De Filippo, A., Musto, C., Milano, M., Semeraro, G.: Towards sustainability-aware recommender systems: analyzing the trade-off between algorithms performance and carbon footprint. In: Proceedings of the 17th ACM Conference on Recommender Systems (Singapore, Singapore) (RecSys 2023), pp. 856–862. Association for Computing Machinery, New York (2023). https://doi.org/10.1145/3604915.3608840

Sun, F., et al.: BERT4Rec: Sequential Recommendation with Bidirectional Encoder Representations from Transformer. arXiv:1904.06690 (2019)

Wang, X., He, X., Wang, M., Feng, F., Chua, T.-S.: Neural Graph Collaborative Filtering. In Proceedings of the 42nd International ACM SIGIR Conference on Research and Development in Information Retrieval (Paris, France) (SIGIR 2019), pp. 165–174. Association for Computing Machinery, New York (2019). https://doi.org/10.1145/3331184.3331267

Wang, X., Na, C., Strubell, E., Friedler, S., Luccioni, S.: Energy and carbon considerations of fine-tuning BERT. In: The 2023 Conference on Empirical Methods in Natural Language Processing (2023)

Wani, F.A., Bucarelli, M.S., Silvestri, F.: Learning with noisy labels through learnable weighting and centroid similarity. In: 2024 International Joint Conference on Neural Networks (IJCNN), pp. 1–9. IEEE (2024)

Wu, S., Sun, F., Zhang, W., Xie, X., Cui, B.: Graph neural networks in recommender systems: a survey. ACM Comput. Surv. 55(5), Article 97, 37 (2022). https://doi.org/10.1145/3535101

Xu, L., et al.: towards a more user-friendly and easy-to-use benchmark library for recommender systems. In: Proceedings of the 46th International ACM SIGIR Conference on Research and Development in Information Retrieval (Taipei, Taiwan)

(SIGIR 2023), pp. 2837–2847. Association for Computing Machinery, New York (2023). https://doi.org/10.1145/3539618.3591889

Yu, J., Yin, H., Xia, X., Chen, T., Cui, L., Nguyen, Q.V.H.: Are graph augmentations necessary? simple graph contrastive learning for recommendation. In: Proceedings of the 45th international ACM SIGIR Conference on Research and Development in Information Retrieval, pp. 1294–1303 (2022)

Zhao, Z., Lu, H., Cai, D., He, X., Zhuang, Y.: User preference learning for online social recommendation. IEEE Trans. on Knowl. and Data Eng. 28(9), 2522–2534 (2016). https://doi.org/10.1109/TKDE.2016.2569096

# 14 Kg of CO2: Analyzing the Carbon Footprint and Performance of Session-Based Recommendation Algorithms

Alejandro Plaza[1]($\boxtimes$), Juan Carlos Gil[1], and Denis Parra[1,2,3]

[1] Pontificia Universidad Catolica de Chile, Santiago, Chile
{aplaza2,denis.parra,juan.gil}@uc.cl
[2] Millenium Institute for Healthcare Engineering, iHealth, Santiago, Chile
[3] National Center for Artificial Intelligence, CENIA, Santiago, Chile

**Abstract.** Green AI aims to develop accurate AI models that are also sustainable without compromising the environment, especially in terms of carbon emissions. There are few studies on this topic in recommender systems, so we analyzed the trade-offs between recommendation performance and carbon footprint in session-based recommender systems. We use five public e-commerce datasets to predict the next item a user will interact with based solely on their past click events. The GRU4Rec algorithm and five unofficial reimplementations in different deep learning frameworks (Theano, PyTorch, TensorFlow, Keras, and Reckpack) are evaluated. The results indicate a strong effect of the loss function and dataset size on the carbon footprint without significantly affecting the accuracy metrics. We show evidence that the implementation choice for the same algorithm strongly affects the $CO_2$ emitted, and optimized implementations do not sacrifice recommendation efficiency, which should be considered when choosing a framework or implementation for an algorithm.

**Keywords:** Information Systems · Ecologic Recommender Systems

## 1 Introduction

In today's digital era, recommender systems have become essential components for enhancing user experience across various platforms, especially in e-commerce. These systems use advanced algorithms to predict user interests and suggest relevant products, which not only increases customer satisfaction but also drives sales. A prominent algorithm in this field is GRU4Rec, a model based on Gated Recurrent Units (GRU) specifically designed for session-based recommendations.

However, implementing GRU4Rec in its original Theano framework presents several challenges today, mainly due to the obsolescence of its dependencies and the lack of updates from the authors, making its use difficult in modern development environments. This situation has led to the creation of numerous unofficial

L. Boratto et al. (Eds.): RecSoGood 2024, CCIS 2470, pp. 123–134, 2025.
https://doi.org/10.1007/978-3-031-87654-7_12

re-implementations in more recent and actively maintained frameworks, such as PyTorch, TensorFlow, and Keras. These re-implementations aim to improve the accessibility, performance, and compatibility of the algorithm with current technologies.

As the research community strives to improve the performance of these systems, a significant concern arises: the environmental impact of deep learning models. Training complex models can consume a considerable amount of energy, thereby contributing to the global carbon footprint. In this context, evaluating not only the accuracy and efficiency of algorithms but also their ecological sustainability becomes crucial.

Recent studies have investigated the environmental impact of using machine learning techniques with deep learning tools [6], the opportunities for $CO_2$ optimization through implementation improvements, such as better GPU utilization [7], and the increased carbon footprint resulting from using complex recommendation algorithms over more basic ones [4]. However, the effect of using different implementations and libraries for the same algorithm has not been analyzed, raising the question of whether there is also an environmental implication in their choice. Recently, this topic has also been investigated in the context of recommender systems, but only considering traditional top-k ranking models [5] and not sequence or session-based methods.

This study focuses on analyzing the unofficial re-implementations of GRU4Rec and their impact both in terms of recommendation performance and carbon footprint. Through experiments using five well-known public datasets, the performance of different GRU4Rec versions in their various deep learning frameworks is measured. The code used can be found in the official repository[1] of the study.

## 2   Methodology

The experiment is based on a previous study on the performance of GRU4Rec re-implementations compared to its original implementation in Theano [2].

### 2.1   Datasets

**Datasets Used.** The experiment uses five public datasets based on real e-commerce sessions, the same ones used in the base research.

*Yoochoose* [2]: This dataset contains user sessions from an unnamed e-commerce site. The data is divided into individual sessions, each containing one or more click events, along with associated purchase events. Given the nature of the task of predicting items within sessions, only the click events are used. The dataset was originally published for the RecSys Challenge 2015 and has been consistently used to evaluate session-based recommenders.

---

[1] https://github.com/Juancagp/RecSys-Project-2024-1.

[2] https://www.kaggle.com/datasets/chadgostopp/recsys-challenge-2015/data.

*Ress46.* [3]: The Rees46 dataset comprises eight months of user behavior data from a multi-category e-commerce site, spanning from October 2019 to April 2020. For the analysis, two months are used, considering only the viewing events for the prediction of the next item, following common practices in real-world recommender systems that train with recent data to avoid trend shifts. Although the dataset includes precomputed sessions [2], the sessions are recalculated due to inconsistencies found, such as events from multiple users in the same session and irregular time gaps. A one-hour threshold is applied to define a new session if the gap between two consecutive events exceeds this time.

*Coveo.* [4]: Published to predict shopper intent from clickstream data as part of the SIGIR Ecom 2021 Challenge. The dataset consists of user sessions using 30 min as the threshold to define the end of a session. The data was collected by Coveo from one of its partners' e-commerce sites. Although there are five types of events present (add, click, detail, purchase, and remove), only the detail event is used to build the sessions, corresponding to the user's visit to an item detail page.

*RetailRocket.* [5]: This dataset contains view, add-to-cart, and transaction events collected over 4.5 months. Similar to the previous datasets, only the view events are used. The dataset was published to encourage research in the field of recommender systems.

*Diginetica.* [6]: This dataset contains user sessions collected over six months, extracted from the search engine logs of an e-commerce site. It includes item page views preceded by search queries. Although it lacks exact timestamps, each event indicates the time elapsed since the session's first query. It was published for the CIKM Cup 2016 Track 2: Personalized E-Commerce Search Challenge.

The original table detailing the amount of data for each dataset used is provided in the appendix.

**Preprocessing.** To obtain the processed datasets for both training and testing, the processing codes defined in the base research are used, with updates made to accommodate the more recent versions of the libraries used in the original work. The update adheres to the same preprocessing, considering the following aspects:

– *Events*: Only view, click, and detail events are used for predicting the next item.

---

[3] https://www.kaggle.com/datasets/mkechinov/ecommerce-behavior-data-from-multi-category-store.
[4] https://github.com/coveooss/shopper-intent-prediction-nature-2020.
[5] https://www.kaggle.com/datasets/retailrocket/ecommerce-dataset.
[6] https://competitions.codalab.org/competitions/11161#learn_the_details-data2.

- *Sessions*: User histories are divided into sessions with a one-hour threshold for Rees46 and RetailRocket; precomputed sessions are used for Yoochoose, Coveo, and Diginetica.
- *Ignored Data*: Only session ID, item ID, and timestamp are retained; in Diginetica, a virtual timestamp is computed.
- *Repeated Item Filtering*: Consecutive repeated items in sessions are reduced to a single occurrence to better align with next-item prediction.
- *Iterative Filtering*: Sessions with fewer than two items and items with fewer than five occurrences are iteratively removed until no changes occur.
- *Training/Test Split*: Time-based splits are used. For Yoochoose, Rees46, and Coveo, the split is one day before the last event; for RetailRocket and Diginetica, it is seven days before. The test set includes sessions that begin after the split, and the training set includes events before the split, truncating sessions that extend beyond it.

### 2.2    $CO_2$ Meter

For carbon footprint measurement, the open-source CodeCarbon tool is used, a package that allows developers to track emissions measured in kilograms of $CO_2$ equivalents ($CO_2eq$) to estimate the carbon footprint of the work performed. $CO_2eq$ is a standardized measure used to express the global warming potential of various greenhouse gases, or in other words, the amount of $CO_2$ that would have an equivalent impact on global warming. In this case, where the pollutant gas is emitted through the electricity consumed, carbon emissions are measured in kilograms of $CO_2$ equivalent per kilowatt-hour.

The carbon dioxide emissions, expressed as kilograms of $CO_2$ equivalent, are the product of two main factors:

**C** : The carbon intensity of the electricity consumed for computation, quantified as grams of $CO_2$ emitted per kilowatt-hour of electricity. For Chile, this variable is equal to 332.612 $kgCO_2/MWh$.

**E** : The energy consumed by the computing infrastructure, quantified as kilowatt-hours. This is measured according to the computational power usage:

$$(GPU + RAM + CPU) \cdot time\_in\_seconds \qquad (1)$$

### 2.3    Implementations

To ensure replicability and to use relevant re-implementations, GRU4Rec re-implementations already studied in previous research [2] are used, and they are tested with two different loss functions: Cross-Entropy and BPR-Max. The implementations used are as follows:

- **GRU4REC-pytorch**[7]: PyTorch re-implementation of the original algorithm, one of the most popular. Its code can utilize both loss functions.
- **Torch-GRU4Rec**[8]: Another PyTorch re-implementation, older and less popular. However, it has better results than its more updated counterpart. It can also utilize both loss functions.
- **GRU4Rec-Tensorflow**[9]: A relatively popular re-implementation in Tensorflow, last updated in 2019.
- **Keras GRU4Rec**[10]: A Keras/Tensorflow re-implementation that continues to be updated annually to remain compatible with Keras versions.
- **Recpack GRU4Rec**[11]: Also implemented with PyTorch, this is an experimentation toolkit listed in the ACM RecSys GitHub repository as a useful framework for evaluation.

For all re-implementations, the best-known hyperparameters and settings according to their recommendation metrics [2] are used. This way, the analysis focuses on the carbon consumption of the best version of each algorithm.

**Hardware resources**. Two laptops with NVIDIA Geforce RTX 4090 and 4060 graphics cards, respectively, are used for training and measuring. As a result, the $CO_2$ measurement results may vary depending on the equipment used.

### 2.4   Experimental Settings

To conduct the experiments and ensure compatibility with the necessary packages for each implementation, it is necessary to create and configure specific virtual environments that meet the different requirements of each framework used, depending on the level of maintenance provided by their authors. Subsequently, to ensure replicability and efficiency in executing the experiments, specific functions are defined to encapsulate and measure the carbon footprint of the training process of each implementation using CodeCarbon. The approach adopted is detailed below:

**Encapsulation of the Training Process**: The training of each algorithm is executed within a function that creates an environment to track the carbon footprint of each iteration and store the obtained data.

**Recommendation Measurement**: MRR@20 and Recall@20 are used as metrics for the performance of the implementations. Since these are the same metrics extracted in the base research, they can be used to verify the correct use of the algorithms.

**Carbon Footprint Measurement**: Each implementation uses five training epochs, and multiple iterations, ranging from two to five, are performed for

---

[7] https://github.com/hungthanhpham94/GRU4REC-pytorch.
[8] https://github.com/yeganegi-reza/Torch-GRU4Rec.
[9] https://github.com/Songweiping/GRU4Rec_TensorFlow.
[10] https://github.com/paxcema/KerasGRU4Rec.
[11] https://gitlab.com/recpack-maintainers/recpack.

greater reliability of the results. For the Coveo, Diginetica, and Retail Rocket datasets, the carbon footprint of each model was measured across up to five independent iterations, with the final carbon footprint being the simple average of these. On the other hand, for the Yoochoose and Rees46 datasets, the number of iterations was reduced to a maximum of two due to the prolonged training time that these datasets represented for each model, reaching over 12 h per iteration. A table with the execution times per epoch for each implementation and dataset is provided in the appendix.

To ensure the accuracy of the carbon footprint measurements, additional precautions are taken. Since CodeCarbon measures the total energy consumption of the device, during the training period, the computers are dedicated exclusively to this task. This involves closing all non-essential applications and processes, ensuring that the carbon footprint measurement reflects only the energy consumption of model training, without external interference.

## 3   Results and Discussion

During the experiments, an issue arose with the Keras GRU4Rec reimplementation. The format for resetting the hidden layer states of the neural network differs from that used in the base research. Attempts to adjust the parameters accepted by the function allowed the training to proceed, but with much lower precision metrics than expected. As a result, the carbon measurements for Keras are considered unreliable.

**Table 1.** Quantitative Analysis of GRURec-pytorch, Torch-GRU4Rec, and Recpack GRU4Rec using Recall@20, MRR@20, and CodeCarbon (in Kg of CO2).

| Data set | GRU4REC-pytorch (Major Fix) | | | Torch-GRU4Rec (Out-of-the-box) | | | Recpack GRU4Rec (Major Fix) | | |
|---|---|---|---|---|---|---|---|---|---|
| | Recall | MRR | $CO_2eq$ | Recall | MRR | $CO_2eq$ | Recall | MRR | $CO_2eq$ |
| Cross-entropy loss | | | | | | | | | |
| Yoochoose | 0.4228 | 0.1191 | 0.159981 | 0.6657 | 0.285 | 0.1677031 | – | – | – |
| Rees46 | 0.2013 | 0.0376 | 0.525542 | 0.4691 | 0.1608 | 0.5361566 | – | – | – |
| Coveo | 0.1796 | 0.051 | 0.003353 | 0.2799 | 0.0877 | 0.0092914 | 0.1525 | 0.0679 | 0.0518763 |
| RetailRocket | 0.279 | 0.0984 | 0.003432 | 0.4127 | 0.1617 | 0.0025393 | 0.2725 | 0.1081 | 0.0102273 |
| Diginetica | 0.2844 | 0.073 | 0.00411 | 0.4494 | 0.1365 | 0.0039825 | 0.3348 | 0.0958 | 0.0073623 |
| BPR-max loss | | | | | | | | | |
| Yoochoose | – | – | – | – | – | – | – | – | – |
| Rees46 | – | – | – | – | – | – | – | – | – |
| Coveo | 0.1545 | 0.0412 | 0.003258 | 0.298 | 0.0917 | 0.002833 | 0.1447 | 0.0402 | 0.03508 |
| RetailRocket | 0.2639 | 0.0973 | 0.002560 | 0.4183 | 0.1608 | 0.002576 | 0.3335 | 0.1152 | 0.026241 |
| Diginetica | 0.2616 | 0.0692 | 0.004233 | 0.4457 | 0.1370 | 0.004033 | 0.3861 | 0.1089 | 0.021795 |

**Table 2.** Quantitative Analysis of GRU4Rec-Tensorflow and Keras GRU4Rec using Recall@20, MRR@20, and CodeCarbon (in Kg of CO2).

| Data set | GRU4Rec-Tensorflow (Minor Fix) | | | Keras GRU4Rec (Major Fix) | | |
|---|---|---|---|---|---|---|
| | Recall | MRR | $CO_2eq$ | Recall | MRR | $CO_2eq$ |
| Cross-entropy loss | | | | | | |
| Yoochoose | 0.4501 | 0.1438 | 1.2332969 | 0.0003 | 0.0003 | 0.0381032 |
| Rees46 | 0.2699 | 0.0661 | 1.8798876 | 0.0001 | 0.00002 | 0.0342054 |
| Coveo | 0.1877 | 0.0533 | 0.2002904 | 0.0018 | 0.0003 | 0.2911515 |
| RetailRocket | 0.3427 | 0.12 | 0.0004678 | 0.0005 | 0.0001 | 0.0706315 |
| Diginetica | 0.3152 | 0.0841 | 0.0004673 | 0.0004 | 0.00005 | 0.076924 |

Additionally, during the experimentation phase, it was decided not to train the Yoochoose and Rees46 datasets using the Recpack implementation with both loss functions, and Keras with the BPR-max loss function. The training times ranged from 0.5 to 2 d per epoch, which was a limitation given the available time.

Initially, an attempt was made to measure the carbon footprint for the original Theano implementation of GRU4Rec. However, due to various configurations and reliance on deprecated libraries, replicating the functionality and training was impossible. Nevertheless, since the other reimplementations were executed and the metrics and training times aligned with those expressed in the base study (except for Keras), it can be theorized that the carbon footprint of the original implementation is lower compared to its counterparts. The resulting metrics and carbon footprints can be seen in Tables 1 and 2 for each respective implementation.

Each table shows the results for the Recall@20 and MRR@20 metrics, along with their carbon footprint represented in $CO_2eq$ for each tested set. It is important to note that the study is based on training the best versions of each implementation from the base study according to their precision metrics.

Based on the results obtained, several interesting points emerge. First, the entire study resulted in a carbon footprint of approximately 14 kg of $CO_2$, which is equivalent to a 56 km drive in a compact natural gas vehicle [3].

## 3.1 Performance vs. Carbon Footprint

Across different implementations, there is a variation of up to 0.2 in Recall and 0.13 in MRR. Except for the Torch-GRU4Rec implementation, there is a small range of variation in the carbon footprint. On the other hand, $CO_2$ emissions vary by up to 0.17 kg, with the effect being solely due to the specific implementation used.

Torch-GRU4Rec generally provides better performance metrics and lower carbon footprints compared to other reimplementations. It also shows better metrics than its more commonly used PyTorch counterpart.

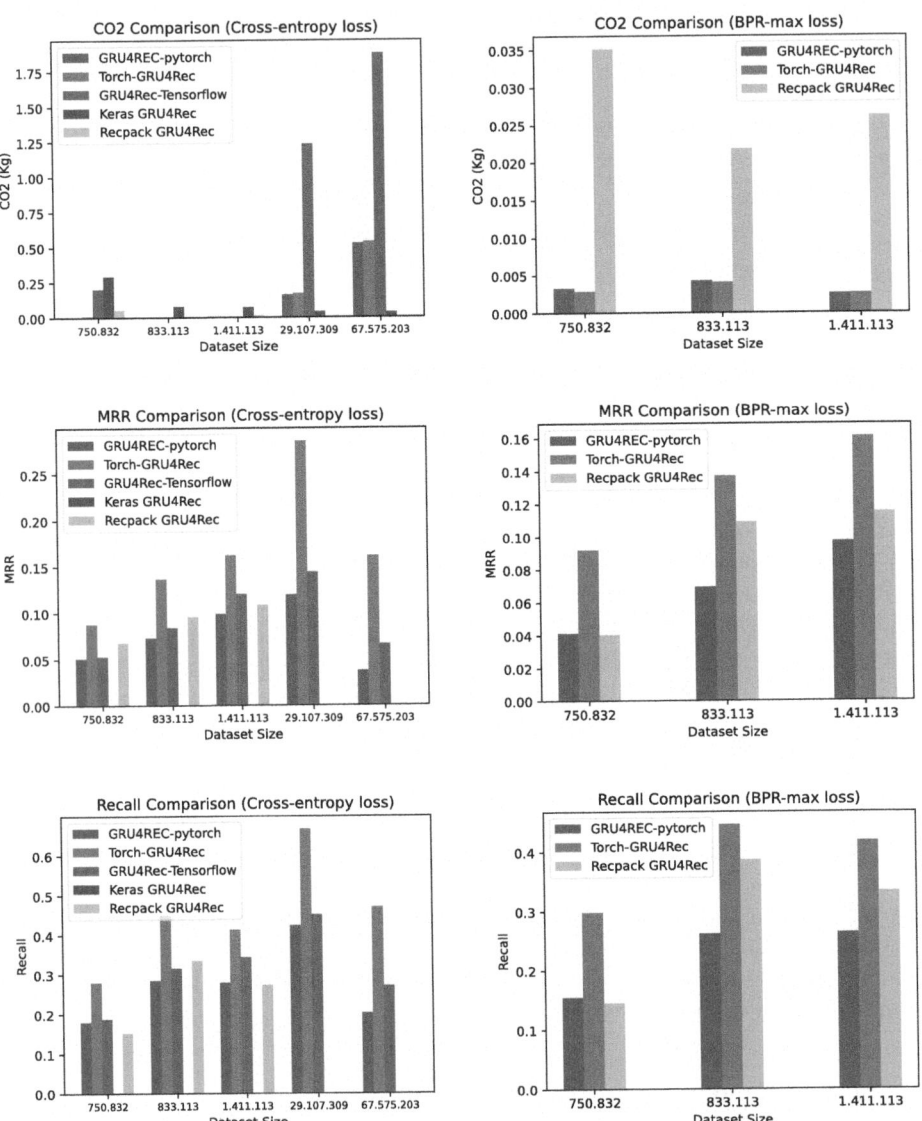

**Fig. 1.** Comparative charts of accuracy metrics and CO2 emissions for different GRU4Rec implementations by dataset size.

## 3.2    Loss Function vs. Carbon Footprint

As seen in the base research, using either of the two loss functions yields fairly close metrics, although some implementations do perform better with one of them. However, using BPR-Max shows a considerably lower $CO_2$ expenditure, indicating that the choice of loss function directly affects the carbon footprint. While Recpack shows significantly higher $CO_2$ expenditure compared to GRU4Rec-pytorch and Torch-GRU4Rec with BPR-Max, it does not reach the levels seen with the Cross-Entropy loss function. This also impacts implementations that only use Cross-Entropy, such as GRU4Rec-TensorFlow, which demonstrate a high environmental impact.

## 3.3    Dataset vs. Carbon Footprint

Fig. 1 illustrate the effect of dataset size on the metrics, ordered from left to right by size. It is not surprising that both Recall and MRR improve with a larger amount of data, but it is also observed that a larger dataset tends to generate a higher $CO_2$ expenditure, though a linear relationship between ecological impact and dataset size is not identifiable. In fact, the largest datasets used are considered medium-sized, so the use of larger datasets could result in much higher $CO_2$ expenditures than expected, potentially exhibiting exponential behavior.

## 3.4    Ease of Use and Compatibility

Some reimplementations are easier to replicate compared to others due to ease of use and maintenance of frameworks by their authors. Training times also affect the feasibility of using certain implementations based on availability. However, if training time is not a limitation, there appears to be a strong correlation between training time and the carbon footprint produced.

## 3.5    General Analysis

Among pairs of reimplementations, the differences in carbon footprint are not very noticeable, but there are significant variations in the evaluation metrics achieved. This finding highlights a previously unconsidered fact: the existence of non-optimal reimplementations that, while generating similar carbon footprints to the optimal versions, do not offer improvements in efficiency. These implementations, which provide no additional benefits in performance but contribute equally to greenhouse gas emissions, represent an unnecessary source of environmental pollution. Therefore, maintaining these reimplementations in circulation and use is unjustifiable from both an ecological and efficiency perspective, as they perpetuate greenhouse gas emissions without offering significant improvements in recommendation system performance.

Based on the experiments conducted, different GRU4Rec implementations can be identified that adapt to various needs, balancing performance and carbon footprint. The following specific recommendations are made:

- **Best Overall Balance**: *Torch-GRU4Rec*. This reimplementation offers an excellent balance between performance and carbon footprint. In most cases, it provides the best precision metrics (*Recall@20* and *MRR@20*) and lower $CO_2$ emissions compared to other versions. Use *Torch-GRU4Rec* if you are looking for a model that maintains high performance while minimizing environmental impact.
- **Focus on Carbon Footprint**: *GRU4Rec-PyTorch*. Although it does not always offer the best performance in terms of precision, this implementation generally produces a lower carbon footprint, especially with the *BPR-Max* loss function. Choose *GRU4Rec-PyTorch* if minimizing carbon emissions is your priority, even if it means sacrificing some precision.
- **Good Precision with Higher Carbon Footprint**: *GRU4Rec-TensorFlow*. This reimplementation may offer good precision metrics but at the cost of a significantly higher carbon footprint. A notable increase in $CO_2$ emissions was observed compared to other versions. If you are not using Torch, opt for *GRU4Rec-TensorFlow* only if precision is absolutely critical and you are willing to accept a greater environmental impact. It can also be used as a comparative framework for other reimplementations.
- **Evaluation and Maintenance**: *Recpack GRU4Rec*. Although this implementation showed good precision metrics, its carbon footprint was considerably higher in some cases. *Recpack GRU4Rec* can be useful for evaluating and comparing different frameworks, but its environmental impact should be considered, and if possible, opt for more efficient reimplementations.

## 4    Conclusions

This study provides a comprehensive view of how to balance efficiency and ecological responsibility in the development of session-based recommendation systems. It is crucial to prioritize algorithms that achieve a balance between ease of execution, model performance, and environmental sustainability. Reimplementations in modern frameworks like PyTorch offer a suitable combination for the first two factors, although they still present challenges in terms of energy consumption.

On the other hand, re-implementations that do not offer significant performance improvements and consume considerable amounts of energy should be addressed from various perspectives, such as requesting the author to maintain or improve the re-implementation. It might even be beneficial to include performance information based on known datasets, as in the present study, in the re-implementation documentation. Maintaining these implementations in circulation without any action contributes unnecessarily to the global carbon footprint without tangible benefits in terms of validation metrics. Moreover, the difficulty of executing the original version underscores the importance of using frameworks that receive updated maintenance with current technologies, not only to improve compatibility but also to ensure that tools remain accessible and usable in the future.

This work promotes more sustainable practices in the research and application of deep learning technologies, highlighting the importance of evaluating both the performance and environmental impact of recommendation algorithms. Future work should continue exploring ways to optimize both the efficiency and ecological footprint of learning models, contributing to a more sustainable technological landscape.

**Acknowledgments.** This research was conducted for the final project of the IIC3633 Recommender Systems course in the semester 2024-1 at Pontificia Universidad Católica de Chile. Author Denis Parra was funded by ANID Chile, Millennium Science Initiative Program, Codes ICN2021_004 (iHealth) and ICN17_002 (IMFD), and by Basal Funds for Center of Excellence FB210017 (CENIA). In addition, we thank Fondecyt grant 1231724.

**Disclosure of Interests.** The authors have no competing interests to declare that are relevant to the content of this article.

# A    Dataset Details

For a better understanding of the composition of the data used, Table 3 presents the basic statistics of the datasets from the base research on re-implementations.

**Table 3.** Basic statistics of the datasets (train/testsplit) [2]. Evts/sess. stands for Events per session.

| Dataset | Trainingset | | | | Testset | | | | #Items |
|---|---|---|---|---|---|---|---|---|---|
| | #Events | #Sessions | #Days. | Evts/sess. | #Events | #Sessions | #Days. | Evts/sess. | |
| Yoochoose | 29,107,309 | 7,597,703 | 181 | 3.83 | 71,849 | 15,854 | 1 | 4.53 | 34,858 |
| Rees46 | 67,575,203 | 10,190,006 | 60 | 6.63 | 1,054,210 | 166,841 | 1 | 6.32 | 172,756 |
| Coveo | 1,411,113 | 165,673 | 17 | 8.52 | 52,501 | 7,748 | 1 | 6.78 | 10,868 |
| RetailRocket | 750,832 | 196,234 | 131 | 3.83 | 29,148 | 8,036 | 7 | 3.63 | 36,824 |
| Diginetica | 833,113 | 177,266 | 146 | 4.70 | 70,164 | 15,040 | 7 | 4.67 | 40,351 |

# B    Training Times

To appreciate the different execution times for each implementation and loss function, Table 4 presents the execution times per epoch for the training sessions from the base research on re-implementations.

**Table 4.** Training time (in seconds) of one epoch of the official and third party GRU4Rec implementations. The value in parentheses show how much longer the training of reimplementation takes over the official version [2].

| Dataset | GRU4Rec | GRU4Rec-pytorch | Torch-GRU4Rec | GRU4Rec_TFlow | KerasGRU4Rec | Recpack |
|---|---|---|---|---|---|---|
| Cross-entropy loss | | | | | | |
| Yoochoose | 452 | 1,948(x4.31) | 2,082(x4.61) | 982(x2.17) | 13,740(x30.4) | 13,458(x29.77) |
| Rees46 | 367 | 7,618(x20.76) | 7,193(x19.6) | 2,382(x6.49) | 123,266(x335.87) | 49,262(x134.23) |
| Coveo | 37 | 85(x2.3) | 91(x2.46) | 55(x1.49) | 568(x15.35) | 663(x17.92) |
| RetailRocket | 2.8 | 10.1(x3.61) | 10.7(x3.82) | 23(x8.21) | 276.3(x98.68) | 122.3(x43.68) |
| Diginetica | 4.5 | 17.7(x3.93) | 17.7(x3.93) | 26.3(x5.84) | 359.3(x79.84) | 115.2(x25.6) |
| BPR-max loss | | | | | | |
| Yoochoose | 488 | 1,855(x3.8) | 2,164(x4.43) | N/A | N/A | 21,270(x43.59) |
| Rees46 | 1,957 | 29,528(x15.09) | 30,690(x15.68) | N/A | N/A | 179,835(x91.89) |
| Coveo | 12 | 23(x1.92) | 32(x2.67) | N/A | N/A | 771(x64.25) |
| RetailRocket | 6.9 | 20.5(x2.97) | 26.4(x3.83) | N/A | N/A | 450.2(x65.25) |
| Diginetica | 8 | 23.2(x2.9) | 36.9(x4.61) | N/A | N/A | 352.2(x44.03) |

# References

1. Bouza Heguerte, L., Bugeau, A., Lannelongue, L.: How to Estimate Carbon Footprint When Training Deep Learning Models? A Guide and Review (2023). https://hal.science/hal-04120582/document
2. Hidasi, B., Tibor, A.: The Effect of Third Party Implementations on Reproducibility (2023). https://dl.acm.org/doi/10.1145/3604915.3609487
3. Myclimate. CO2 emissions calculator for your car (2024). https://co2.myclimate.org/en/car_calculators/new
4. Spillo, G., De Filippo, A., Musto, C., Milano, M., Semeraro, G.: Towards Sustainability-aware Recommender Systems: Analyzing the Trade-off Between Algorithms Performance and Carbon Footprint (2023). https://web.archive.org/web/20231011120445id_. https://dl.acm.org/doi/pdf/10.1145/3604915.3608840
5. Vente, T., et al.: From Clicks to Carbon: The Environmental Toll of Recommender Systems. arXiv preprint arXiv:2408.08203 (2024)
6. Wright, D., Igel, C., Samuel, G., Selvan, R.: Efficiency is Not Enough: A Critical Perspective of Environmentally Sustainable (2023). http://arxiv.org/2309.02065
7. Wu, C., et al.: Sustainable AI: Environmental Implications, Challenges and Opportunities (2022). https://arxiv.org/pdf/2111.00364

# From Explanation to Exploration: Promoting DivErsity in Recommendation Systems

Antonino Ferraro[1] , Antonio Galli[1] , Valerio La Gatta[2]([envelope]) ,
Marco Postiglione[2] , Diego Russo[1,2] , Gian Marco Orlando[1,2] ,
Giuseppe Riccio[1,2] , Antonio Romano[1,2] , and Vincenzo Moscato[1]

[1] University of Naples Federico II, Department of Electrical Engineering
and Information Technology, via Claudio 21, 80125 Naples, Italy
{antonino.ferraro,antonio.galli,vincenzo.moscato}@unina.it,
{diego.russo,gian.orlando,giuseppe.riccio9,
antonio.romano45}@studenti.unina.it
[2] Department of Computer Science, McCormick School of Engineering and Applied
Science, Northwestern University, 2233 Tech Dr, 60208 Evanston, IL, USA
{valerio.gatta,marco.postiglione}@northwestern.edu

**Abstract.** Contemporary recommender systems excel in personalizing content based on user preferences, yet concerns persist regarding recommendation diversity and the ensuing *rabbit hole* effect. Prior research on *explanation-driven diversification* indicates the importance of analyzing the similarity of explanations for different items within a single recommendation list to promote recommendation diversity. However, it is equally crucial to assess each item's potential impact on guiding recommendations towards a *rabbit hole* over time. This paper delves into the dynamic relationship between explanations and diversity across multiple interactions within a recommender system. We introduce FEEDERS (From Explanation to Exploration: promoting DivErsity in Recommendation Systems), a framework designed to leverage explanations for enhancing recommendation diversity and mitigating the rabbit hole effect in repeated interactions with a recommender system. Specifically, FEEDERS leverages an explainable recommender system and enables multiple corrective actions, such as item re-ranking and modification of item importance before recommendation. Our experiments using the PGPR framework [39] and the MovieLens1M dataset demonstrate FEEDERS' effectiveness in enhancing recommendation diversity, achieving a notable up to 10% increase compared to its closest competitor, while maintaining competitive accuracy performance. In contrast to all baselines, FEEDERS consistently exhibits or increases diversity trends across consecutive interactions with the recommender system, indicating resilience against the rabbit hole effect.

**Keywords:** Recommendation Diversity · Explanation-Driven Diversity · Rabbit Hole Effect

© The Author(s), under exclusive license to Springer Nature Switzerland AG 2025
L. Boratto et al. (Eds.): RecSoGood 2024, CCIS 2470, pp. 135–150, 2025.
https://doi.org/10.1007/978-3-031-87654-7_13

# 1   Introduction

Recommender systems have become indispensable across various domains, including music recommendation [21,30], social networks [2,10], and cultural heritage platforms [12,35], where they provide users with personalized content that aligns with their unique preferences. By offering highly relevant recommendations, these systems have significantly enhanced user satisfaction and engagement, strengthening audience loyalty across digital platforms [28]. However, alongside these advancements, the increasing complexity of recommendation algorithms has raised concerns regarding their transparency, fairness, and long-term effects on user behavior. These concerns are further compounded by the challenge of maintaining diversity in recommendations, particularly as systems become more deeply personalized. Ensuring attributes like diversity and explainability, in addition to recommendation accuracy, is critical to developing robust and trustworthy recommender systems that align with broader media and information ethics [23,36]

Current research has explored these aspects individually, particularly diversity and explainability, which are often treated as independent goals in recommendation research [6,20,38,43,45]. Explainability is essential for fostering trust, as users want to understand the rationale behind recommendations, while diversity helps broaden the content they encounter, minimizing potential filter bubbles. Interestingly, the explanations themselves can provide valuable clues about recommendation diversity. For example, content-based explanations may highlight strong tendencies towards particular categories of content, while collaborative filtering explanations might reveal a bias towards what is popular among similar users. These biases, if unexamined, could limit exposure to a wider array of content, indicating the potential of explanations to serve as early indicators of diversity decline. Inspired by this concept, research has suggested *explanation-driven diversification*, a process of diversifying recommendations by analyzing the similarity in explanations across items [41]. For instance, [40] proposed a post-hoc algorithm that adjusts recommendations by assessing the diversity of explanations, optimizing for both relevance and content variety.

Despite these contributions, most approaches remain limited to single interactions, assessing diversity within individual recommendation rounds. They overlook the cumulative effect of repeated interactions, where content alignment with a user's previous choices can lead to the *rabbit hole effect*, an escalating focus on narrow content aligned with past preferences [44]. Furthermore, recent studies highlight the risk of recommender systems actively guiding users down paths toward increasingly extreme or biased content, a trend that has raised concerns about algorithmic influences on radicalization [11,14,24,31]. This calls for strategies to monitor diversity not just within single interactions but also across the broader recommendation experience to mitigate the risks of content homogenization over time and address potential long-term impacts on users' media and information consumption.

To address this, we introduce FEEDERS (From Explanation to Exploration: promoting DivErsity in Recommendation Systems), a framework that leverages explanations over multiple interactions to counter the narrowing effects of repeated recommendations. FEEDERS utilizes an explainable recommender system (*ER*) to examine the dissimilarity of explanations across interactions, using this information to gauge each item's influence in potentially leading users toward a rabbit hole. By monitoring the diversity of explanations across time, FEEDERS dynamically re-ranks recommended items or adjusts item weights based on their potential impact, balancing recommendation accuracy with diversity. To the best of our knowledge, FEEDERS is the first framework to quantify the risk of polarization within a recommender system using explanations and to apply corrective measures directly informed by these findings.

In our experiments, we implemented FEEDERS using the Policy-Guided Path Reasoning (PGPR) framework [39] as our explainable recommender system. Evaluations on the *MovieLens1M (ML1M)* dataset [15] against several baselines indicate that FEEDERS significantly improves diversity-by up to 10% compared to the nearest baseline-while maintaining strong accuracy. Notably, in simulations across multiple interactions, FEEDERS consistently maintains or increases diversity, contrasting with the declining diversity observed in other methods

Beyond enhancing the technical performance of recommender systems, FEEDERS aligns with broader societal objectives, particularly those related to social responsibility and inclusivity. By promoting the recommendation of diverse content and actively reducing algorithmic bias, FEEDERS supports Sustainable Development Goal (SDG) 10: Reduced Inequalities. This approach helps to create digital environments that resist the formation of echo chambers and minimize the risk of content polarization, addressing the long-term effects of recommender systems on media and information ecosystems.

## 2 Related Works

### 2.1 Diversity in Recommender Systems

The trend towards heightened personalization in recommender systems has undeniably enhanced their efficacy, yet it has also triggered concerns regarding the potential decline in recommendation diversity resulting from excessive personalization [23]. Consequently, researchers have turned their attention towards developing novel strategies that strike a balance between recommendation relevance and content diversity [45]. These strategies can be broadly classified into three categories based on when they are integrated into the recommendation process [38]: *pre-processing* methods, *in-processing* methods, and *post-processing* methods. *Pre-processing* techniques aim to address diversity concerns prior to the optimization or training phase of the recommender system. They often encompass methods such as data augmentation [46] and feature engineering [9] to introduce diversity-enhancing factors into the recommendation process. *In-processing* methods operate during the optimization phase and involve integrating diversity constraints directly into the optimization objective or loss function [25].

Finally, *post-processing* methods are applied after the recommender system's optimization phase. These methods often involve the implementation of sophisticated learning-to-rank strategies [37], which re-rank the initially generated recommendation list to prioritize diverse items while maintaining relevance [45].

Despite the advancements in diversification methods, the above-mentioned studies primarily focus on diversifying items recommended within a single interaction with the recommender system. This narrow focus fails to consider the dynamic evolution of recommendations across multiple interactions, a phenomenon closely associated with the *rabbit hole effect* [44]. Essentially, even if a single interaction introduces diversity in recommendations, the ongoing reinforcement of specific content types in subsequent interactions may lead users to experience a gradual narrowing of content exposure over time. Moreover, recent investigations [14,24,31] highlight the significant role of recommendation algorithms in guiding users towards radicalized pathways characterized by increasingly extreme or biased content. Intriguingly, these tendencies persist regardless of the diversity observed during individual interactions with the system.

Our proposal directly tackles the challenge of diversifying content across multiple user interactions within the system. Specifically, we measure the *segregation score* of an item based on its capacity to steer recommendations towards a rabbit hole. Our framework, FEEDERS, utilizes this metric to deploy precise corrective measures aimed at enhancing not only the diversity within a single interaction but also the overall diversity and trajectory of recommendations over time.

## 2.2   Explainable Recommender Systems

The demand for explainable recommender systems stems from the growing complexity and opacity inherent in modern recommendation strategies [42]. Within these systems, explanations can take various forms, such as path reasoning techniques that elucidate the reasoning behind a particular recommendation [39], and text-based explanations [8] that, for example, align the reviews of recommended items with user interests [7]. From a broader perspective, explanations serve to enhance user trust in recommendations, consequently increasing the likelihood of user adherence to these recommendations [1]. Moreover, this explanation-driven transparency empowers users to further personalize the recommender system according to their individual needs and preferences [13,22].

The primary objective of all these systems is to prioritize explanations, ultimately directed towards rendering recommendations transparent [6,36]. Nevertheless, explanations potentially serve purposes beyond elucidating the rationale behind a recommendation to the user. For example, [29] have showcased how model's explanation could be used to promote a fairer recommendation. In the context of diversity, *explanation-driven diversification* suggests utilizing explanations' similarity to promote diverse items. The underlying assumption is that if the explanations for recommended items are too similar, it indicates low diversity. Building upon this premise, [40] introduced a post-hoc greedy algorithm that refines recommendation lists iteratively by assessing dissimilarities among explanations, thus identifying the most relevant items. Similarly, [32] have recently reframed the recommendation problem by generating explanation chains comprising potentially relevant items. Diversity is enforced by balancing the inclusion of new elements with their differences from those already in the chain.

In this paper, we leverage explainable recommender systems to address the challenge of content diversification. Unlike the above-mentioned work that concentrate on utilizing explanations to construct a single diverse list of recommendations, our approach pioneers the utilization of explanations to measure the segregation effect of recommending an item. Specifically, we utilize the dissimilarity between explanations provided during consecutive interactions with the recommender system as an indicator of the item's capacity to guide subsequent interactions towards a rabbit hole.

# 3  Methodology

## 3.1  Problem Formulation

Let's define the user-item graph $\mathcal{G} = (\mathcal{V}, \mathcal{E})$, where $\mathcal{V}$ comprises users and items, $\mathcal{V} = \mathcal{U} \cup \mathcal{I}$, and $\mathcal{E} = \{(u, i, w) | u \in \mathcal{U}, i \in \mathcal{I}, w \in \mathbb{R}\}$ represents weighted relationships between users and items. Depending on the application domain, the edge weight $w$ can signify various factors, such as movie ratings or product purchase frequencies. Additionally, we consider an explainable recommender system $ER$ that not only performs recommendations but also provides justifications for each recommended item. Formally,

$$ER : (u, \mathcal{G}) \to RL^u = [(i_1^u, exp_{i_1}^u), (i_2^u, exp_{i_2}^u), \cdots, (i_n^u, exp_{i_n}^u)],$$

where $n$ is the number of recommended items, and $exp_{i_k}^u$ represents the explanation for item $i_k$ recommended to user $u$. Specifically, $exp_{i_k}^u$ represents $ER$'s reasoning path that has driven the recommendation of item $i_k$:

$$exp_{i_k}^u = \{u \to \hat{e}_1 \to \hat{e}_2 \to \cdots \to i_k | \hat{e}_j \in \mathcal{V}\}$$

In other words, $exp_{i_k}$ is a walk on $\mathcal{G}$ starting from $u$ and terminating at $i_k$. Hereafter, we omit the dependence from the user to simplify the notation, i.e., $exp_{i_k}^u = exp_{i_k}$ and $RL^u = RL$.

Our goal is to evaluate each item's potential impact on steering recommendations toward a rabbit hole. Essentially, we seek to learn a function:

$$g : (\mathcal{G}, ER, RL) \to [s_1, s_2, \cdots, s_n]$$

where $s_k \in \mathbb{R}$ represents the segregation score for item $i_k \in RL$. Subsequently, we aim to utilize the segregation scores for items in $RL$ to deploy a corrective action $\eta$ that generates a new recommendation list $\hat{RL}$ for the user. Formally,

$$\eta : (\mathcal{G}, RL, [s_1, s_2, \cdots, s_n]) \to \hat{RL}$$

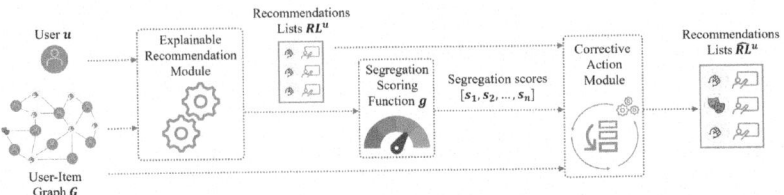

**Fig. 1.** Our framework comprises three primary modules: (i) Explainable Recommendation, where each user is provided with a personalized list of recommendations accompanied by explanations; (ii) Segregation Scoring, where the segregation score for each recommended item is computed; and (iii) Corrective Action, where a new recommendation list is generated to balance the relevance of the recommended items and their segregation score.

$\hat{RL}$ being a new recommendation list for the user $u$. In particular $\hat{RL}$'s generation balances the relevance of the items in $RL$ with their segregating effects its items. Importantly, this formalization remains adaptable to various corrective actions, such as re-ranking $RL$'s items or updating $\mathcal{G}$'s weights before a brand-new inference on $ER$.

## 3.2 Framework

Figure 1 illustrates the inference flow executed by FEEDERS. Initially, given the user $u$ and the user-item graph $\mathcal{G}$, an off-the-shelf *explainable recommendation module* performs the recommendation task and delivers $RL$, which comprises the recommended items along with their respective explanations. Subsequently, the *segregation scoring* function determines the segregation scores $s_1, s_2, \cdots, s_n$ for each item in $RL$. Finally, the *corrective action* module utilizes these segregation scores to generate the final recommendation $\hat{RL}$. We provide detailed descriptions of each component in the subsequent sections.

**Explainable Recommender System.** We adopt the Policy-Guided Path Reasoning (PGPR) framework [39] as our explainable recommender system. PGPR is specifically chosen for its inherent explainability, achieved through a combination of reinforcement learning and multi-hop graph reasoning. This framework is suitable for our use case as it identifies the most relevant items for a given user input while training a policy-guided graph search algorithm to select informative reasoning paths that support the recommendation process. The transparency of explanation generation in PGPR is a key advantage, particularly when contrasted with other recommender systems relying on post-hoc explanation methods that may be susceptible to instabilities and perturbations [5]. Additionally, PGPR's adaptability to integrate supplementary graph-structured knowledge, such as actor-movie relationships or songs-album associations [3,4], enhances its versatility across various domains, accommodating additional entities and relationships within the user-item graph. However, while FEEDERS is initially designed around PGPR, it is worth noting its flexibility to accommodate other explainable recommender systems, provided they generate explanations represented as sequences of nodes within the user-item graph.

**Segregation Scoring.** This module is responsible for computing the segregation score $s_k$ for each recommended item $i_k$ for a given user $u$. To achieve this, we simulate a scenario where the user adopts the recommendation of item $i_k$. This simulation involves updating the user-item graph $\mathcal{G}$ by introducing a new edge linking $u$ and $i_k$, followed by another round of inference on the explainable recommender system. Consequently, we generate a revised recommendation list that includes $i_k$ along with its updated explanation $\hat{exp}_{i_k}$. Formally, the segregation score $s_k$ for item $i_k$ is defined as the Jaccard distance metric between the aforementioned explanations:

$$s_k = \frac{|exp_{i_k} \cup \hat{exp}_{i_k}| - |exp_{i_k} \cap \hat{exp}_{i_k}|}{|exp_{i_k} \cup \hat{exp}_{i_k}|}$$

where $exp_{i_k}$ and $\hat{exp}_{i_k}$ are the original and revised explanations for item $i_k$, respectively. Notably, a higher distance value indicates greater diversity observed between two successive interactions, reflecting a reduced segregating effect stemming from the initial recommendation of item $i_k$. By iteratively applying this process to all items in the recommendation list $RL$, we derive the segregation scores $[s_1, s_2, \cdots, s_n]$ for every item recommended by the explainable recommender system.

**Corrective Action.** This module is responsible for determining a new recommendation to balance the relevance of the recommended items and their segregation scores. In particular, we have devised two strategies: (i) re-ranking the original recommendation $RL$ and (ii) updating the original user-item graph $\mathcal{G}$ to penalise the most segrating items before running a new recommendation step. In both cases, the trade-off between accuracy and diversity is controlled via an exponential moving average mechanism based on a parameter $\theta$.

**Re-ranking (RR).** Re-ranking methods have received considerable attention because of their flexibility in balancing the recommendation accuracy, with other properties, including diversity [26]. Our framework leverages the formulation proposed by [45]:

$$RR(RL, [s_1, s_2, \cdots, s_n], \theta) = \frac{1 - \theta}{n} \sum_{i \in RL} f_{rec}(i) + \theta * s_i,$$

where $f_{rec}(i)$ denotes the position of item $i_k \in RL$, $s_i$ is the segregation score of the item $i_k \in RL$, and $\theta$ is the coefficient to control the trade-off between relevance and diversity. Using this formula, we determine the new position of each item $i_k$ in the original recommendation list $RL$, yielding an updated list $\hat{RL}$ for each user.

Notably, re-ranking methods are model-agnostic, operating independently of specific recommender systems, and offer time efficiency by circumventing the need for re-training computations.

**Adjusting Item-Related Weights (MW).** This technique involves adjusting edge weights within the user-item graph $\mathcal{G}$ to promote diversity, focusing on the connections that contribute to the explanation. Specifically, we employ a weight decay mechanism [27] to penalize the relationships associated with items having the highest segregation scores:

$$MW(\mathcal{G}, [s_1, s_2, \cdots, s_n], \theta) = w_{u,i} - \theta$$

where $w_{u,i}$ denotes the weight of the edge linking user $u \in \mathcal{U}$ and item $i \in \mathcal{I}$, and $\theta$ represents the penalty factor used to decrease the edge weight. A higher $s_k$ value indicates a higher likelihood of segregating items not appearing prominently in the revised recommendation list $\hat{RL}$. Once the edge weights in $\mathcal{G}$ have been adjusted for all nodes, it will be possible to generate the new recommendation list $\hat{RL}$.

Notably, this method differs from re-ranking and may require periodic model retraining, especially when multiple consecutive iterations occur.

## 4   Experiments

### 4.1   Dataset and Metrics

We utilized *MovieLens 1M (ML1M)* [15], which is widely utilized in movie recommendation research. Specifically, we selected a subset of 750 users, each with at least 25 recorded ratings. This subset encompasses 2430 items and a total of 22838 interactions. To evaluate recall, we partitioned the ratings into training and test sets prior to commencing the simulations. The training set constituted 70% of the data, while the test set comprised 30%.

For evaluating diversity, we utilize the *Jaccard distance* to assess the system's capability to recommend a diverse set of items to users over two consecutive iterations. Formally,

$$D@k = \frac{|RL \cup RL'| - |RL \cap RL'|}{|RL \cup RL'|}$$

where $RL$ and $RL'$ represent two lists of items recommended in distinct iterations and $k$ is the length of the recommended list. Moreover, we measure Recall@k to assess the accuracy performance of the system.

### 4.2   Implementation Details

All experiments have been conducted on a computational platform equipped with an 8th Gen Intel Core i7-8750H processor running at 2.20 GHz, 16 GB of

RAM, and an NVIDIA GeForce GTX 1050 Ti. Performance evaluations involving multiple interactions with the recommender system were executed over 30 iterations, each iteration taking approximately 9 h to complete.

During each iteration, users selected recommended items according to a geometric distribution i.e., the probability for user $u$ to select an item in $RL^u$ depends on its position. This probabilistic selection mechanism aimed to mimic real-world user behavior, where items higher in the ranking are more likely to be chosen.

Moreover, we utilized the original implementation of PGPR[1] and trained the model for 30 epochs using default hyper-parameters. While the RR strategy did not necessitate any additional updates to the recommender system, we periodically fine-tuned the graph embedding algorithm within PGPR when applying the MW corrective action. This fine-tuning was necessary to accommodate new edges added to the original user-item graph as part of the simulation process.

### 4.3   Evaluating Optimal Configuration

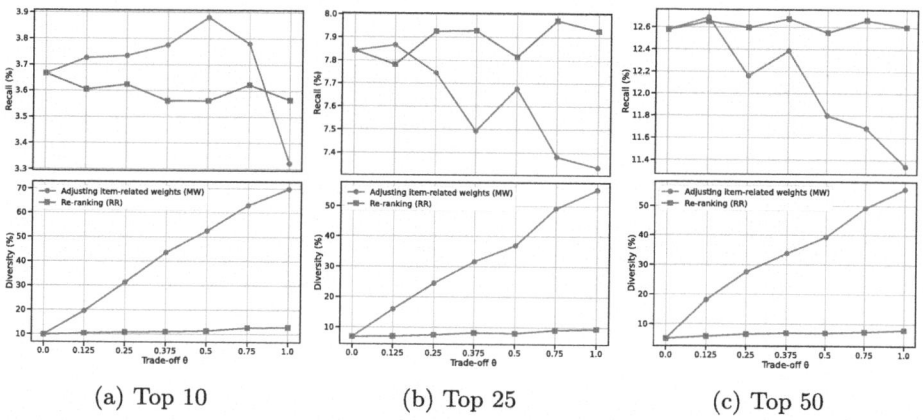

(a) Top 10          (b) Top 25          (c) Top 50

**Fig. 2.** Evaluating Optimal Configuration: recall and diversity considering the top-10, top-25 and top-50 items, by varying $\theta$ to balance recommendation relevance and diversity.

To determine the optimal configuration that balances recommendation relevance and diversity, we focus on the type of corrective action (RR vs MW) and the value of $\theta$ within the *corrective action* module.

Figures 2a, 2b and 2c illustrate the recall and diversity metrics for the top-10, top-25, and top-50 recommended items, respectively, while varying the $\theta$ parameter. As anticipated, both the RR and MW strategies exhibit an enhancement in

---

[1] https://github.com/orcax/PGPR.

recommendation diversity, evident from the upward trend in the diversity metric across all cases. Notably, the MW corrective strategy demonstrates superior effectiveness compared to RR, as indicated by its steeper diversity curve when $\theta$ is varying.

Remarkably, the pursuit of diversity does not necessarily lead to a decline in recall. For recall@10, the MW strategy even yields improvements when $\theta \leq 0.5$. Moreover, the RR strategy generally maintains the relevance of recommended items at a consistent level compared to scenarios without corrective actions. These findings likely stem from the fact that, while both actions involve adjusting the positions of recommended items, RR preserves the overall items in the original recommendation. In contrast, MW introduces new items, leading to more pronounced changes in the final outcomes and potentially higher variability in recall and diversity metrics.

Our optimal configuration selection involves setting $\theta = 0.125$ with the MW strategy as the corrective action to promote diversity. This decision is well-supported by the observed trends in Figs. 2a, 2b and 2c, where this configuration consistently boosts diversity while ensuring a recall value surpassing the baseline ($\theta = 0$).

### 4.4 Comparison with Baselines

To evaluate the performance of FEEDERS, a comprehensive comparative analysis was conducted, encompassing a variety of recommender system algorithms representing diverse methodological families: (i) collaborative filtering algorithms, i.e., *Singular Value Decomposition (SVD)* [19], *Alternating Least Squares (ALS)* [17] and *Bayesian Personalized Ranking (BPR)* [33]; (ii) content-based recommender systems, i.e., *Item-based k-Nearest Neighbors (Item KNN)* [34]; (iii) hybrid recommender systems, i.e., *LightGCN* [16] and *Policy-Guided Path Reasoning (PGPR)* [39]; (iv) diversity-aware recommender systems, i.e., *DivMF* [18].

**Results.** Firstly, we investigate FEEDERS' performance when varying the number of interactions with the recommender system. As previously mentioned, we leverage a geometric distribution to simulate item selection across different iterations. Figure 3 illustrates recall@10 and diversity@10 across these iterations. Our observations reveal a distinct trend among all baselines, showcasing a diminishing (resp. escalating) trajectory for diversity (resp. recall) metrics. This outcome underscores the foundational hypothesis of our research, emphasizing that ensuring item diversity within a singular interaction with the recommender system is insufficient. The potential of an item to guide recommendations down a *rabbit hole* pathway holds significant importance. Indeed, although some baselines (e.g., ItemKNN, DivMF) initially exhibit robust diversity metrics (even surpassing FEEDERS in some instances), their diversity performance swiftly declines, indicative of recommendations converging towards similarity across successive

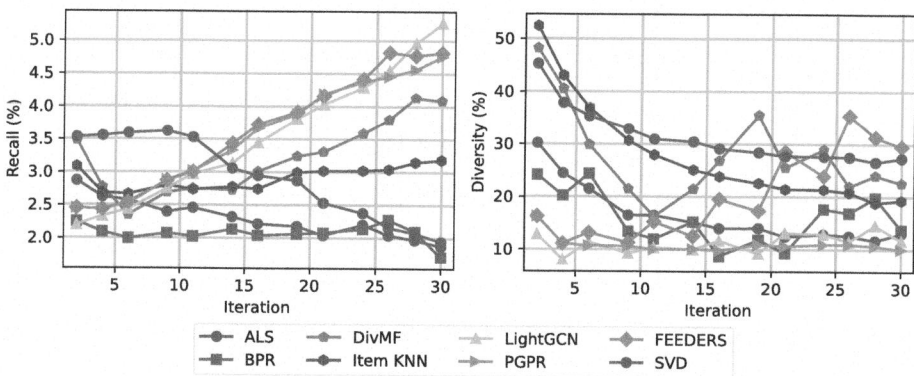

**Fig. 3.** Comparison with Baselines: recall@10 and diversity@10 by simulating consecutive interactions with the recommender system.

interactions with the system. This trend aligns with the escalating recall metrics, driven by these systems' inclination towards heightened personalization for maximizing relevance.

Conversely, FEEDERS stands out as the only method showcasing increasing trends in both recall and diversity metrics over time. This outcome underscores the efficacy of the adopted corrective measures, which actively promote diverse items without compromising performance over extended usage periods.

To further evaluate FEEDERS' performance, Fig. 4 depicts the recall and diversity metrics by varying numbers of items $K$ in the recommendation lists assuming a fixed interaction step. We observe that FEEDERS exhibits competitive recall performance, aligning with top-performing methods like LightGCN and PGPR. Notably, in terms of diversity, FEEDERS surpasses all competitors in most cases. For instance, FEEDERS achieves a substantial 10% increase in diversity@3 compared to the runner-up method (DivMF), with only a minor 2.5% recall decrease compared to the best-performing method (LightGCN).

Interestingly, top performers in recall (such as LightGCN) lag in diversity metrics, even under-performing simple baselines like SVD and ItemKNN. This observation supports the general intuition that models emphasizing personalization, as seen in LightGCN and PGPR, often sacrifice diversity in recommendations. These results demonstrate that FEEDERS strikes a balance between relevance and diversity, leveraging the strengths of both worlds. It maintains commendable relevance performance while significantly enhancing result diversity, offering a promising solution to the challenge of personalized yet diverse recommendations.

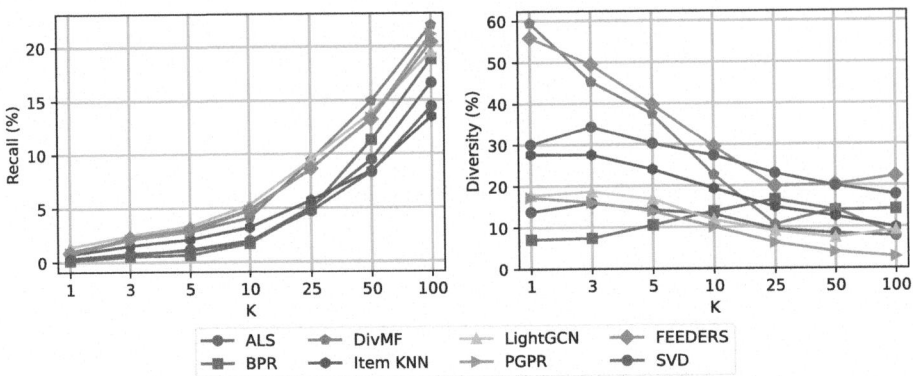

**Fig. 4.** Comparison with Baselines: recall and diversity by varying the number of items ($K$) in the recommendation list.

## 5   Conclusion and Future Works

In this paper, we introduced FEEDERS (From Explanation to Exploration: promoting DivErsity in Recommendation Systems), a novel framework designed to enhance recommendation diversity using explanations. Specifically, we defined the segregation score of an item to quantify its propensity to guide users towards a rabbit hole. FEEDERS leverages an explainable recommender system to determine this score by assessing the (dis-)similarity between consecutive interactions with the recommender system. Subsequently, the proposed approach employs corrective actions based on these segregation scores to strike a balance between recommendation relevance and diversity. Our preliminary results validate the efficacy of FEEDERS, showcasing its ability to achieve top-tier accuracy while ensuring a higher level of diversity compared to several existing recommender systems. Importantly, FEEDERS prevents recommendations from steering users towards a rabbit hole, maintaining a high level of diversity even across multiple interactions with the recommender system. These findings highlight the importance of considering not only diversifying recommendations within a single interaction but also acknowledging the potential polarizing effects of recommending an item over the long term.

Looking ahead, we envision expanding the application of FEEDERS to diverse explainable recommender systems, transcending its current domain of movie recommendations. Our primary objective is to evaluate its efficacy across various domains such as social networks and e-commerce platforms, thereby broadening its utility and relevance.

Additionally, we plan to delve deeper into exploring alternative corrective actions based on segregation scores, aiming to fine-tune recommendation outcomes. By identifying and implementing effective strategies, our goal is to strike an optimal balance between recommendation relevance and diversity, ultimately enhancing user engagement and loyalty.

# References

1. Abdollahi, B., Nasraoui, O.: Explainable matrix factorization for collaborative filtering. In: Bourdeau, J., Hendler, J., Nkambou, R., Horrocks, I., Zhao, B.Y. (eds.) Proceedings of the 25th International Conference on World Wide Web, WWW 2016, Montreal, Canada, 11-15April 2016, Companion Volume, pp. 5–6. ACM, Montreal, Canada (2016). https://doi.org/10.1145/2872518.2889405
2. Amato, F., Moscato, V., Picariello, A., Piccialli, F.: Sos: a multimedia recommender system for online social networks. Futur. Gener. Comput. Syst. **93**, 914–923 (2019)
3. Bollacker, K.D., Evans, C., Paritosh, P.K., Sturge, T., Taylor, J.: Freebase: a collaboratively created graph database for structuring human knowledge. In: SIGMOD Conference, pp. 1247–1250 (2008). https://doi.org/10.1145/1376616.1376746
4. Cao, Y., Wang, X., He, X., Hu, Z., Chua, T.: Unifying knowledge graph learning and recommendation: Towards a better understanding of user preferences. In: Liu, L., White, R.W., Mantrach, A., Silvestri, F., McAuley, J.J., Baeza-Yates, R., Zia, L. (eds.) The World Wide Web Conference, WWW 2019, San Francisco, CA, USA,13-17 May 2019. pp. 151–161. ACM, San Francisco, CA, USA (2019). https://doi.org/10.1145/3308558.3313705
5. Chanson, A., Labroche, N., Verdeaux, W.: Towards local post-hoc recommender systems explanations. In: Stefanidis, K., Marcel, P. (eds.) Proceedings of the 23rd International Workshop on Design, Optimization, Languages and Analytical Processing of Big Data (DOLAP) co-located with the 24th International Conference on Extending Database Technology and the 24th International Conference on Database Theory (EDBT/ICDT 2021), Nicosia, Cyprus, March 23, 2021. CEUR Workshop Proceedings, vol. 2840, pp. 41–50. CEUR-WS.org, Nicosia, Cyprus (2021). https://ceur-ws.org/Vol-2840/paper6.pdf
6. Chatti, M.A., Guesmi, M., Muslim, A.: Visualization for recommendation explainability: A survey and new perspectives. CoRR arXiv: abs/2305.11755 (2023). https://doi.org/10.48550/ARXIV.2305.11755
7. Chen, H., Chen, X., Shi, S., Zhang, Y.: Generate natural language explanations for recommendation. CoRR abs/ arXiv: 2101.03392 (2021)
8. Cheng, H., Wang, S., Lu, W., Zhang, W., Zhou, M., Lu, K., Liao, H.: Explainable recommendation with personalized review retrieval and aspect learning. In: Rogers, A., Boyd-Graber, J.L., Okazaki, N. (eds.) Proceedings of the 61st Annual Meeting of the Association for Computational Linguistics (Volume 1: Long Papers), ACL 2023, Toronto, Canada, 9-14 July 2023, pp. 51–64. Association for Computational Linguistics, Toronto, Canada (2023). https://doi.org/10.18653/V1/2023.ACL-LONG.4
9. Cheng, P., Wang, S., Ma, J., Sun, J., Xiong, H.: Learning to recommend accurate and diverse items. In: Barrett, R., Cummings, R., Agichtein, E., Gabrilovich, E. (eds.) Proceedings of the 26th International Conference on World Wide Web, WWW 2017, Perth, Australia, 3-7 April 2017, pp. 183–192. ACM, Perth, Australia (2017). https://doi.org/10.1145/3038912.3052585
10. Eirinaki, M., Gao, J., Varlamis, I., Tserpes, K.: Recommender systems for large-scale social networks: a review of challenges and solutions. Futur. Gener. Comput. Syst. **78**, 413–418 (2018)
11. Fabbri, F., Wang, Y., Bonchi, F., Castillo, C., Mathioudakis, M.: Rewiring what-to-watch-next recommendations to reduce radicalization pathways. In: Proceedings of the ACM Web Conference 2022, WWW 2022, pp. 2719-2728. Association for Computing Machinery, New York (2022). https://doi.org/10.1145/3485447.3512143

12. Fiorucci, M., Khoroshiltseva, M., Pontil, M., Traviglia, A., Del Bue, A., James, S.: Machine learning for cultural heritage: a survey. Pattern Recogn. Lett. **133**, 102–108 (2020)

13. Guesmi, M., Chatti, M.A., Joarder, S.A., Ain, Q.U., Alatrash, R., Siepmann, C., Vahidi, T.: Interactive explanation with varying level of details in an explainable scientific literature recommender system. (2023). https://doi.org/10.48550/ARXIV.2306.05809

14. Haroon, M., Chhabra, A., Liu, X., Mohapatra, P., Shafiq, Z., Wojcieszak, M.: Youtube, the great radicalizer? auditing and mitigating ideological biases in youtube recommendations (2022)

15. Harper, F.M., Konstan, J.A.: The movielens datasets: history and context. ACM Trans. Interact. Intell. Syst. **5**(4), 19:1–19:19 (2016). https://doi.org/10.1145/2827872

16. He, X., Deng, K., Wang, X., Li, Y., Zhang, Y., Wang, M.: Lightgcn: Simplifying and powering graph convolution network for recommendation. In: Huang, J.X., Chang, Y., Cheng, X., Kamps, J., Murdock, V., Wen, J., Liu, Y. (eds.) Proceedings of the 43rd International ACM SIGIR conference on research and development in Information Retrieval, SIGIR 2020, Virtual Event, China, 25-30 July 2020, pp. 639–648. ACM (2020). https://doi.org/10.1145/3397271.3401063

17. Hu, Y., Koren, Y., Volinsky, C.: Collaborative filtering for implicit feedback datasets. In: Proceedings of the 8th IEEE International Conference on Data Mining (ICDM 2008), 15-19 December 2008, Pisa, Italy. pp. 263–272. IEEE Computer Society (2008). https://doi.org/10.1109/ICDM.2008.22

18. Kim, J., Jeon, H., Lee, J., Kang, U.: Diversely regularized matrix factorization for accurate and aggregately diversified recommendation. In: Kashima, H., Idé, T., Peng, W. (eds.) Advances in Knowledge Discovery and Data Mining - 27th Pacific-Asia Conference on Knowledge Discovery and Data Mining, PAKDD 2023, Osaka, Japan, 25-28 May 2023, Proceedings, Part III. LNCS, vol. 13937, pp. 361–373. Springer (2023). https://doi.org/10.1007/978-3-031-33380-4_28

19. Koren, Y., Bell, R.M., Volinsky, C.: Matrix factorization techniques for recommender systems. Computer **42**(8), 30–37 (2009)

20. Kunaver, M., Pozrl, T.: Diversity in recommender systems - a survey. Knowl. Based Syst. **123**, 154–162 (2017)

21. La Gatta, V., Moscato, V., Pennone, M., Postiglione, M., Sperlí, G.: Music recommendation via hypergraph embedding. IEEE Trans. Neural Netw. Learn. Syst. **34**(10), 7887–7899 (2022)

22. La Gatta, V., Moscato, V., Postiglione, M., Sperlì, G.: Castle: Cluster-aided space transformation for local explanations. Expert Syst. Appl. **179**, 115045 (2021)

23. Lathia, N., Hailes, S., Capra, L., Amatriain, X.: Temporal diversity in recommender systems. In: Crestani, F., Marchand-Maillet, S., Chen, H., Efthimiadis, E.N., Savoy, J. (eds.) Proceeding of the 33rd International ACM SIGIR Conference on Research and Development in Information Retrieval, SIGIR 2010, Geneva, Switzerland, 19-23 July 2010, pp. 210–217. ACM, Geneva, Switzerland (2010). https://doi.org/10.1145/1835449.1835486

24. Ledwich, M., Zaitsev, A.: Algorithmic extremism: Examining youtube's rabbit hole of radicalization. First Monday **25** (2019). https://api.semanticscholar.org/CorpusID:209460683

25. Li, S., Zhou, Y., Zhang, D., Zhang, Y., Lan, X.: Learning to diversify recommendations based on matrix factorization. In: 15th IEEE Intl Conf on Dependable, Autonomic and Secure Computing, 15th Intl Conf on Pervasive Intelligence and

Computing, 3rd Intl Conf on Big Data Intelligence and Computing and Cyber Science and Technology Congress, DASC/PiCom/DataCom/CyberSciTech 2017, Orlando, FL, USA, 6-10 November 2017, pp. 68–74. IEEE Computer Society, Orlando, FL, USA (2017). https://doi.org/10.1109/DASC-PICOM-DATACOM-CYBERSCITEC.2017.26

26. Liu, X., Wang, G., Bhuiyan, M.Z.A.: Personalised context-aware re-ranking in recommender system. Connect. Sci. **34**(1), 319–338 (2022)

27. Loshchilov, I., Hutter, F.: Decoupled weight decay regularization. In: 7th International Conference on Learning Representations, ICLR 2019, New Orleans, LA, USA, 6-9 May 2019. OpenReview.net, New Orleans, LA, USA (2019). https://openreview.net/forum?id=Bkg6RiCqY7

28. Masłowska, E., Malthouse, E., Hollebeek, L.: The role of recommender systems in fostering consumers' long-term platform engagement. J. Service Manag. **33** (05 2022). https://doi.org/10.1108/JOSM-12-2021-0487

29. Medda, G., Fabbri, F., Marras, M., Boratto, L., Fenu, G.: GNNUERS: fairness explanation in gnns for recommendation via counterfactual reasoning. CoRR (2023). https://doi.org/10.48550/ARXIV.2304.06182

30. Moscato, V., Picariello, A., Sperli, G.: An emotional recommender system for music. IEEE Intell. Syst. **36**(5), 57–68 (2020)

31. O'Callaghan, D., Greene, D., Conway, M., Carthy, J., Cunningham, P.: Down the (white) rabbit hole: the extreme right and online recommender systems. Soc. Sci. Comput. Rev. **33**, 459–478 (2015)

32. Rana, A., D'Addio, R.M., Manzato, M.G., Bridge, D.: Extended recommendation-by-explanation. User Model. User Adapt. Interact. **32**(1–2), 91–131 (2022)

33. Rendle, S., Freudenthaler, C., Gantner, Z., Schmidt-Thieme, L.: BPR: bayesian personalized ranking from implicit feedback. CoRR abs/ arXiv: 1205.2618 (2012)

34. Sarwar, B.M., Karypis, G., Konstan, J.A., Riedl, J.: Item-based collaborative filtering recommendation algorithms. In: Shen, V.Y., Saito, N., Lyu, M.R., Zurko, M.E. (eds.) Proceedings of the Tenth International World Wide Web Conference, WWW 2010, Hong Kong, China, 1-5 May 2001, pp. 285–295. ACM (2001). https://doi.org/10.1145/371920.372071

35. Su, X., Sperlì, G., Moscato, V., Picariello, A., Esposito, C., Choi, C.: An edge intelligence empowered recommender system enabling cultural heritage applications. IEEE Trans. Industr. Inf. **15**(7), 4266–4275 (2019)

36. Vultureanu-Albisi, A., Badica, C.: Recommender systems: an explainable AI perspective. In: International Conference on INnovations in Intelligent SysTems and Applications, INISTA 2021, Kocaeli, Turkey, 25-27 August 2021, pp. 1–6. IEEE, Kocaeli, Turkey (2021). https://doi.org/10.1109/INISTA52262.2021.9548125

37. Wasilewski, J., Hurley, N.: Incorporating diversity in a learning to rank recommender system. In: Markov, Z., Russell, I. (eds.) Proceedings of the Twenty-Ninth International Florida Artificial Intelligence Research Society Conference, FLAIRS 2016, Key Largo, FL, USA, 16-18 May 2016, pp. 572–578. AAAI Press, Key Largo, FL, USA (2016). http://www.aaai.org/ocs/index.php/FLAIRS/FLAIRS16/paper/view/12944

38. Wu, H., Zhang, Y., Ma, C., Lyu, F., Diaz, F., Liu, X.: A survey of diversification techniques in search and recommendation. CoRR (2022). https://doi.org/10.48550/ARXIV.2212.14464

39. Xian, Y., Fu, Z., Muthukrishnan, S., de Melo, G., Zhang, Y.: Reinforcement knowledge graph reasoning for explainable recommendation. In: Piwowarski, B., Chevalier, M., Gaussier, É., Maarek, Y., Nie, J., Scholer, F. (eds.) Proceedings of the 42nd

International ACM SIGIR Conference on Research and Development in Information Retrieval, SIGIR 2019, Paris, France, 21-25 July 2019, pp. 285–294. ACM, Paris, France (2019). https://doi.org/10.1145/3331184.3331203

40. Yu, C., Lakshmanan, L.V.S., Amer-Yahia, S.: It takes variety to make a world: diversification in recommender systems. In: Proceedings of the 12th International Conference on Extending Database Technology: Advances in Database Technology, EDBT 2009, pp. 368-378. Association for Computing Machinery, New York (2009). https://doi.org/10.1145/1516360.1516404

41. Yu, C., Lakshmanan, L.V.S., Amer-Yahia, S.: Recommendation diversification using explanations. In: Ioannidis, Y.E., Lee, D.L., Ng, R.T. (eds.) Proceedings of the 25th International Conference on Data Engineering, ICDE 2009, 29 March 2009 - 2 April 2009, Shanghai, China, pp. 1299–1302. IEEE Computer Society, Shanghai, China (2009). https://doi.org/10.1109/ICDE.2009.225

42. Zhang, Y., Chen, X.: Explainable recommendation: a survey and new perspectives. Found. Trends Inf. Retr. **14**(1), 1–101 (2020)

43. Zhang, Y., Lai, G., Zhang, M., Zhang, Y., Liu, Y., Ma, S.: Explicit factor models for explainable recommendation based on phrase-level sentiment analysis. In: andAndrew Trotman, S.G., Bruza, P., Clarke, C.L.A., Järvelin, K. (eds.) The 37th International ACM SIGIR Conference on Research and Development in Information Retrieval, SIGIR 2014, Gold Coast, QLD, Australia - 06 - 11 July 2014, pp. 83–92. ACM, Gold Coast, QLD, Australia (2014). https://doi.org/10.1145/2600428.2609579

44. Zhao, X., Zhu, Z., Caverlee, J.: Rabbit holes and taste distortion: distribution-aware recommendation with evolving interests. In: Leskovec, J., Grobelnik, M., Najork, M., Tang, J., Zia, L. (eds.) WWW '21: The Web Conference 2021, Virtual Event / Ljubljana, Slovenia, 19-23 April 2021, pp. 888–899. ACM / IW3C2, Ljubljana, Slovenia (2021). https://doi.org/10.1145/3442381.3450099, https://doi.org/10.1145/3442381.3450099

45. Zhao, Y., Wang, Y., Liu, Y., Cheng, X., Aggarwal, C.C., Derr, T.: Fairness and diversity in recommender systems: A survey. CoRR (2023). https://doi.org/10.48550/ARXIV.2307.04644

46. Zheng, Y., Gao, C., Chen, L., Jin, D., Li, Y.: DGCN: diversified recommendation with graph convolutional networks. In: Leskovec, J., Grobelnik, M., Najork, M., Tang, J., Zia, L. (eds.) WWW 2021: The Web Conference 2021, Virtual Event / Ljubljana, Slovenia, 19-23 April 2021, pp. 401–412. ACM / IW3C2, Virtual Event / Ljubljana, Slovenia (2021). https://doi.org/10.1145/3442381.3449835

# Effects of Representation Nudges on the Perception of Playlist Recommendations

Shah Noor Khan[1]([✉])[iD], Eelco Herder[1][iD], and Diba Kaya[2]

[1] Utrecht University, Utrecht, The Netherlands
{s.n.khan1,e.herder}@uu.nl
[2] Jstor, New York, USA

**Abstract.** Music plays a significant role in social interactions across cultures, carrying diverse meanings and serving various personal and global purposes. Therefore, it is crucial that music platforms ensure that users from diverse groups feel recognized, fairly treated, and satisfied with their recommendations. This study examines how "representation" nudges influence playlist selection and user attitudes towards different minority groups. The results indicate that users appreciated the labels, provided that they recognized the associated user group as a minority that needs attention. In some cases, users changed their playlists accordingly, particularly when they are in line with their personal preferences.

**Keywords:** Music recommendation · Playlists · Minority representation · Nudges

## 1 Introduction

Music is an integral part of social interactions and experiences in diverse cultures [36]. It carries significant social meanings and serves various functions, from fostering self-awareness and creating social bonds to conveying emotions [18]. Music is a potent medium for expressing local concerns, with teenagers especially using their music preferences to shape and define their identities [25,30].

Recommender Systems (RS) process large volumes of choices to suggest the most appropriate and relevant items to users. However, these systems tend to favor certain items, recommending them more frequently, while other items receive less attention [22]. As a result, the group with the least coherence to popular tastes is most affected, often receiving poorer recommendations [1].

Research shows that users who prefer non-mainstream music have more extensive profiles and listen to a wider variety of artists than those who favor mainstream music. This highlights the need to improve recommendations for these users [22]. Recommending less popular, long-tail items is also beneficial to diversify recommendations for mainstream users and to increase exposure of lesser known artists and songs [3,29]. Platforms like Music recommender system

© The Author(s), under exclusive license to Springer Nature Switzerland AG 2025
L. Boratto et al. (Eds.): RecSoGood 2024, CCIS 2470, pp. 151–160, 2025.
https://doi.org/10.1007/978-3-031-87654-7_14

(MRS) use techniques such as nudging [11] to subtly guide user decisions toward better outcomes without enforcing specific choices [35].

For this study, we tailored playlists for user dimensions like age, origins, gender, and sexual orientation, and used representation nudges to inform users – who may or may not belong to the associated user groups – about these dimensions, in order to assess their acceptance. These dimensions have been previously explored in evaluating biases in recommender systems [12,14]. Also, the study aimed to determine whether the nudges associated with various minority groups influenced the participants' playlist preferences.

## 2   Literature Review

In RS, fairness and equity are increasingly considered important. Research [21, 32] on fairness often defines fairness uniformly across all groups. However, it is essential to recognize that fairness should be defined differently for different groups [6]. Freeman et al. [16] view fairness as a dynamic state, where current relations between advantaged and disadvantaged groups are not considered as a given, but as dynamics that should be explicitly shaped by system decisions. Researchers have recently explored rich sub-group fairness, aiming for fairness across multiple intersecting subgroup categories [21].

Within recommender systems, nudges are interface elements that aim to steer user choices in directions that are considered more desirable [20]. Nudging has proven effective in various areas, including sustainable transportation [2], energy conservation [33], green transportation [5], eco-friendly clothing [8], healthier eating [13,34], and privacy awareness [28]. In music recommendations, for instance, nudges may help users explore new genres, encouraging them to go beyond their usual preferences [23].

Playlists are vital to online music listening, with most users creating them for personal and shared use. Platforms like Spotify offer tools for creating and curating playlists based on user preferences. The curation of playlists highlighting specific themes serves as a form of self-expression, a feature of identity, and contributes to the expansion of public culture [26,27]. This curation can also raise awareness about inequality and help unite minority communities [37]. Another study demonstrates that identity plays a crucial role in the creation of playlists on streaming platforms [17].

Studies [15,24] highlight concerns about gender balance and bias, with women often receiving less accurate recommendations. Also, recommending ethnic or region-specific music is challenging due to its poor fit with Western-based methods and small user bases [7,9]. Research [10] examines how LGBTQ-themed playlists influence and reflect LGBTQ identities and cultures.

In our current study, we aim to apply nudging strategies to highlight minority groups in recommender systems, thereby fostering a more inclusive platform. This research could potentially alter user directions and increase awareness of minority groups within the majority.

# 3    Methodology

This section describes the method and study design. We utilized the vignettes method [4], which is effective in HCI studies. This technique involves presenting participants with specific scenarios or stories and then asking them questions to understand their reactions, attitudes, or decision-making processes. Participants were provided with different scenarios introducing nudges and were asked to select playlists and answer questions related to their choices in the study.

The purpose of the study was to explore whether playlist adaptations affect participants' choices in terms of playlist selection. There were two rounds in this study. In each round, participants were presented with four sets of three playlists, with each playlist consisting of 15 songs. Each set of three playlists was presented on a separate screen, and in each set, there was one playlist with a specific equity-focused optimization and two generic, base-line playlists.

All playlists included a balanced mix of songs selected from the current charts[1], popular songs from the 2010 s[2], and popular R&B songs[3]. Additionally, each optimized playlist contained 4 songs selected for users from a particular age group, origin, gender, or orientation, selected from reputable national and international song collections: a 40+ Retro Playlist with popular classic rock songs[4], a Europeanized Playlist including Dutch, German and French songs[5], a Gender-Balanced Playlist featuring Power Women songs[6], and a Rainbow Playlist boasting songs popular among the queer community[7].

We created an interactive website for this study[8], with the aim to entertain the participants and to solicit their reactions. The study was carried out either in person or online via Teams, with the experimenter guiding the participants through the study. Participants consented to be recorded.

In the first round, participants were consecutively presented with four web pages, each containing a set of three playlists. Their task was to simply select the playlist they preferred from the set of three. An example selection screen is displayed in Fig. 1.

Participants were not given any indication about possible playlist interventions and were asked to think aloud during the process. Each interface contained one optimized playlist and in order to keep conversations comparable, the order of optimized playlists and associated user groups (age, origin, gender,

---

[1]  https://www.top40.nl/top40/2024/week-4.

[2]  https://open.spotify.com/playlist/6JpGyIjFccZ6COElPnDZKu.

[3]  https://thefortyfive.com/opinion/best-r-and-b-songs-of-all-time/.

[4]  https://www.arrow.nl/wp-content/uploads/2023/10/Arrow-Classic-Rock-500-2023-100-11.pdf.

[5]  https://www.nporadio2.nl/nieuws/npo-radio-2/31f4a2a2-32fc-4e75-88f1-b6e73a283f5d/dit-is-de-koninklijke-500-van-2022,    https://www.muziekweb.nl/en/Link/HCX1490/De-40-bekendste-Duitse-liedjes,   https://www.top40.nl/overig-nieuws-de-grootste-franstalige-hit.

[6]  https://www.seventeen.com/celebrity/music/g22878449/girl-power-songs/.

[7]  https://www.timeout.com/music/best-gay-songs.

[8]  https://www.projects.science.uu.nl/ics-playlistselection/.

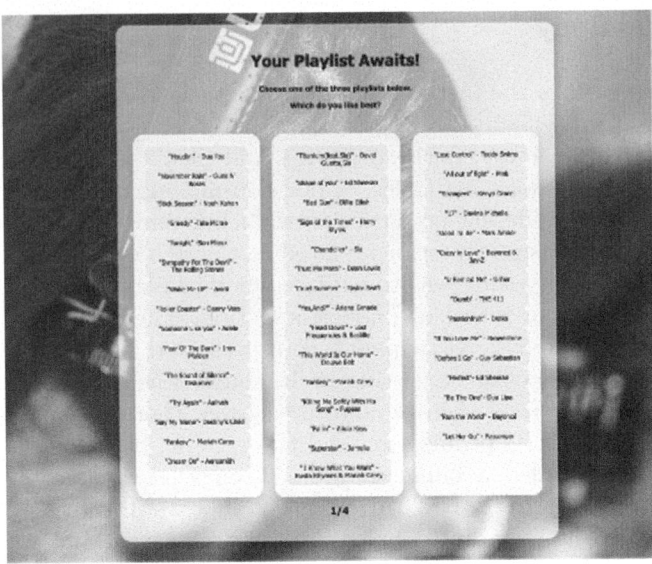

**Fig. 1.** Playlist selection in the first round. All playlists, including the optimized one, are presented equally, in randomized order.

orientation) was fixed, ordered by the expected increasing controversy. Within each interface, the order of the playlists was randomized to avoid middle-option bias [31], but the altered playlist remained the same.

In the second round, four types of labels were used, each referring to the user group dimensions mentioned above. The labels were intended to serve as nudges to raise attention for the suggested disadvantages that user groups may experience within the platform. The labels of the optimized playlists had a different pastel background color compared to the other two playlists. The pastel colors were used to reduce any bias caused by color. In addition, the songs associated with the user group dimensions were highlighted with a different pastel background color, demonstrating how these user groups could be better accommodated. In Fig. 2, there is an example of the optimized playlist, the label suggests that it is a Europeanised playlist and the highlighted songs with different background are the songs associated with this dimension.

At the end of the second round, participants were asked questions related to how comfortable they are with the optimizations, how well they rated the adaptations to the user groups, as well as their familiarity and association with each of the four user groups. Finally, participants were asked to comment upon the optimized playlist and they were invited to change their choice or to indicate that they would stick to their initial choice with this additional knowledge.

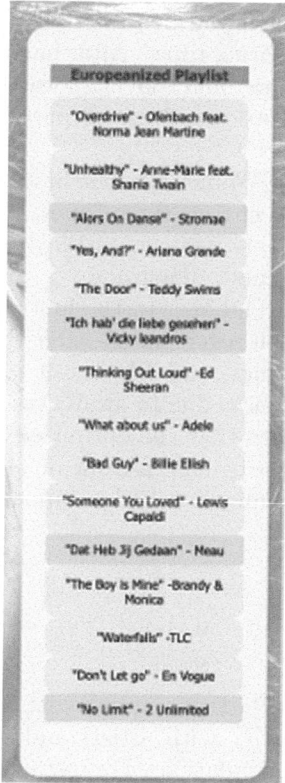

**Europeanized Playlist**

"Overdrive" - Ofenbach feat. Norma Jean Martine

"Unhealthy" - Anne-Marie feat. Shania Twain

"Alors On Danse" - Stromae

"Yes, And?" - Ariana Grande

"The Door" - Teddy Swims

"Ich hab' die liebe gesehen" - Vicky leandros

"Thinking Out Loud" -Ed Sheeran

"What about us" - Adele

"Bad Guy" - Billie Eilish

"Someone You Loved" - Lewis Capaldi

"Dat Heb Jij Gedaan" - Meau

"The Boy is Mine" -Brandy & Monica

"Waterfalls" -TLC

"Don't Let go" - En Vogue

"No Limit" - 2 Unlimited

**Fig. 2.** An optimized playlist in the second round, with user group label and highlighted songs associated with this user group.

## 4    Results

The study was qualitative in nature and, since it was a preliminary study, we initially aimed to have 10 participants. However, after 8 participants, we found that we had reached the intended saturation level.

### 4.1    User Interaction and Playlist Choices

The playlist selection in the first round and the playlist confirmation or change in the second round served as a basis for the interviews, reported in the next subsection. Therefore, we start with a summary of these results. The numbers presented are indicative and used for interpretation. The participants saw the playlists in random order, but for convenience, in this section, the optimized playlist is always Playlist 1.

*Age Dimension* (40+ Retro): In both rounds, Playlist 1 and Playlist 2 were picked four times each, showing no particular preference. Playlist 3 was not selected at all. Apparently, the optimization did not affect participants' choices.

*Origin Dimension* (Europeanized): In the first round, Playlist 1 was chosen twice, and Playlist 3 was chosen six times. After having seen the nudges in round 2, Playlist 1 was chosen six times, and Playlist 3 was chosen twice. This indicates that awareness of the optimization influenced participants to choose Playlist 1 more.

*Gender Dimension* (Power Women): In the first round, Playlist 1 was chosen five times, and Playlist 3 was chosen three times. After having seen the representation nudges, all participants had chosen Playlist 1, apparently indicating a strong association with the gender dimension.

*Orientation Dimension* (Rainbow): In the first round, Playlist 1 was chosen once, and Playlist 3 was chosen seven times. After the nudges have been shown, Playlist 1 was chosen five times, and Playlist 3 was chosen three times: five participants changed their choices due to awareness of the optimization.

Overall, the results indicate that the optimized playlists influenced participants' choices, especially for the gender, European, and sexual orientation dimensions. The age dimension optimization had no apparent effect.

## 4.2   Interviews

All interviews were transcribed and coded. This section is structured based on the most important and frequent codes.

**Initial Selection Criteria:** Participants' playlist selections were influenced by factors that included familiarity with artists and songs, personal preferences, situational needs, and recommendations. For instance, P1 and P4 prefer familiar artists like Kensington, Ed Sheeran and Dua Lipa, while P1 and P3 avoid Justin Bieber. Further, P2 and P4 chose playlists based on specific goals or situations, whereas P1 and P7 rely on Spotify's recommendations. Nostalgia also plays a role, with P1 and P4 mentioning songs from their teenage years.

**Affiliation with User Groups/Dimensions:** Participants showed reluctance to choose the optimized playlist for the 40+ demographic, as they felt this playlist did not resonate with their personal identity or music tastes. For example, P3 and P8 noted that such playlists felt irrelevant to them, with P7 humorously remarking that a 40+ label made them feel old, despite being only 30.

There was a strong tendency towards supporting European artists, with participants highlighting the importance of promoting local talent over dominant American artists. P6 and P4 mentioned choosing playlists featuring European artists to align with their tastes and support regional music scenes.

The discussion also highlighted benefits of playlists optimized for queer or female artists, seeing these as opportunities to explore diverse perspectives and support underrepresented groups. P7, who does not identify as queer, still expressed a desire to support queer artists, because they enjoy the positive and self-affirming messages in their music.

In conclusion, while demographic labels on playlists can influence music selection, personal identity and significance related to those identities play a significant role in playlist selection. Participants preferred playlists that align with their cultural and regional affiliations and that promote diversity and inclusion, but at the same time showed hesitation in selecting playlists for a age group with whom they do not identify and which don't consider as relevant.

**Effects of the Optimization:** Participants described varied responses to the effects of playlist optimizations, reflecting their individual preferences and decision-making processes. P1 and P6 stated that awareness of the optimizations did not significantly change their choice. They mentioned that they would have chosen the playlist quicker with the label that served as representation nudge, but would still go for the same one regardless of the label.

P2, P5, and P7 found the labels interesting, making the playlists seem less generic. They liked the categorization and felt it helped them discover new music. P5 felt that the labels provided an extra reason to listen to the playlist and made them more aware of inclusivity. P7 appreciated the variety and the opportunity to discover new music from female artists, mentioning that the labels influenced their initial choice, but would still consider the songs in the playlist.

P3 and P4 had mixed feelings about the labels. P3 shared that while they usually choose based on the title of the playlist, the additional information made them consider the gender balance and variety within the playlist. They found the new dimension of variety appealing and felt it increased the likelihood of choosing the playlist. P4 felt that while the labels provided a new perspective, they did not always resonate with their personal preferences. P8 felt that the labels did not resonate with them personally and preferred playlists that focused on the music genre rather than the audience's age or underrepresented groups.

**Acceptance of Highlighting Minorities:** Several participants expressed a desire for the inclusion of various categories to cater to different tastes and groups. P1 stated that being part of a minority group influences their interest in such playlists, while P6 emphasized the potential for these playlists to become mere token gestures if not implemented sincerely. The idea of supporting one's minority group through algorithmic boosts was seen positively by P5.

There was also a concern about potential backlash from highlighting minority groups, especially from right-wing movements. Despite this, P2 felt that representation is crucial and that having visible categories for minority communities is beneficial. P3 was interested in seeing if exposure to minority-focused playlists could change perceptions among those not identifying with those communities.

## 5    Discussion

In the first round of playlist selection without any labels, the majority of participants mainly based their choices on familiarity with artists and their liking towards the songs. The context in which they were listening also influenced their selections. These results are expected and in line with current literature [19]. In the second round, the participants were shown the optimization labels, along with the highlighting of the optimized tracks. This affected their selection criteria, as described in the interview results.

Our participants, all between 20 and 30, found it hard to associate themselves with the optimized playlist for 40+ users, also because they did not consider this group a user group that lacks representation. By contrast, the European dimension did prompt participants to change their choices, as they are aware of the issues faced by these artists and consider them a minority on the platform.

For the dimension of gender and orientation, there was a significant effect as well. Since the participants were already familiar with these groups being discriminated, they felt that promoting these groups would create a more positive and inclusive atmosphere. Their familiarity with these groups is also a result of these groups being discussed on a broader level in the current society.

However, the participants' decision to select a different playlist was affected by personal preferences as well. Although a couple of participants considered the minority representation an important aspect, they still preferred to go with the option they originally selected. This may be interpreted as a potential *conflict of interest* between the wish (or social desirability) to appreciate values like inclusivity on the one hand and the wish to enjoy songs of their own preference on the other hand – in cases where these two factors do not align.

Furthermore, participants emphasized that superficial labeling would not be helpful. There was a mention of backlash as well from groups that do not like minorities being represented, but still considered visibility to be important and beneficial, as this could also help in changing perceptions among such users.

## 6    Conclusion

In this study, we aimed to investigate whether optimized playlists and associated labels for four different minority groups (age group, origin, gender and orientation) had any effect on the choice selection of participants. The results indicated that these labels did influence participants' choices, but only if they identified with or sympathized with the respective minority group, emphasizing the importance of meaningful labels over superficial ones. The second aspect of the study focused on whether participants would be comfortable with a platform that highlights minority preferences. Participants indeed showed positive attitudes, although they raised questions about potential backlash.

This preliminary study, being qualitative in nature, could be expanded into a more quantitative study by using the interface as a survey tool to gather responses from a larger sample group, in order to analyze patterns in playlist selection. Systematic variations and planned comparisons could also provide specific strategies to solve potential conflicts of interest between users wanting to show their sympathy with specific non-mainstream user groups – by accepting (or even embracing) the associated songs and genres in their choice architecture – and the desire to still have playlists and recommendations optimized for their own preferences.

# References

1. Abdollahpouri, H., Mansoury, M., Burke, R., Mobasher, B.: The connection between popularity bias, calibration, and fairness in recommendation. In: Proceedings of the 14th ACM Conference on Recommender Systems, pp. 726–731 (2020)
2. Anagnostopoulou, E., et al.: From mobility patterns to behavioural change: leveraging travel behaviour and personality profiles to nudge for sustainable transportation. J. Intell. Inform. Syst. **54**, 157–178 (2020)
3. Anderson, C.: Debating the long tail. Harvard Business Review (2008)
4. Atzmüller, C., Steiner, P.M.: Experimental vignette studies in survey research. Methodology (2010)
5. Bothos, E., Apostolou, D., Mentzas, G.: Recommender systems for nudging commuters towards eco-friendly decisions. Intell. Decision Technol. **9**(3), 295–306 (2015)
6. Burke, R., Mattei, N., Grozin, V., Voida, A., Sonboli, N.: Multi-agent social choice for dynamic fairness-aware recommendation. In: Adjunct Proceedings of the 30th ACM Conference on User Modeling, Adaptation and Personalization, pp. 234–244 (2022)
7. Cornelis, O., Lesaffre, M., Moelants, D., Leman, M.: Access to ethnic music: advances and perspectives in content-based music information retrieval. Signal Process. **90**(4), 1008–1031 (2010)
8. Cossalin, A.G., Mauro, N., Ardissono, L.: Promoting green fashion consumption through digital nudges in recommender systems. IEEE Access (2024)
9. Davidson, J., et al.: The youtube video recommendation system. In: Proceedings of the Fourth ACM conference on Recommender systems, pp. 293–296 (2010)
10. Dhaenens, F., Burgess, J.: 'press play for pride': The cultural logics of lgbtq-themed playlists on spotify. New Media & Society **21**(6), 1192–1211 (2019)
11. Dolgopolova, I., Li, B., Roosen, J.: Do nudges matter? consumer perception and acceptance of recommender systems with different types of nudges. In: 3rd FAccTRec Workshop: Responsible Recommendation at The ACM Conference Series on Recommender Systems RECSYS 2020 (2020)
12. Ekstrand, M.D., et al.: All the cool kids, how do they fit in?: Popularity and demographic biases in recommender evaluation and effectiveness. In: Conference on fairness, accountability and transparency, pp. 172–186. PMLR (2018)
13. El Majjodi, A., Starke, A.D., Trattner, C.: Nudging towards health? examining the merits of nutrition labels and personalization in a recipe recommender system. In: Proceedings of the 30th ACM Conference on User Modeling, Adaptation and Personalization, pp. 48–56 (2022)
14. Farnadi, G., Kouki, P., Thompson, S.K., Srinivasan, S., Getoor, L.: A fairness-aware hybrid recommender system. arXiv preprint arXiv:1809.09030 (2018)
15. Ferraro, A., Serra, X., Bauer, C.: Break the loop: gender imbalance in music recommenders. In: Proceedings of the 2021 Conference on Human Information Interaction and Retrieval, pp. 249–254 (2021)
16. Freeman, R., Zahedi, S.M., Conitzer, V.: Fair social choice in dynamic settings. In: Proceedings of the 26th International Joint Conference on Artificial Intelligence (IJCAI), pp. 4580–4587. International Joint Conferences on Artificial Intelligence Marina del Rey, CA (2017)
17. Hagen, A.N.: The playlist experience: personal playlists in music streaming services. Pop. Music Soc. **38**(5), 625–645 (2015)

18. Hallam, S., Cross, I., Thaut, M.: Oxford handbook of music psychology. Oxford University Press (2009)
19. Jannach, D., Lerche, L., Jugovac, M.: Item familiarity effects in user-centric evaluations of recommender systems. In: RecSys Posters (2015)
20. Jesse, M., Jannach, D.: Digital nudging with recommender systems: survey and future directions. Comput. Human Behav. Rep. **3**, 100052 (2021)
21. Kearns, M., Neel, S., Roth, A., Wu, Z.S.: Preventing fairness gerrymandering: auditing and learning for subgroup fairness. In: International Conference on Machine Learning, pp. 2564–2572. PMLR (2018)
22. Kowald, D., Schedl, M., Lex, E.: The unfairness of popularity bias in music recommendation: a reproducibility study. In: Jose, J.M., et al. (eds.) ECIR 2020. LNCS, vol. 12036, pp. 35–42. Springer, Cham (2020). https://doi.org/10.1007/978-3-030-45442-5_5
23. Liang, Y., Willemsen, M.C.: Promoting music exploration through personalized nudging in a genre exploration recommender. Inter. J. Hum.-Comput. Interact. **39**(7), 1495–1518 (2023)
24. Mansoury, M., Abdollahpouri, H., Smith, J., Dehpanah, A., Pechenizkiy, M., Mobasher, B.: Investigating potential factors associated with gender discrimination in collaborative recommender systems. In: The Thirty-third International Flairs Conference (2020)
25. North, A.C., Hargreaves, D.J.: Music and adolescent identity. Music. Educ. Res. **1**(1), 75–92 (1999)
26. Potter, J.: Digital media and learner identity: the new curatorship. Springer (2012)
27. Potter, J., Gilje, Ø.: Curation as a new literacy practice (2015)
28. Salem, R.B., Aïmeur, E., Hage, H.: A nudge-based recommender system towards responsible online socializing. In: OHARS@ RecSys, pp. 23–39 (2020)
29. Shani, G., Gunawardana, A.: Evaluating recommendation systems. Recommender Systems Handbook, pp. 257–297 (2011)
30. Simon, F.: Sound effects: Youth, leisure and the politics of rock 'n'roll. Constable, London (1981)
31. Simons, A., Weinmann, M., Tietz, M., vom Brocke, J.: Which reward should i choose? preliminary evidence for the middle-option bias in reward-based crowdfunding (2017)
32. Sonboli, N., Eskandanian, F., Burke, R., Liu, W., Mobasher, B.: Opportunistic multi-aspect fairness through personalized re-ranking. In: Proceedings of the 28th ACM Conference on User Modeling, Adaptation and Personalization, pp. 239–247 (2020)
33. Starke, A., Willemsen, M., Snijders, C.: Effective user interface designs to increase energy-efficient behavior in a rasch-based energy recommender system. In: Proceedings of the Eleventh ACM Conference on Recommender Systems, pp. 65–73 (2017)
34. Starke, A.D., Asotic, E., Trattner, C., Van Loo, E.J.: Examining the user evaluation of multi-list recommender interfaces in the context of healthy recipe choices. ACM Trans. Recommender Syst. **1**(4), 1–31 (2023)
35. Thaler, R.H., Sunstein, C.R., Balz, J.P.: Choice architecture. The behavioral foundations of public policy (2014)
36. Turino, T.: Music as social life: The politics of participation. University of Chicago Press (2008)
37. Wargo, J.M.: # donttagyourhate: Reading collecting and curating as genres of participation in lgbt youth activism on tumblr. Digital Culture & Educ. **9**(1) (2017)

# Author Index

L. Boratto et al. (Eds.): RecSoGood 2024, CCIS 2470, pp. 161–162, 2025.
https://doi.org/10.1007/978-3-031-87654-7

The manufacturer's authorised representative in the EU is Springer
Nature Customer Service Centre GmbH, Europaplatz 3, 69115 Heidelberg,
Germany. If you have any concerns regarding our products, please
contact ProductSafety@springernature.com

Printed and bound by CPI Group (UK) Ltd, Croydon, CR0 4YY

28/04/2026

02098542-0009